WITHDRAWN

The Literature of Travel, Exploration and Empire

Series Editors: Iain McCalman and Nicholas Thomas

There is now an unprecedented level of interest in travel, cross-cultural relations and colonial histories. Scholars in cultural history, literary studies, art history, anthropology and related fields have become increasingly interested in the history of encounters between Europeans and other peoples, in the intellectual and scientific dimensions of exploration and travel, and in the development of travel-writing genres.

Despite this burgeoning scholarly interest, many important texts are unavailable, or available only in expensive facsimiles that lack up-to-date commentary. This new series will make key texts more widely available. It will include not only remarkable but previously unpublished or poorly known texts, but also new editions of well-known works. Accessible introductions will situate the works in the light of recent historical and anthropological research, and theoretical developments in the understanding of travel and colonial representation. Annotations will provide relevant contextual information and emphasize questions of interpretation.

Forthcoming titles include

George Barrington, *A Voyage to New South Wales* (c. 1793), edited by
 Suzanne Rickard
George Keate, *An Account of the Pelew Islands* (1788), edited by Nicholas
 Thomas and Karen Nero
F. E. Maning, *Old New Zealand and Other Writings* (1863), edited by Alex
 Calder
Hester Lynch Piozzi, *Observations and Reflections made in the Course of a
 Journey Through France, Germany and Italy* (1789), edited by Chloe Chard
Ada Pryor, *A Decade in Borneo* (1894), edited by Susan Morgan
David Samwell, *The Death of Captain Cook and other Writings* (1786), edited
 by Iain McCalman, Martin Fitzpatrick and Nicholas Thomas
C. F. Volney, *Ruins, or a Survey of the Revolutions of Empire* (c. 1791), edited
 by Iain McCalman

For further information, see
 www.anu.edu.au/culture/projects/cultural_history.html

MAIDEN VOYAGES AND INFANT COLONIES

Plate 1

'This Elegant Design represents History Writing Narratives of the respective Voyages and Travels contained in this Work, & the emblematical representations of the Four Quarters of the World, surrounding the Globe, point out the Extensive Nature of this Undertaking ...'. Frontispiece to William Portlock's *A New Collection of Modern Voyages and Travels* (1794). *Source:* State Library of Victoria.

Maiden Voyages and Infant Colonies

Two Women's Travel Narratives of the 1790s

Edited by Deirdre Coleman

Leicester University Press
London and New York

Leicester University Press
A Cassell imprint
Wellington House, 125 Strand, London WC2R 0BB
370 Lexington Avenue, New York NY 10017–6550

First published 1999

British Library Cataloguing-in-Publication Data
A catalogue record for this book is available from the British Library.

ISBN 0-7185-0149-7 (hardback)
       0-7185-0150-0 (paperback)

Editorial work towards this publication has been supported by

the centre for cross-cultural research

AN AUSTRALIAN RESEARCH COUNCIL SPECIAL RESEARCH CENTRE
THE AUSTRALIAN NATIONAL UNIVERSITY, CANBERRA, ACT 0200
www.anu.edu.au/culture

Typeset by BookEns Limited, Royston, Hertfordshire
Printed and bound in Great Britain by Biddles Ltd, Guildford and King's Lynn

CONTENTS

Illustrations   ix

Acknowledgements   xiii

Chronology   xv

Introduction   1

Note on Texts   43

Anna Maria Falconbridge, *Two Voyages to Sierra Leone* (1794)   45

Editor's Notes   156

Mary Ann Parker, *A Voyage Round the World* (1795)   169

Editor's Notes   221

Bibliography   227

Index   235

ILLUSTRATIONS

Plate 1
Frontispiece to William Portlock's *A New Collection of Modern Voyages and Travels* (1794).
Source: State Library of Victoria.

Plate 2
Sample pages of Falconbridge's *Two Voyages to Sierra Leone* (1794).
Source: State Library of Victoria.

Plate 3
Title-page of George Thompson's *Slavery and Famine, Punishments for Sedition* (1794).
Source: Mitchell Library, State Library of New South Wales.

Plate 4
Two Wedgwood medallions from Erasmus Darwin, *The Botanic Garden* (1791).
Source: Rare Book and Special Collections Library, University of Sydney.

Plate 5
Title-page of *The Voyage of Governor Phillip to Botany Bay* (1789) depicting the Wedgwood medallion.
Source: Rare Book and Special Collections Library, University of Sydney.

Plate 6
'A View of the Governor's House at Rose-Hill, in the Township of Parramatta', from David Collins, *An Account of the English Colony in New South Wales* (1798).
Source: Rare Book and Special Collections Library, University of Sydney.

Plate 7
'Representation of the Coin introduced into the Sierra Leona Colony', from Carl Wadstrom, *An Essay on Colonization* (1794).
Source: Social Sciences and Humanities Library, University of New South Wales.

Plate 8
'Nautical Map', from Carl Wadstrom, *An Essay on Colonization* (1794).
Source: Cambridge University Library; by permission of the Syndics of Cambridge University Library.

Plate 9
'La Nature' (Anonyme, *c.* 1790), Musée Carnavalet, Paris.
Source: Photothèques des Musées de la Ville de Paris; photographer Lyliane Degraces.

Plate 10
'Plan of the Island of Bulama', from Carl Wadstrom, *An Essay on Colonization* (1794).
Source: Cambridge University Library; by permission of the Syndics of Cambridge University Library.

Plate 11
'A Representation of my first Conference with the Natives', from John Matthews, *A Voyage to the River Sierra-Leone* (2nd edn, 1791).
Source: Cambridge University Library; by permission of the Syndics of Cambridge University Library.

Plate 12
Juan Ravenet (*c.* 1766–?), 'Convictos enla Nueva Olanda' (1793).
Source: Dixson Galleries, State Library of New South Wales.

Plate 13
Portrait of Bennelong (*c.* 1795).
Source: Mitchell Library, State Library of New South Wales.

Plate 14
Title-page of Anna Maria Falconbridge's *Two Voyages to Sierra Leone* (1794).
Source: State Library of Victoria.

Plate 15
'A View of the entrance into Sierra-leone River', from John Matthews, *A Voyage to the River Sierra-Leone* (2nd edn, 1791).
Source: Cambridge University Library; by permission of the Syndics of Cambridge University Library.

Plate 16
'Prospect of Bense Island and Fort', from Thomas Astley, *A New General Collection of Voyages and Travels*, vol. 2 (1745).
Source: Cambridge University Library; by permission of the Syndics of Cambridge University Library.

Plate 17
'A View of Ya, Ma, Cooba's Town in White Man's Bay, Sierra-Leone', from John Matthews, *A Voyage to the River Sierra-Leone* (2nd edn, 1791).
Source: Cambridge University Library; by permission of the Syndics of Cambridge University Library.

Plate 18
'The Banjon, or African Guitar', from John Matthews, *A Voyage to the River Sierra-Leone* (2nd edn, 1791).
Source: Cambridge University Library; by permission of the Syndics of Cambridge University Library.

Plate 19
'A method whereby the Men of Guinea oblige their Wives to purge themselves from the accusation of Adultery', from William Portlock's *A New Collection of Modern Voyages and Travels* (1794).
Source: State Library of Victoria.

Plate 20
'A View of Sierra-Leone River, from St. George's Hill, where the Free Black settlement was made in the year 1787', from John Matthews, *A Voyage to the River Sierra-Leone* (2nd edn, 1791).
Source: Cambridge University Library; by permission of the Syndics of Cambridge University Library.

Plate 21
Title-page of Mary Ann Parker's *A Voyage Round the World* (1795).
Source: Australian National Library.

Plate 22
Juan Ravenet (*c.* 1766–?), 'Ingleses enla Nueva Olanda' (1793).
Source: Dixson Galleries, State Library of New South Wales.

Plate 23
'A direct North General View of Sydney-Cove' (1794), oil painting based on a drawing by Thomas Watling.
Source: Dixson Galleries, State Library of New South Wales.

Plate 24

'By water to Parramatta; with a distant view of the western mountains, taken from the Windmill-hill at Sydney', from *The Voyage of Governor Phillip* (1789).
Source: Rare Book and Special Collections Library, University of Sydney.

Plate 25

'A non-descript Bird found at Botany Bay, in New South Wales. From a Drawing made on the spot' (1791).
Source: Mitchell Library, State Library of New South Wales.

ACKNOWLEDGEMENTS

I am grateful to the Series Editors, Iain McCalman and Nicholas Thomas, for their invitation to contribute a volume to *The Literature of Travel, Exploration and Empire*. Jenny Newell, research and editing assistant to the series at the Centre for Cross-Cultural Research, Canberra, is also to be thanked for her wonderfully efficient back-up support on all fronts, but particularly in the time-consuming task of tracking down some of the more elusive illustrations. Gerard Goggin spent a good part of last summer scanning the texts to disk, researching footnotes, and overseeing the formatting of the whole, a job which was in turn double-checked by Carol Willock immediately before submission. Their accuracy, expertise and speed have been invaluable.

At the institutional level, this edition has been supported by an Australian Research Council Grant and by the Centre for Cross-Cultural Research in Canberra. I am grateful to both these bodies for providing research assistance and access to interstate and overseas libraries. Amongst my colleagues at the University of Sydney and elsewhere, I wish to thank Judith Barbour, Anette Bremer, Hilary Fraser, Bruce Gardiner, Melissa Hardie, Philip Hardie, Dorothy Jones, Kate Lilley, Judy Quinn and Elizabeth Webby for their comments and contributions. Special thanks to Debra Adelaide, who possesses, in addition to her many other remarkable talents, a wide knowledge of early Australian colonial writing. Richard Neville, Picture Curator at the State Library of New South Wales, mounted an inspired and (for me) timely exhibition entitled 'A Rage for Curiosity', offering all kinds of fresh slants on the records of the early colony at Port Jackson.

For help with the Sierra Leone section I thank Susan Griffith, who cheerfully performed a survey for me of possible illustrations in Cambridge University Library. Susan's recent work, and mine over the past four years, owes a great deal to librarian Terry Barringer, whose friendly helpfulness and specialist knowledge of the important Royal Commonwealth Society Collection, now in Cambridge University Library, has opened many doors for scholars from all over the Commonwealth. Brian Hubber, Rare Books

Acknowledgements

Librarian at the State Library of Victoria, was also most helpful and efficient on the occasions I worked in Melbourne, as were librarians Sara Hilder at the University of Sydney, and Margot Zeggelink at the University of New South Wales. Finally, I acknowledge my indebtedness to the scholarship of Christopher Fyfe, A. P. Kup and Ellen Gibson Wilson; their many fine books and editions have fascinated me over the last few years.

On the domestic front I thank Vince for his quick wit and good humour, and his tolerance of the extent to which my working life absorbs evenings and weekends. My greatest debt of all is, however, to my friend and neighbour Mary Jolly. Without Mary's loving and steady devotion to Susanna and Benjamin, and her generosity, wisdom and thoughtfulness about all areas of our day-to-day lives, I would never have had the chance to complete this book on time.

Deirdre Coleman
University of Sydney
January 1998

CHRONOLOGY

Date	Lives of Falconbridge and Parker	Other publications	Historical events
1786		Thomas Clarkson, *On the Slavery and Commerce of the Human Species*	Granville Sharp sets up 'Committee for the Relief of Black Poor' in London
1787		Ottobah Cugoano, *Thoughts and Sentiments on ... the Slavery and Commerce of the Human Species*	First Fleet departs England First settlers sail to Sierra Leone
1788		John Matthews, *Voyage to the River Sierra-Leone*	January: First Fleet arrives at Port Jackson
		Alexander Falconbridge, *An Account of the Slave Trade on the Coast of Africa*	Societé des Amis des Noirs established in France for abolition of slave trade
		Thomas Clarkson, *Essay on the Impolicy of the African Slave Trade*	
1789		Olaudah Equiano, *Interesting Narrative*	Fall of the Bastille
		The Voyage of Governor Phillip to Botany Bay	November–December: Second Fleet preparing to sail for Botany Bay

Date	Lives of Falconbridge and Parker	Other publications	Historical events
1789 *(cont'd)*		Watkin Tench, *A Narrative of the Expedition to Botany Bay*	
1790		John White, *Voyage to NSW*	June: Second Fleet arrives in Port Jackson
		Edmund Burke, *Reflections on the Revolution in France*	
		Mary Wollstonecraft, *Vindication of the Rights of Men*	
1791	January: Falconbridge sets out on first voyage to Sierra Leone	Thomas Paine, *Rights of Man*	January: Third Fleet departs England
	February: Falconbridge arrives in Sierra Leone	John Matthews, *Voyage to the River Sierra-Leone* (2nd edn)	France abolishes slavery
	March: Parker departs England		April: House of Commons rejects Wilberforce's first abolition bill but approves a charter for the Sierra Leone Company
	June: Falconbridge departs Sierra Leone, taking Naimbana's second son (the Black Prince) back to England for education		June: Louis XVI tries to flee France, but is arrested and forced to accept the new constitution
			August: Third Fleet begins to arrive in Port Jackson
			August: Large slave uprising on French-controlled St Domingo
	September: Parker arrives in Port Jackson		

Date	Lives of Falconbridge and Parker	Other publications	Historical events
1792		Mary Wollstonecraft, *Vindication of the Rights of Woman*	January: Nova Scotian blacks depart from Halifax, under command of John Clarkson
	February: Falconbridge arrives in Sierra Leone		March: Nova Scotian blacks arrive in Sierra Leone
	June: Parker arrives back in England		Sugar boycott in Britain
	December: Alexander Falconbridge dies		August: Royal family imprisoned in Paris
			December: John Clarkson departs Sierra Leone. William Dawes takes over as governor
1793	January: Falconbridge marries Isaac DuBois	Olaudah Equiano, *Interesting Narrative* (6th & 7th edns)	January: Louis XVI executed
			February: France declares war on Britain; black loyalists arrive in Sierra Leone
	July: Falconbridge and DuBois return to England via Jamaica	John Hunter, *Historical Journal of Port Jackson* Watkin Tench, *Complete Account*	July: Terror begins in France under Robespierre
	September: Falconbridge sees Wilberforce and Paine burnt together in effigy in Kingston, Jamaica		Emancipation of slaves in St Domingo confirmed

Date	Lives of Falconbridge and Parker	Other publications	Historical events
1793 *(cont'd)*			Decline in Britain of public agitation for abolition
			October: Marie-Antoinette executed
1794	August: Capt. John Parker dies	*Two Voyages to Sierra Leone*	April: Scottish martyrs sentenced to transportation
	December: Parker's last child born	William Henry Portlock, *A New, Complete, and Universal Collection of Voyages and Travels*	September: Freetown destroyed by the French
		Carl Wadstrom, *An Essay on Colonization*	October: Treason trials begin against leading reformers
		Olaudah Equiano, *Interesting Narrative* (9th edn)	
1795	Parker narrative published	*A Voyage Round the World*	Britain takes possession of the Cape of Good Hope
			Maroon uprising in Jamaica
			November: Gagging Acts introduced into British Parliament

INTRODUCTION

Doth a fountain send forth at the same place sweet water and bitter?
Ottobah Cugoano [and Olaudah Equiano] (1787)

ithin two months of each other in 1791, two English women set
sail with their husbands on relief missions to two recently
established and far-flung British colonies, Botany Bay on the east
coast of New Holland, and Sierra Leone, West Africa. Both settlements were
established in the wake of the revolt of the old colonies in America, a revolt
which had raised two new problems for Britain. Where would Britain now
send her excess convicts, and what accommodation could be afforded dis-
possessed loyalist refugees? As the crisis of overflowing gaols and hulks
deepened through the 1780s, the British Government canvassed a range of
options for the unwanted felons. These options included several sites on the
West African coast (including Sierra Leone) and Botany Bay.[1] Initially the
Government favoured an African solution to the convict problem, with
Botany Bay a possible destiny for the loyalist refugees.[2] Accordingly,
several small consignments of convicts were sent to Africa from the hulks,
but the mortality was terrible, and those who survived harassed the
natives and disrupted established trade. In the end, with all its African
options ruled out, the Government approved Botany Bay. Given the
'absolute necessity' of finding a remedy as soon as possible, the east coast
of New Holland suddenly seemed the most eligible choice.[3] Justifications
for the decision followed shortly afterwards. It was further away, for a
start; the climate was believed to be more friendly to Europeans than the
African coast, and the soil sufficiently fertile for the settlement to be
independent of the 'mother country' after the first year. Improbably, the
natives were also considered unlikely to mind, let alone resist. Finally, it
was argued, should the colony thrive, it would prove a most useful market
for many European commodities; and of course there was speculation
about the cultivation of raw materials, such as flax, hemp and timber for
the use of Britain's navy.

Africa's possible usefulness to Britain did not, however, fade from view
once the surplus convicts were allocated to Botany Bay. From the 1770s
onwards, there had been intermittent speculation about the possibility of a

joint philanthropic and commercial venture on the west coast of Africa, a free, sugar-growing settlement which would eventually undermine the thriving slave trade to the West Indies. Emmanuel Swedenborg, a Swedish visionary, had even claimed that, in the heart of Africa, there existed a New Jerusalem, with a race of people living according to a new spiritual revelation, a vision which spawned at least one blueprint from his followers for a 'free community' at Sierra Leone.[4] A more pressing, less obscure role for the west coast of Africa arose, however, from the loyalist problem generated by post-war dislocation. The most conspicuous manifestation of this was the influx into Britain of thousands of displaced blacks from America, many of whom had emancipated themselves from slavery by joining the British army and navy during the War of Independence. These loyalist ex-slaves swelled the number of 'black poor' already living in ghettos, particularly in areas of London, causing a growing mixture of concern and alarm throughout the 1780s. Such were the numbers and poverty of this group that Granville Sharp, philanthropist and abolitionist, together with other members of the 'Committee for the Relief of the Black Poor', decided that short-term charitable measures were no longer adequate to deal with the problem.[5] Accordingly, the idea of a self-governing 'Province of Freedom' for ex-slaves, to be established at Sierra Leone, began to gain ground. No territory had been negotiated with the natives, of course, but this did not in the least deter Government from lending its financial support to the Committee's scheme. Charity payments to the blacks soon became conditional upon signed agreements to go, and in 1786 the first shipment of colonists was rounded up from the London ghettos.[6] Since the majority of those who sailed were men, a number of white women were also taken on board, 'chiefly women of the lowest sort, in ill health, and of bad character', according to a later report of the Sierra Leone Company.[7]

In 1791, both settlements, now four years old, were in extreme difficulties. In the widely used trope of the day, independence from the mother country for these 'infant' colonies was still a very dim prospect. It was the task of Mary Ann Parker's husband, commander of the *Gorgon*, to salvage what he could from the supply ship the *Guardian*, shipwrecked off Cape Town en route to the starving convict colony at Port Jackson, near Botany Bay. Captain Parker was then to proceed to the new colony, carrying much needed provisions and the first contingent of the New South Wales Corps. Also on board were Lieutenant-Governor Philip Gidley King and his wife, destined for the new penal settlement on Norfolk Island, plus 31 hand-picked young convicts, chosen for their knowledge of farming. It was essential that the colony be weaned from its dependence upon supply ships like the *Guardian* and the *Gorgon*. To this end, Parker included in her narrative her husband's report on the excellent prospects for whale fishing on the New Holland coast. If whalers could be induced to prefer this coast to the American one, the costs of transportation would come down and the colony cease its 'continually accumulating burthen to the mother-country'. In the short term, though, the *Gorgon*'s mission was to stave off starvation. The fear that the colony was almost at the end of its provisions was confirmed by reports reaching the *Gorgon* at Cape Town. Six months' provisions, at full allowance, were all that remained – a cruel hardship, Mary Ann Parker reflected, on top of all the other difficulties of a colony 'in its infant state'. Nevertheless, confirmation that the colony was near desperation raised her anticipation of the joy that their arrival would bring: 'What then could afford us more heart-felt pleasure than the near event of relieving them? for it is surely happiness to succour the distressed'. Another source of anticipated delight was the greeting they would receive from the 85 members of the Royal Marines who, together with their families, would hail the arrival of the *Gorgon* as their release from the colony. William Dawes, later Governor of Sierra Leone, was one such marine officer.[8] His friend, Captain Watkin Tench, was another. In the book about the colony he published in 1793, Tench confessed to no 'mingled sensations' at the approach of the *Gorgon* in September 1791. Instead, he and his fellow officers 'hailed it with rapture and exultation'.[9]

Anna Maria Falconbridge's husband had an even more difficult mission than Captain Parker. Alexander Falconbridge's task was to re-establish at Sierra Leone the colony of free blacks begun four years earlier, a job which would involve intensive negotiations with several powerful native brokers and careful handling of the local white slave traders. Of the original 411 settlers who sailed, almost one hundred had died in the first wet season of 1787. Over the next two years, the rest either joined the slave trade or worked in the numerous factories established for that purpose; some were even kidnapped and sold into slavery. Within only the first year of its establishment, Sharp was referring ruefully to the 'Province of Freedom' as his 'poor little ill-thriven swarthy daughter', a phrase which boded ill for the colony's future prospects of political independence and self-government.[10]

Eventually, with his own funds exhausted, Sharp handed over the colony to the management of a group of business-minded, evangelical philanthropists, keen for abolition but also hopeful of commercial success to off-set the huge expenses involved in colonization. By the time the new managers took over, the settlement was faring badly, caught between the slave traders on the coast, and the natives with whom they did business. When Falconbridge sailed early in 1791, the settlement contained barely sixty people, and this motley remnant had been burnt out of their houses and dispersed by King Jemmy, one of the local native chieftains. In order to rehabilitate Sharp's sickly off-spring and transform it into a 'thriving settlement',[11] the Sierra Leone Company, as the new trading body called itself, employed Falconbridge as a commercial agent. Formerly a surgeon in the slave trade, Falconbridge had no commercial background, but he knew the west coast well and knew something about dealing with the natives; he was also passionate in his detestation of slavery.[12] Shortly after Falconbridge set out with his young, new bride, the Company engaged John Clarkson, younger brother of the abolitionist Thomas Clarkson, to repatriate another group of loyalist Africans, many of them ex-slaves, from their first 'home' in Nova Scotia.[13] Their number and skills would, it was hoped, secure the vulnerable settlement.

Mary Ann Parker's motive for publishing *A Voyage Round the World* (1795) is clearly stated on the title-page; naming herself as 'widow', she presents her text to the public as written 'for the advantage of a numerous family' (*Plate 21*). An attractively produced book, it only ever saw one edition. Presumably it answered the financial purpose for which it was published, for it is dedicated to the Princess of Wales, and boasts a 'List of Subscribers' almost as long as that achieved by the publisher John Stockdale for his *Voyage of Governor Phillip to Botany Bay*, the first official account of the new settlement, an expensively produced quarto with 55 plates.[14] Structurally, Parker's narrative is a simple retrospect, probably written up from a journal, and incorporating selections from her husband's official papers – his letters and reports, and the ship's log. We do not have any certain biographical knowledge of the author, but the subscription list suggests that she probably came from a military family in the North of England.[15] Certainly, her presentation of herself conforms to the convention of the essentially private, financially embarrassed, and reluctant woman writer. The Preface apologizes in advance for the book's 'brevity and other greater demerits', faults due to her predicament 'as a nurse, and being obliged to attend so much to her domestic concerns'. The competing claims of mother, wife and author begin and end the narrative of her fifteen-month journey, during which one son dies in England, only to be replaced by another four days after arriving back. Furthermore, in a striking vignette at the close, the fatherless children of the title-page and Preface reappear at the very end of the narrative, where the author presents herself as dandling on her left arm 'an infant of *seven* months', whilst writing with her right. The narrative we encounter between these apologetic, domestic frames creates, however, a rather different impression – of a well-educated and well-travelled woman who leapt at the opportunity of accompanying her husband to the 'remotest parts of the globe', although (regretfully) it meant leaving behind her two young children, and her mother from whom she had never been separated for more than a fortnight.

Like the convict colony at Botany Bay, the Sierra Leone 'free' colony of (principally) black settlers had generated a good deal of public interest, not to say controversy.[16] 'The Eyes of England are upon you & this Infant Colony', Thomas Clarkson wrote to his younger brother John. 'No Establishment has made such a Noise as this in the Papers or been so generally admired'. He also urged his brother to keep a journal, reminding him of the vogue for 'histories of new countries', and promising to get him £500 for the manuscript when he returned.[17] John Clarkson kept a very full diary of his frustrating experience as Governor of Sierra Leone but, probably out of loyalty to the Sierra Leone Company, he never published it. More importantly, he would never have done anything to hinder the anti-slavery cause he so passionately supported.[18] Anna Maria Falconbridge did not share her friend's scruples. Casting her *Two Voyages to Sierra Leone* as a series of letters to a friend (*Plate 14*), she bluntly flouts the 'threadbare prevailing custom' of the reluctant 'Authoress', candidly declaring that, in penning her letters, she had in fact had some idea of publishing them. After this initial boast, she then succumbs, rather unconvincingly, to the dictates of modesty, complaining of the 'inability', indeed the 'infancy', of her pen, limitations which kept her in uncertainty about proceeding until the beginning of April 1794. Without a doubt, the date provides us with an important clue as to what precipitated her into print: the Sierra Leone Company's recent publication of its latest *Report* on the colony, in which her late husband's 'habits of intoxication, idleness, and irregularity' were held responsible for the infant colony's 'first difficulties' and 'commercial disappointments'. The *Report* also impugns the character of the Nova Scotian blacks 'repatriated' to Sierra Leone in 1792, representing them as disobedient, disrespectful and ungrateful children. Finally, the Directors blame the blacks' general unruliness and hostility to whites on Falconbridge's second husband, Isaac DuBois, recently dismissed from the Company's service.[19] Here was plenty of inflammable material for any woman to address, let alone such a markedly spirited woman as Falconbridge appears to have been. Accordingly, in her Preface she throws down the gauntlet, challenging the entire Court of the Directors of the Sierra Leone Company 'to contradict one *tittle*' of what she has advanced.

Unlike Parker's *Voyage Round the World*, Falconbridge's book was reprinted twice within the space of a year, then re-issued in a new edition in 1802. It was a cheap production, with numerous typographical errors, written 'in a sprightly manner' as one commentator politely put it. The same reviewer confessed to surprise 'that the writer's success should not have induced her to present the reader with a little better paper and type' (*Plate 2*).[20] Despite evidence of hasty publication, Falconbridge's book is by no means an unsophisticated one. Like many travel writers, she works the epistolary mode for a number of advantages, not least of which is the identification of privacy with authenticity and truthfulness. Making no promises of 'elegant or modish diction', the letter writer claims to offer just 'a rigid adherence to truth ... without embellishment', a ploy which succeeded with at least one reviewer who praised Falconbridge's 'plain and artless language', and the 'credibility' generated by the letters' 'internal evidence'.[21] A more careful reading would, in fact, have revealed some internal inconsistencies, all of which suggest that the book was, at least in part, cobbled together shortly before publication.[22] Most important, though, in the creation of her authorial self, is that notion of the 'infancy' of her pen, a trope which naturalizes discourse in such a

(4)

LETTER II.

SPITHEAD, *Jan.* 12, 1794.

My dear Friend,

CONTRARY winds prevented us from proceeding directly out of the channel, and made it necessary to put into this place. We have been here two days, but I am told there is an appearance of the wind changing, and that it is probable we shall make the attempt to get away some time this day; therefore I think it best not to defer performing my promise of writing to you, least we fail, and I am disappointed.

We embarked at Gravesend between eleven and twelve o'clock, the night after I wrote you: every thing seemed in dreadful confusion; but this I understand is commonly the case on board ships when on the eve of failing: besides the captain had several friends who came from London to bid him farewell.　　　　You

(5)

You may guess my mind, in spite of all the resolution a young girl is capable of mustering, could not be undisturbed; but I would not give way to any melancholy reflections, and endeavoured to smother them as often as they intruded; although I must confess they sometimes caught me off my guard, and my heart, for the moment, was ready to burst with the thoughts of what I had to encounter, which was pictured to me by almost every one in the worst of colours.

However I went to bed, and being much fatigued, was in hopes every care would be buried for the night in delightful sleep; but in this I was disappointed, for although my eyes were closed as soon as I got my head on the pillow, yet it was not of long continuance.

I had slept perhaps two hours, when the shocking cries of murder awoke me! I did not at the instant recollect where I was, but the first thoughts which occurred upon remembering myself on ship-board, were, that a gang of pirates had attacked the ship, and would put us all to death.

All the cabin was by this time alarmed; the cries of murder still continuing while
B

Plate 2　Sample pages of Falconbridge's narrative, showing the quality of type and lay-out, and the erroneous date at the head of the letter.
Source: State Library of Victoria.

way that Falconbridge appears unable to do anything other than give us a truthful, spontaneous, first-hand view of history in the making. To this end, writing itself is often thematized, usually the writing performed on ship-board, a 'fatiguing job', she tells her correspondent at one point, 'being obliged to sit in bed with a book placed on my knee, which serves for a writing desk'. Furthermore, that the friend to whom she writes is a woman allows Falconbridge to be frankly autobiographical, with a particular focus upon issues to do with their sex. For instance, the first letter alludes to her voyage as a type of self-exile, penitentially performed to expiate for the wilfulness of marrying hastily, against the wishes of her friends; subsequent letters contain several highly personal allusions to the difficulties of managing her first husband.

But as Falconbridge's contemporary, Anna Laetitia Barbauld, argued, the epistolary mode is 'highly fictitious', being at one and the same time 'the most natural and the least probable way of telling a story'.[23] Falconbridge's ready admission that she penned the letters with an eye to their possible publication alerts us to the text's double nature, a duplicity further highlighted by an editorial apparatus of dedication, preface, footnotes and appendix, all of which generate the fiction of real, private letters embedded in the heart of a published, impersonal book. Falconbridge's juxtaposition of so-called 'manuscript' and print also underscores the way in which the epistolary genre is central to the construction and definition of the categories of public and private. Falconbridge's letters may be emblematic of the private – of the intimate female body – mapping as they do a sentimental story of moving from a first, unhappy marriage through to a second, happy one. But she is also the 'citizen–critic', a member of a republic of letters determined to achieve three public ends.[24] The first is self-vindication; Falconbridge is 'an injured Woman' seeking redress for the shabby treatment dealt out to her (and her two husbands) by the Directors of the Sierra Leone Company. The second is vindication of the Nova Scotian blacks, whose sense of betrayal she shared; by publishing their account of futile petitioning to the Directors in 1793, her book becomes the vehicle for publicizing their side of the story. The third end is public exposure; Falconbridge is determined to publicize the bungling, hypocrisy and greed of a Government-sponsored colonial venture, run entirely by white, male philanthropists.[25]

BOTANY BAY AND SIERRA LEONE

In the popular imagination of late eighteenth-century Britain, nothing seemed so terrible as the fate of transportation to Botany Bay, unless of course you were black, in which case being kidnapped into slavery was an even worse fatality. White apologists for the slave trade like Lieutenant John Matthews, whose book on Sierra Leone appeared in 1788, even argued that

there was in essence no difference between enslavement and transportation –
'between the African condemned for some offence against the laws of his
country, to be sold to a white man, and the English felon transported to a
wild uncultivated country; for such Botany Bay is represented, and whose
distance for ever excludes the hope of returning'.[26] Indeed, in the same year
that Falconbridge published her narrative, a radical little book appeared
with the large-gestured, gothic title, *Slavery and Famine, Punishments for
Sedition; or, an Account of the Miseries and Starvation at Botany Bay*
(*Plate 3*).[27] And just in case some might protest that there was indeed a
difference between the slave and the transportee, apologists for slavery
could always argue, as Matthews did, that by far the greater proportion
of pain lay on the side of the white transportee: 'the affliction of the
African at parting from his native country, very probably may be felt with
redoubled force by the more enlightened European'.[28] The insertion of
slavery into some kind of equation with transportation is only one of
several such rhetorical equivalences bandied around in the 1790s, all of
which are highly unstable and open to manipulation by advocates at both
ends of the political spectrum.[29] Another popular pro-slavery argument,
which again attempts to map the exotic of slavery onto more familiar
terrain, was the cliché that there really was no difference in the condition
of West Indian slaves and Britain's labouring poor, an analogy which
invited the comically seditious inversion given it by Coleridge in an anti-
slavery lecture of 1795, delivered in the slaving port of Bristol: 'I appeal to
common sense whether to affirm that the Slaves are as well off as our
Peasantry, be not the same as to assert that our Peasantry are as bad off as
Negro Slaves – and whether if the Peasantry believed it there is a man
amongst them who [would] not rebel? and be justified in Rebellion?'[30]

Granville Sharp's blueprint for Sierra Leone may have been drawn up
along the most generous, even utopian, lines of justice, equality and self-
governance,[31] but the horrors of slavery and transportation, and their
connection with one another, shadow many of the early perceptions of
this colony. Falconbridge's narrative is no exception. At Spithead in
January 1791, as she waited to set sail, full of anxiety and foreboding, she
nevertheless confessed to her correspondent that she had witnessed a sight
which challenged her to re-assess some of her fears regarding her voyage:

> The only thing that has attracted my notice in the harbour, is the fleet
> with convicts for Botany Bay, which are wind bound, as well as
> ourselves.
>
> The destiny of such numbers of my fellow creatures has made what I
> expect to encounter, set lighter upon my mind than it ever did before;
> nay, nothing could have operated a reconciliation so effectually: for as
> the human heart is more susceptible of distress conveyed by the eye,
> than when represented by language however ingen[i]ously pictured
> with misery, so the sight of those unfortunate beings, and the thoughts

SLAVERY AND FAMINE,

PUNISHMENTS FOR SEDITION;

OR,

AN ACCOUNT

OF THE

MISERIES AND STARVATION

AT

BOTANY BAY.

By GEORGE THOMPSON,
Who failed in the ROYAL ADMIRAL, May, 1792,

WITH SOME

PRELIMINARY REMARKS.

By GEORGE DYER, B. A.
LATE OF EMANUEL COLLEGE, CAMBRIDGE;
AUTHOR OF THE COMPLAINTS OF THE POOR.

PRINTED FOR J. RIDGWAY, YORK STREET,
ST. JAMES'S SQUARE.

MDCCXCIV.

Plate 3 Title-page of George Thompson's *Slavery and Famine, Punishments for Sedition* (1794).
Source: Mitchell Library, State Library of New South Wales.

of what they are to endure, have worked more forcibly on my feelings, than all the accounts I ever read or heard of wretchedness before.

In 1791 it is the Third Fleet which emotionally complicates Falconbridge's historical understanding of her voyage, but from the First Fleet onwards transportation had played a bedevilling part in shaping ideas about the Sierra Leone enterprise. Instead of appearing as opposites – a haven for poor blacks and a hell for white felons – Sierra Leone and Botany Bay looked troublingly similar. According to Granville Sharp, instead of the 700 (mainly) poor blacks who agreed to go out to Sierra Leone, only 439 embarked in the Royal Navy ships in February 1787, the rest scared off by the fact that the ships for Africa were fitting out at the same time as the First Fleet.[32] The other deterrent for black colonists was Sierra Leone itself. With its estuary, deep channels, and well-populated adjacent territories, it had long been a centre for British and other European slave traders. The distrust of Sharp's black 'orphans' was well summarized at the time by two outspoken 'Sons of Africa', Ottobah Cugoano and Olaudah Equiano. Despite their friendship with Sharp, and their initial enthusiasm for the idea of a 'Province of Freedom', these two ex-slaves came quickly to question the motives of a Government which simultaneously sanctioned slavery and sponsored an attempt to abolish it. They asked: '*Doth a fountain send forth at the same place sweet water and bitter?* ... can it be readily conceived that government would establish a free colony for them nearly on the spot, while it supports its forts and garrisons, to ensnare, merchandize, and to carry others into captivity and slavery.'[33] A similar scepticism could be applied to the simultaneous creation of Sierra Leone and Botany Bay – the first supposedly founded upon the noblest principles, the second so obviously an expedient, cruel and unjust measure.

Falconbridge's shudder at the uncomfortable proximity of Botany Bay and her own destination – the haphazard, even serendipitous distinction between their fates as colonies – is very much a harbinger of the way in which her narrative destabilizes and brings into ironic conjunction notions of transportation and of repatriation, exile and return, the convict and the free. Even the ship hired by her husband's abolitionist employers to carry them to Sierra Leone belonged to a prosperous London slave trading firm, whose proprietors had only recently justified to Parliament their sale in Sierra Leone of five of Sharp's original black settlers to a French slaver.[34] For the moment, though, as Falconbridge looks across at the Third Fleet, she takes comfort from the contrast between her own freely chosen exile and that of the miserable felons. As it turned out, her pity for the miserable fate of the Third Fleet's transportees was to prove well-founded. Since the *Gorgon* sailed into Port Jackson at the same time as this fleet, Mary Ann Parker gives us a graphic eye-witness account of the convicts' shocking condition upon arrival. So appalling was the spectacle of the dead and dying that Captain Parker was commissioned to write a report, part of which is inserted into his wife's narrative. According to Parker's report on the *Queen*, the explanation for the high mortality of its Irish transportees lay in the nature of the Government's contracts with private firms, such that 'the more of them that die, the more it redounds to the interest of the ship-owners and masters, who are paid so much a-head by government, for each individual, whether they arrive in the colony or not'. Although the method differed, the net result bore an uncanny resemblance to the worst excesses of the insurance claims wielded by ship-owners in the slave trade.[35]

The juxtaposition and interconnection of Botany Bay and Sierra Leone in this period can be seen in Erasmus Darwin's *Botanic Garden*, published in 1792, which reproduced on the same page engravings of two Wedgwood cameos (*Plate 4*).[36] The larger of the two is an allegorical design which had also been used on the title-page of *The Voyage of Governor Phillip to Botany Bay* (1789) (*Plate 5*), where it was explicated by the legend: 'Hope encouraging Art and Labour, under the influence of Peace, to pursue the employments necessary to give security and happiness to an infant settlement'. This idealized cameo was accompanied by a strikingly optimistic and visionary poem, 'Visit of Hope to Sydney-Cove, near Botany-Bay', in which Darwin imagines an illustrious civilization arising on the site of the new colony. Lulling to sleep 'the troubled air' and 'tossing deep' of this turbulent new infant colony, Hope magisterially proclaims a new birth, in a manner foreshadowing Kubla Khan's decree for reclaiming the wilderness of Xanadu. The new birth imagined by Darwin is one which involves a type of forgetting, a willed amnesia about the origins and grim purpose of Botany Bay:

> *There* shall broad streets their stately walls extend,
> The circus widen, and the crescent bend;
> *There*, ray'd from cities o'er the cultur'd land,
> Shall bright canals, and solid roads expand.–
> *There* the proud arch, Colossus-like, bestride
> Yon glittering streams, and bound the chafing tide;
> Embellish'd villas crown the landscape scene,
> Farms wave with gold, and orchards blush between.–
> *There* shall tall spires, and dome-capt towers ascend,
> And piers and quays their massy structures blend;
> While with each breeze approaching vessels glide,
> And northern treasures dance on every tide![37]

Despite the up-to-date specificity of the location referred to in the title – Sydney Cove – Darwin's poem is happily unconstrained by personal acquaintance with the colony. Written before the First Fleet annalists published their decidedly ambivalent, first-hand encounters with the colony, the allegory forms part of a long-standing fantasy about a great southern

Copied from Capt. Phillip's Voyage
to Botany Bay, by permission of the Proprietor.

Plate 4 Two Wedgwood medallions from Erasmus Darwin, *The Botanic Garden* (1791),
opp. p. 87.
Source: Rare Book and Special Collections Library, University of Sydney.

THE
VOYAGE
OF
GOVERNOR PHILLIP
TO
BOTANY BAY;

with an

Account of the Establishment of the Colonies of

PORT JACKSON & NORFOLK ISLAND;

compiled from Authentic Papers,

which have been obtained from the several Departments.

to which are added,

The Journals of Lieut.ᵗ Shortland, Watts, Ball, & Cap.ᵗ Marshall,

with an Account of their New Discoveries

embellished with fifty five Copper Plates.

The Maps and Charts taken from Actual Surveys,

& the Plans & Views drawn on the Spot,

by Capt. Hunter, Lieut.ᵗ Shortland, Watts, Dawes, Bradley, Capt. Marshall, &c.

LONDON
Printed for John Stockdale, Piccadilly.

MDCCLXXXIX.

Plate 5 Title-page of *The Voyage of Governor Phillip to Botany Bay* (1789) depicting the Wedgwood medallion: 'Hope encouraging Art and Labour, under the influence of Peace, to pursue the employments necessary to give security and happiness to an infant settlement'. *Source:* Rare Book and Special Collections Library, University of Sydney.

land mass, a place of the future 'call'd the *South-Sea*' in Daniel Defoe's fictional *A New Voyage round the World*: 'new Worlds, new Nations, and new inexhaustible Funds of Wealth and Commerce, such as never were yet known to the Merchants of *Europe*'.[38] Mary Ann Parker's own flattering account of the colony is not untouched by this legend; for instance, of the new settlement at Parramatta she records that she was 'surprised to find that so great a progress had been made', but the description she gives us puts into more modest perspective Darwin's vision of the colony's promising commercial, agricultural and architectural prospects. 'There is a very good level road,' she writes, 'of great breadth, that runs nearly a mile in a straight direction from the landing place to the Governor's house, which is a small convenient building, placed upon a gentle ascent, and surrounded by about a couple of acres of garden ground: this spot is called Rose-Hill. On both sides of the road are small thatched huts, at an equal distance from each other' (*Plate 6*). Watkin Tench, weary of the colony and eager to be home, joked that Parramatta's main street was 'of such breadth as will make Pall-Mall and Portland-Place "hide their diminished heads" '.[39]

The second cameo, 'the poor fetter'd SLAVE on bended knee/ From Britain's sons imploring to be free', needed little introduction or explanation from Darwin.[40] As the emblem of the abolitionist movement, the kneeling slave had adorned thousands of seals and cameos throughout the late 1780s; women wore the design on pins in their hair, men sported it on rings, on shirt-pins, or as coat-buttons. It is, of course, a problematic image; the manacled and supplicating slave seems doubly captured by chains and by discourse, the ventriloquized Christian motto floating above his head: 'Am I not a man and a brother'. Carl Wadstrom's enthusiastic *Essay on Colonization*,[41] the first volume of which was published the same year as Falconbridge's *Two Voyages*, reproduces the image of the kneeling slave in his book, suggesting that the Wedgwood cameo would make a good seal for the Bulama colony, the rival West African 'free' settlement going forward at the same time as Sierra Leone (*Plate 7*). However, in the 'Nautical Map' Wadstrom designed for his *Essay*, he frees up the slave's kneeling posture, and his hands are no longer joined together in prayer but extended towards Europe (*Plate 8*). But if Europe resembles Wedgwood's Hope, by 1794 she has been re-conceived as a revolutionary Liberty, offering the slave freedom via the symbols of civilization (the small temple) and agriculture (the horse and spade).[42] A less conditional promise of liberation to blacks can be seen in the engraving 'La Nature' (*c*. 1790), where a bountiful maternal France devotes one breast each to her black and white infants, whose fraternal, twinned, bonds are reinforced by their tiny hand-shake across her abdomen (*Plate 9*).

Wadstrom's 'Nautical Map' thus brings together Wedgwood's kneeling slave and his figure of Hope, with Liberty as the bridge spanning the gulf

Plate 6 'A view of the Governor's House at Rose-Hill, in the Township of Parramatta', from David Collins, *An Account of the English Colony in New South Wales* (1798), opp. p. 125. According to Collins, the thatched huts, made of wattle and plaster, were placed at a distance of sixty feet from each other as a 'useful precaution against fire' (p. 126).
Source: Rare Book and Special Collections Library, University of Sydney.

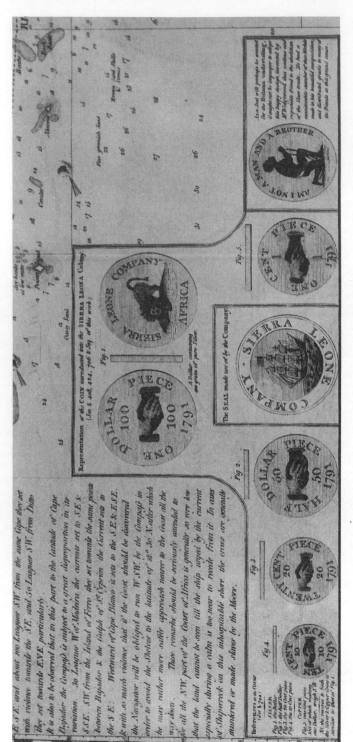

Plate 7 'Representation of the Coin introduced into the Sierra Leona Colony', from Carl Wadstrom, *An Essay on Colonization* (1794). The illustration also shows the seal made use of by the Company, and the Wedgwood kneeling slave as a possible seal for Bulama.
Source: Social Sciences and Humanities Library, University of New South Wales.

Plate 8 'Nautical Map', from Carl Wadstrom, *An Essay on Colonization* (1794).
Source: Cambridge University Library; by permission of the Syndics of Cambridge University Library.

Plate 9 'La Nature' (Anonyme, *c.* 1790), Musée Carnavalet, Paris.
Source: Photothèques des Musées de la Ville de Paris; photographer Lyliane Degraces.

between the two continents of Africa and Europe. The map exemplifies the central argument of Wadstrom's *Essay*, that liberty and civilization in Africa could only be achieved through colonization and 'legitimate' trade; not the trade in human flesh, that wicked 'illegitimate' off-spring of white and black contact on the coast, but a new trade, fuelled by fanciful speculation as to the viability and export potential of African produce, and the vision of ship-loads of European manufactures, Darwin's 'northern treasures', dancing on every tide. For passionate abolitionists like Wadstrom the argument was a simple one, and it was exemplified by the design of the Sierra Leone coins – a black hand clasping a white one (*Plate 7*). This hand-shake was indeed a symbol of fraternity, but it was also a symbol of commercial transaction. British traders would make more money if they treated Africans as fellow traders and customers rather than as merchandise – instead of selling them, the idea was to buy their native produce, and sell them goods,[43] an argument which reflected Britain's new interest in importing raw materials and exporting domestic manufactures. Such a mutually beneficial exchange of raw materials and domestic manufacture was also envisaged for Botany Bay. The Wedgwood medallion of Hope at Sydney-Cove neatly exemplified the process: fashioned from Botany Bay clay sent home by Governor Phillip for analysis, copies of the porcelain medallion were sent out to the colony 'to shew the inhabitants what their materials would do'.[44]

Wadstrom's fantasy of brotherhood, colonization and trade can be seen in his utopian sketch of the stately avenues of trees and orderly warehouses on an imaginary pier at Bulama (*Plate 10*). The settlement as actually planned was a much more sordid affair, grasped at eagerly by 'half-pay officers, decayed gentlemen and dissolute adventurers',[45] many of whom had applied (unsuccessfully) to go out to Sierra Leone. Subscriptions for funding the cost of the settlement were called for in 1791, with the island auctioned off in a London coffee-house at the rate of 500 acres for each £30 subscribed. As one sceptical commentator noted, with £9000 eagerly paid in within a month, the trustees 'were to grant to the subscribers *one hundred and fifty thousand acres of land* in a country of which they had not obtained *one inch* of territory'.[46] If this was a bad beginning, matters were only to get worse, for unlike the Directors of the Sierra Leone Company who at least employed some personnel familiar with Africa, the leaders of the Bulama expedition had no such qualifications. In the end, 275 would-be colonists set sail, some of whom imprudently went ashore on the beautiful island, 'strolling about night and day, wherever they chose; some seeking crabs and muscles, others taking oysters from the mangrove branches; while many were inland botanizing, or hunting after lizards; and others chasing butterflies, and some elephants'.[47] Inevitably they were attacked. Six were killed, four badly injured, seven women and children kidnapped, and the rest dispersed. The almost laughable absurdity of this badly planned venture did not go unremarked in

Plate 10 'Plan of the Island of Bulama', from Carl Wadstrom, *An Essay on Colonization* (1794).
Source: Cambridge University Library; by permission of the Syndics of Cambridge University Library.

England, with one commentator writing sarcastically of the colonists' taking possession 'by hoisting the British flag': 'The natives, not understanding *this mode* by which their property was conveyed to strangers, made an unexpected attack on the newcomers'.[48]

In addition to an economy of commodity exchange, Wadstrom shared many abolitionists' hopes of extensive agricultural cultivation in Africa, undertaken by 'free' or wage labour. Natives and colonists could together cultivate the sugar-cane and other crops, he argued, thus undermining the plantation system of the West Indies. At several points in his *Essay*, Wadstrom imagines West Africa as a giant plantation, with black labourers (free natives and black settlers) ruled over by white overseers. In many ways this was essentially the vision underpinning the Sierra Leone Company's so-called 'mutual interchange of commodities'.[49] To the dismay of the 'free' Nova Scotians who sailed in the belief that they would own their own land, the Company imposed annual quit-rents on their allotments, thus effectively owning their labour.[50] Instead of finding the independence and equality with whites which had eluded them in Nova Scotia, the loyalist blacks soon saw themselves as utterly dependent upon the whims and prejudices of their paternalist employers. The bitter experience of betrayed promises in Nova Scotia was to be re-played in Sierra Leone. It might also be argued that the Company's policy in West Africa was writ large in the choice of Clarkson's two successors, William Dawes and Zachary Macaulay. Dawes had just served three voluntary years in Botany Bay; Macaulay had recently returned from overseeing a slave plantation in Jamaica.[51] Of the latter appointment Anna Maria Falconbridge wrote sarcastically: 'Tis not to be questioned that the prejudices of such an education must impress him with sentiments favorable to the slave trade, and consequently I should not suppose him qualified for a member of Administration in a colony, formed mostly of *blacks*, founded on principles of *freedom*, and for the *express purpose* of abolishing the slave Trade'. In effect Falconbridge is asking the same question as Cugoano and Equiano: can a fountain send forth at the same place sweet water and bitter? By the end of 1794, some of the more disaffected Nova Scotians were answering this question emphatically in the negative. Freetown was re-named 'A Town of Slavery', and when the French destroyed the settlement some of the black settlers welcomed the attack as a liberation.[52] For this group of settlers Falconbridge's *Two Voyages* was to become a 'favourite book'. Isaac Anderson, one of the black petitioners to London in 1793, made himself obnoxious to the authorities in Freetown by reading aloud relevant passages during arguments over the quit-rents in 1797. He was later executed for his part in the uprising of 1800.[53]

ANNA MARIA FALCONBRIDGE, *TWO VOYAGES* TO *SIERRA LEONE*

> *for the Authoress is open to conviction, and if convicted on this occasion, she will with all due deference* kiss the rod of correction.

As her narrative makes plain, Anna Maria Falconbridge had no intention whatsoever of venting her rage by kissing the rod which had punished her. Indeed, the image of such a double chastisement, dealt out by patriarchal authority to children and other subordinates, is ironically positioned at the opening of a text in which the author's 'infant pen' rises up rebelliously against a misguided and oppressive paternalism. If the infant colony of Sierra Leone was growing up to be a refractory child rather than a docile and obedient one, then the responsibility for that lay wholly, she argues, at the feet of its absentee 'father' in London, the Directors of the Sierra Leone Company. It could even be argued that, from the start, this particular colonial infant was destined to be a turbulent and dissatisfied child. Sharp's trope of the 'ill-thriven swarthy daughter' reminds us of the inequality built into the paternalist, colonial relationship – the inequality of his unquestioned authority as a wealthy white male, and the disenfranchised, dependent condition of women and blacks in the late eighteenth century. Falconbridge was acutely aware of her relative insignificance, her subordinated 'child' status vis-à-vis the prestigious Company, with its board of prominent, wealthy abolitionists, several of whom, like Wilberforce, were amongst the most powerful men in the land. Realistically, she chose irony as the best weapon to brandish at the outset, whilst prudently seeking 'protection' for her 'infant pen' from her native, slave-trading port of Bristol.[54]

John Clarkson, who brought the loyalist blacks from Nova Scotia to Sierra Leone, is the good father figure of Falconbridge's story, a mild and kindly first governor who did his best, in unpromising circumstances, to fulfil the promises which he in good faith believed had been made to the loyalists by the Company's Directors. His rule in Sierra Leone did not go unchallenged by the blacks,[55] and there is more than a hint of arrogance in his belief, reported by Falconbridge, that by lifting up his finger he could do what he pleased with them. Nevertheless, he prized the settlers as potentially first-rate colonists, and despaired when they grew disaffected by the mismanagement and corruption of the petty white officers placed over them.[56] Surviving letters from the Nova Scotians often refer to his sweet and gentle behaviour, 'as kind and tender to us as if he was our Father'.[57] In contrast, Botany Bay's William Dawes was the bad father figure, both for Falconbridge and for the black settlers. His severe demeanour and remote, autocratic behaviour, whilst suitable, Falconbridge wrote, 'for a Colony formed wholly of Convicts, and governed by the iron rod of despotism, should be scrupulously guarded against in one like this, whose *basis is Liberty and Equality'*. Clarkson held similar reservations about Dawes's appointment, noting in his journal that the 'arbitrary proceedings' of a penal colony would never do as a model for Sierra Leone because the Nova Scotians required careful handling, having been 'deceived through life' by whites.[58] Later, incensed by the news that the Company had dismissed Clarkson, and that Dawes was to be their new governor, the Nova Scotians lost no time in capitalizing on the recent sensational news from France. With some glee, Falconbridge tells us they intimidated their new ruler by 'reminding him of the recent melancholy fate of Louis XVI. and threat[e]ning something similar to him, if he did not instantly acquiesce with some demand they made relating to provisions'.

If bad, despotic fathers abound in this tale, we also have in Alexander Falconbridge the tyrannical, capricious husband. This marriage seems to have been a mistake from the start, with Falconbridge unsympathetically presenting her new husband as a hot-tempered and argumentative zealot in the anti-slavery cause. There is no doubt that he was a courageous man, an invaluable ally in Thomas Clarkson's campaign to lay first-hand evidence of the slave trade's barbarity before the House of Commons. But he had a weakness for drink, and by all accounts was brutal to his wife.[59] Thus, when he obligingly killed himself with drink on the second trip out, Falconbridge bluntly informs her correspondent that she has no regrets, and promptly re-marries another Company employee – Isaac DuBois, a cotton-planter and prosperous American loyalist from a southern slave-holding family.[60] Indeed, her two marriages, the first in 1791, the second in 1793, reflect the waning popularity of abolitionism as it became more closely associated with radicalism. Towards the end of 1793, after leaving Sierra Leone for the last time, Falconbridge hears that Wilberforce and Tom Paine have been burnt together in effigy at Kingston, Jamaica. Although ostensibly offended by the bracketing of Wilberforce with that 'incendiary' Paine, she nevertheless couples them as extremists. Wilberforce's abolitionist zealotry springs, she writes, from 'too keen notions of humanity, and too zealous a desire of doing good.'

While the Company's *Report* of 1794 may have provided the immediate provocation for Falconbridge's *Two Voyages*, there is no doubt that her book seeks to undermine the authoritative moral position of her first husband's well-known *Account of the Slave Trade*, published in 1788.[61] Certainly one reviewer of *Two Voyages* made the connection between husband and wife, cross-referencing her book with his horrifically detailed and explicit description of the sufferings of the middle passage.[62] Clearly, six years later, the *Account* still had currency in any discussion of Africa or of the slave trade. On the first of her two journeys to Sierra Leone, Falconbridge begins to complicate her first husband's anti-slavery case by dramatically positioning herself between the English slave traders on Bance Island and an abolitionist husband who, in refusing to fraternize with those 'diabolical' traders, imprisons her on board the Company's trading vessel. Placing herself in the position of the captive slave, she describes herself as 'pent up in a floating cage, without room, to walk about, stand erect, or even to lay at length'. Ironically, socializing with the 'genteel' slave traders on Bance Island seems like freedom compared to the coarse slavery of her marriage to an abolitionist.[63] Furthermore, by the time of her happy second marriage she has won through, she says, to a new independence of mind, one which argues that slavery is the only efficient and rational economy for the present (in this she proves herself to be a true daughter of Bristol). Two years later, with second husband in tow, she leaves Sierra Leone for good on the *Nassau*, a Bristol slave ship commanded by her brother, Captain Morley.[64] Complete with human cargo en route to England via Jamaica, the *Nassau* sounds like the eighteenth-century equivalent of a luxury liner. Although Falconbridge is apprehensive of being 'exposed to indelicacies, too offensive for the eye of an English woman' she is 'agreeably disappointed' by the excellent food, accommodation and care given to the slaves. Yet again the aim is to subvert her first husband's well-known description of the slaves' appallingly cramped conditions and inedible food.[65]

Falconbridge's encounter with Africa is relatively unique in offering us the story of a woman's attempt to find her feet in an infant, rather than settled, colonial venture. Unlike later wives who accompanied their husbands to far-flung places where the hierarchies of gender, race and class appeared to be rigidly in place, and where racial segregation and the public/private spheres were more clearly delineated, Falconbridge finds herself in a more fluid and unformed environment. Motivated primarily by an appetite for new and exciting adventure, she does not view herself as the standard-bearer of civilization to a benighted world. Quite the contrary: if anything, she is something of a rogue, conspicuously lacking in the stricter codes of propriety familiar to us in English women travellers of a later period. Adultery, polygamy, male gullibility and female wit, the difficulties of reading other cultures: all these topics crop up humorously in the narrative. One of the funniest incidents begins with a self-parodying moment of reversal, when the female spectator is suddenly transformed into the spectacle: 'The people on the island crowded to see me; they gazed with apparent astonishment—I suppose at my dress, for white women could not be a novelty to them, as there were several among the unhappy people sent out here by government'. While the people on the island stare at Falconbridge's attire, she stares back at their 'native garbs'. The offence against 'delicacy' caused by their nakedness gives way, she writes, to the supposedly more comforting sight of other black women apparently 'of superior rank, at least I concluded so from the preferable way in which they were clad; nor was I wrong in my conjecture, for upon enquiring who they were, was informed one was the *woman* or *mistress* of Mr. ——, another of Mr. B ——, and so on: I then understood that every gentleman on the island had his *lady*'. Falconbridge's satirical play here with notions of delicacy and indelicacy, non-dress and European dress, the white lady and the black lady: all this is part of a sharp-eyed narrative which enjoys exposing the arbitrariness and unreliability of codes, such as those associated with dress and manners.

Dress figures largely in Falconbridge's narrative, as it does throughout many of the late eighteenth-century records of cross-cultural encounters on this part of the coast. One of the reasons for this was the need to keep up appearances in situations fraught with racial and political tension. Throughout his journal, John Clarkson stressed the importance of appearing confident and in command of the situation, even when there was reason to feel quite otherwise.[66] For instance, he went to great lengths to prepare for his first meeting with the local head-man, Naimbana, whom he regarded as an 'absolute' ruler,[67] ordering the Company's ships to fire off their cannons upon his approach, and placing the whole colony under arms to salute him upon landing. His purpose was twofold: to pay due deference to Naimbana, but also (nervously) to impress upon him some idea of the colony's fire-power.[68] Both men decked themselves out in ceremonial dress: Clarkson 'in a full-dress Windsor uniform, with a brilliant star, etc., etc.', Naimbana with

> a sky-blue silk jacket with silver lace, striped cotton trowsers, ruffled shirt, green morocco slippers, a cocked-hat with gold lace, and a white cotton cap, for which a large old judge's wig was afterwards substituted. He had a belt round his neck from which hung the figure of a lamb bearing a cross set with rays formed of paste.[69]

If Clarkson thought the king cut a comical figure, he kept his thoughts to himself, which was more than could be said for Naimbana who could barely restrain himself from laughing out loud at the sight of his counterpart, exclaiming: 'That he had never seen so young a king before'.[70] That Naimbana was an experienced and clever negotiator, well-accustomed to making the whites dance to his tune, is evident in this and all the other records which survive of him. Clarkson noted, for instance, that although Naimbana spoke and understood a little English, 'on matters of business, he always spoke through his interpreter', a process drawn out to such fatiguing length and complexity 'as to occasion strong hysterics' in Clarkson as soon as he got away. Alexander Falconbridge also found the palavers protracted and stressful, believing at one point that Naimbana and the other chiefs were only 'bamboozling' him. Naimbana spelt out his position bluntly to Falconbridge, saying 'he liked the English in preference to all white men, tho' he considered every white man as a *rogue*, and consequently saw them with a jealous eye'. Like other prosperous coastal chiefs he prized education as the essential key to his people's ability to trade equally with the Europeans, but he also believed in keeping his options open: one son he sent to France, another to

A Representation of my first Conference with the Natives.

Plate 11 'A Representation of my first Conference with the Natives', from John Matthews, *A Voyage to the River Sierra-Leone* (2nd edn, 1791). 'Imagine to yourself the shore of a little sandy bay covered with black men, women, and children. Under the shade of a tree sat the king in an arm-chair, dressed in a suit of blue silk, trimmed with silver lace, with a laced hat and ruffled shirt, and shoes and stockings. On each side sat his principal people, and behind him two or three of his wives' (p. 4).

Source: Cambridge University Library; by permission of the Syndics of Cambridge University Library.

England, a third he entrusted to Muslim clerics. In the lore of a coastal people who had dealt with Europeans for centuries: ' "Read book, and learn to be *rogue* so well as white man;" for they say, if white men could not read, or wanted education, they would be no better rogues than *black gentlemen'*.

Falconbridge's first encounter with Naimbana resembles Clarkson's in its theatricality, and in its highly wrought, even dangerous comedy. Unlike Clarkson, though, she did not have to conduct serious business with the old king, so her account is more satirical. At first, when they arrive in Robana town, they catch Naimbana in undress, 'in a loose white frock and trowsers'. Half an hour later he re-appears, attired for the occasion 'in a purple embroidered coat, white sattin waistcoat and breeches, *thread stockings*, and his left side emblazoned with a flaming star; his legs to be sure were *harliquined*, by a number of holes in the stockings, through which his black skin appeared' (*Plate 11*). Naimbana's real self, anything but regal in Falconbridge's eyes, peeps clownishly through the worn-out stockings, puncturing all illusion of ceremony and reducing the scene to the level of pantomime. Naimbana appears before her as just another of Robana town's 'raree-shows', a term evocative of the world of popular fairs where freaks and oddities, such as hermaphrodites, dwarfs, giants and other 'curiosities', were displayed, including, of course, Hottentots and American Indians.[71]

The parti-coloured, 'harliquined' stockings are the one constant feature of what are to be no less than three costume changes in a single afternoon; at one point, when he reappears in a black velvet suit, Falconbridge writes:

> I often had an inclination to offer my services to close the holes: but was fearful least my needle might blunder into his *Majesty*'s leg, and start the blood, for drawing the blood of an African King, I am informed, whether occasioned by accident or otherwise, is punished with death: the dread of this only prevented me.

Naimbana may be a figure of fun for Falconbridge, but as the stockings remind us, he is a harlequin too, with a mischievous, dangerous edge to his performance.[72] In some ways her description of him fits Bakhtin's notion of the carnival-grotesque: buffoon-like and comic, this 'King of Kings' is also formless and a bit terrifying, an unfinished body whose apertures cannot be closed.[73] The parti-coloured appearance of his lower body, part black skin, part pale fabric, also reflects his mixed-blood ancestry: 'the features of his face resemble a European more than any black I have seen', comments Falconbridge; 'he was seldom without a smile on his countenance, but I think his smiles were suspicious'. So convinced did Falconbridge become of Naimbana's malign intentions towards the settlement that she 'swooned into hystericks' at one of the natives' initial, lengthy palavers. The inadvertent revelation of her fear and suspicions severely impeded the course of negotiations, as her husband was quick to point out to her.

Falconbridge's *Two Voyages* is relatively unmarked by the commonplaces of racist hostility so often applied by travellers to African natives: that they were lazy, treacherous and revengeful.[74] On the contrary, it is a point of pride in her narrative that she enjoyed such friendly, even flirtatious, relations with the local chiefs. King Jemmy, for instance, in some respects the settlement's greatest enemy, she regarded as a man of his word, and a man of sensibility. That he always came to see her before anyone else exposed the bogus authority of the men supposedly in charge. She even agreed to stand hostage for him when he stipulated that this was the only condition on which he would consent to go on board one of the Company's ships.[75] With Naimbana she is on less certain ground, as we have seen, but in one of her early 'courtly encounters' with him she triumphs in the knowledge that she is the only woman ever to sit down and eat with him.[76] They are also the only ones to eat dinner with silver forks, and this flattering notice is further enhanced by Naimbana's gift of 'two beautiful pines'.

Falconbridge was not shy of emphasizing the sensational and unprecedented nature of her voyage to the 'inhospitable Coast of Africa'. This was her maiden voyage, she tells us, and her story is chequered throughout 'with such a complication of disasters as I may venture to affirm have never yet attended any of my *dear Country Women*, and such as I sincerely hope they never may experience'. In some ways, though, because her authorship is proof of her survival, we are less impressed by the physical dangers she encounters than by those moments of psychological danger, when inadvertently and unexpectedly she is ensnared by some twist or complication in the threads of her narrative. One of these disconcerting moments occurs at Bance Island House, where she is about to dine with her new friends, the slave traders. Happening to stroll to one of the windows, she looks out only to find herself confronted by the Dantesque vision of the slave yard, with 'between two and three hundred wretched victims, chained and parcelled out in circles, just satisfying the cravings of nature from a trough of rice placed in the centre of each circle'. So horrible is the sight, and yet so insatiable her 'female curiosity', that she assures her correspondent that she 'avoided the prospects from this side of the house ever after'.[77]

MARY ANN PARKER, *A VOYAGE ROUND THE WORLD*

Nothing very extraordinary is related, for nothing extraordinary happened: but, if the particulars do not fill us with astonishment, neither do they excite our incredulity by the marvellous, with which travellers are so apt to embellish their relations.

(*Monthly Review*, May–August, 1796, p. 112)

It is not at all true that nothing extraordinary happened on Mary Ann Parker's voyage round the world. The return journey alone was remarkable for a number of incidents, not least of which was the captured shark with the First Fleet convict's prayer book in its belly. Another serendipitous connection with First Fleet convicts occurred at the Cape where the *Gorgon* took on board the escaped convict Mary Bryant and some of her surviving fellow fugitives, all of whom had sailed from Port Jackson in an open boat to Timor. Tench, for one, was simply astounded by these escapees' 'heroic struggle for liberty'. Also, having travelled out with these convicts to the colony four years earlier, he reflected as well on the strange combination of circumstances which had brought them together once again, circumstances which could only 'baffle human foresight, and confound human speculation'.[78] Parker makes little of these and other incidents, but despite her best intentions of maintaining a smooth, uninterrupted surface, full of witty accounts of pleasant excursions, dinner parties and picnics, her travel narrative is, like Falconbridge's, occasionally troubled by 'female curiosity'. For instance, on the journey out, after arriving safely at the Cape, and having had a good night's sleep on shore, Parker arises in the morning 'particularly thankful to Providence for His protection'. Her prayers of gratitude are, however, immediately greeted by the disturbing sight of the *Gorgon*'s ship-wrecked predecessor:

> Curiosity then directed my steps to a window, whence I beheld the small remains of his Majesty's ship the Guardian ... To avoid as much as possible any disagreeable reflections which might arise from the idea of a probability of our sharing the fate of the above vessel ... I hastened to my companions, and was, for the first time, surprized with a Cape breakfast ...

Similarly, near the Falkland Islands on its return journey, the *Gorgon* encountered numerous ice-islands, whose 'pleasing and grotesque' shapes would have been more thoroughly enjoyed, she tells us, had she been able to divest her mind of the 'horror' occasioned by reflections on the number of navigators 'arrested and frozen to death in the midst of these tremendous masses'.

Having found her sea-legs on earlier travels in France, Spain and Italy, Parker is much more low-keyed than Falconbridge about her journey, even though she describes it as one 'to the remotest parts of the globe'. Of course, unlike Falconbridge, who had only Matthews's book to precede her, Parker was writing amidst a spate of recent publications on the colony at Botany Bay.[79] There were, however, aspects of her book she might have capitalized on, such as its being the first account of the colony written by a woman; there was also the 'rare circumstance', as one reviewer put it, of seeing 'a female name in the list of circumnavigators.'[80] But bolstered by her ample and distinguished list of subscribers, Parker no doubt felt it would be beneath her dignity to puff her own work; self-advertisement would also have jarred somewhat with the genteel persona of the retired, impecunious widow. So, rather than dwell on the many discomforts associated with the journey out, she alludes briefly to 'a fortnight's seasoning and buffeting', after which she begins to enjoy herself: 'with the polite attention of the officers on board, and my amiable companion Mrs. King, we glided over many a watery grave with peace of mind, and uninterrupted happiness'. Similarly, on the return journey, we hear little of the ship's encounters with wild storms, and virtually nothing of the terrible mortality amongst the marines' children. In contrast, other surviving accounts of the *Gorgon*'s return journey comment movingly on the many children ill and dying: 'the children are going very fast – the hot weather is the reason of it', wrote one marine officer.[81]

Throughout her brisk and entertaining narrative, Parker displays the 'little dash of satire' in her composition noted by one of her husband's officers.[82] Marvelling at the bulk of the Cape Town women, she attributes their fatness to 'going without stays', together with a total neglect of their persons after marriage. Of one of her hostesses, Mrs de Witt, she jokes that her size 'was nearly equal to that of a Dutch man of war'.[83] That her own figure is a good one, we learn from one of the many excursions at the Cape, when a downpour requires her to borrow a jacket, 'one half of which I could have spared with great convenience'. But her most glorious moment in the narrative is the stay at Teneriffe, where her fluency in Spanish enlivened many dinner parties and procured her 'unusual attention' from the people she met. Perhaps the most astonished of all was her muleteer, who when he discovered that she spoke his language, seems to have regarded his charge with almost superstitious reverence. Prior to entering any town or village, he 'with great form, requested me to sit up-right, and then spread my hair very curiously over my shoulders', wishing, she supposed, to show her person off 'to the greatest advantage'.

Parker devotes approximately a third of the book to her stay in Port Jackson. Apart from the appalling glimpse of the dead and dying convicts unloaded from the Third Fleet, she gives a positive view of the colony's infancy. She and her husband enjoyed 'the fatherly attention of the good Governor upon all occasions'; nor, on her optimistic view, were the convicts themselves denied Governor Phillip's benevolent paternalism. No doubt inspired by Phillip's devotion to the Crown (even the *Gorgon* 'dressed ship as well as her scanty allowance of colours would permit' for the anniversary of the King's accession), Parker dubbed him '*The Father of his People*', adding that 'the Convict, who has forsaken the crimes that sent him to this country, looks up to him with reverence, and enjoys the reward of his industry in peace and thankfulness'.[84] This idealized and abstract picture of the redeemed convict as grateful, docile child stands in contrast to Parker's many particularized descriptions of exotic birds, about which she appears to have been quite knowledgeable. But if Parker never gets close enough to the felons to describe them to us, she is very much aware of them as a brooding, invisible presence, for instance during the night she spends at Parramatta where she finds 'every thing perfectly quiet, although surrounded by more than one thousand convicts' (*Plate* 12).

Similarly, if Parker learnt during her stay at Port Jackson of the fear, isolation and deprivation some of the free settlers had been experiencing, she does not speak of these, choosing instead to focus upon the 'pleasant excursions' up the river to Parramatta with her friend Mrs King and other 'Ladies' residing at the colony. One of these ladies was Elizabeth Macarthur, who only the year before had complained in a letter to England of 'having no female friend to unbend my mind to, nor a single Woman with whom I could converse with any satisfaction to myself'.[85] Mrs Parker obviously went some way towards alleviating that want. Describing her new friend as 'a very amiable intelligent Woman', Macarthur now spent 'many pleasant days together' with the new visitor. Indeed, since the arrival of the *Gorgon* and the Third Fleet, she could boast that her 'little Circle has been of late quite brilliant; we are constantly making little parties in boats up & down the various inlets of the Harbour, taking refreshments with us, & dining out under an awning upon some pleasant point of Land, or in some of the Creeks or Coves in which for Twenty miles together these waters abound'. These pleasant 'excursions', as Elizabeth Macarthur called them, were never entirely safe, however, 'a Soldier or two always attending' because of sporadic and hostile 'incursions' by the natives.[86]

The isolation which Elizabeth Macarthur experienced before the arrival of the *Gorgon* was of course not confined to women. In the first year of settlement Watkin Tench complained of 'the listlessness' of camp evenings at Port Jackson, where all was 'quiet and stupid'. Eager for variety of company, and for some news from home, his heart would leap at 'every fleeting speck which arose from the bosom of the sea'.[87] But if the *Gorgon* was rapturously welcomed for its delivery from boredom and isolation, it also brought release from the spectre of starvation. Reactions to the loss of the supply ship *Sirius* in 1790 are indicative of the psychological as well as physical toll this remote and precarious new settlement often took upon its inhabitants. David Collins wrote that the news of the supply ship's loss 'was of itself almost sufficient to have deranged the strongest intellect among us. A load of accumulated evils, seemed bursting at once upon our heads'.[88] Writing of the same episode, Elizabeth Macarthur confessed that 'a Chill seems to overpower my faculties ... a dread comes over me, which I am unable to describe'.[89]

At several points, Parker dips into and transcribes verbatim small sections from Tench's two books on the colony, *A Narrative of the Expedition to Botany Bay* (1789) and *A Complete Account of the Settlement at Port Jackson* (1793). In one topographical passage on 'the face of the country' she names Tench as her source; at other times she simply takes what she needs.[90] Her

Plate 12　Juan Ravenet (*c.* 1766–?), 'Convictos enla Nueva Olanda' (1793), a rare depiction of the colony's convicts.
Source: Dixson Galleries, State Library of New South Wales.

chapter on the natives is also indebted to Tench in the way in which it begins with a 'general view' of a negative kind, especially concerning the natives' physical appearance, then descends to 'particular inspection' of an individual (Banalong, in Parker's case),[91] a scrutiny which paradoxically results in a general 'rise in estimation'.[92] This progress from negative to positive, from height to depth, is also, in both authors, interrupted by an exception-to-the-rule of the natives' physical unattractiveness – in Tench's case the remarkable passage on the 'attractions' of Gooreedeeana; in Parker's text an encounter with an unnamed man of 'a most engaging deportment' and 'pleasing' countenance, to whom she gives her 'travelling knife and fork'. But the passage on Banalong which concludes the chapter marks a significant departure from her source. Whereas for Tench Banalong is war-like and untrustworthy, for Parker he is a creature of exquisite sensibility and 'natural goodness', a tear trickling down his check at the sight of a portrait of Captain Parker, at that time away on duty. Written in London, where Banalong was being paraded around, dressed in the clothes of his civilizers (*Plate 13*), Parker's set-piece on the native's sensibility, together with a quotation from one of the period's best known abolitionist poems, is very much a metropolitan vignette.[93] As such, it forms a striking contrast to her decidedly more ambivalent encounters with natives in the colony, such as the time when she finds herself 'seated in the woods with twelve or fourteen of them, men, women, and children'. Despite being repelled by their unfamiliar appearance, she does not feel fear, she says, being accompanied by a party 'more than sufficient for my protection'. At the same time, however, she confesses that her ease and confidence are a pretence, for should her real feelings of disgust have appeared, the natives 'would have rendered my being in their company not only unpleasant, but unsafe'. Again, as at Sierra Leone, we see the importance for white intruders of keeping up appearances in these new settlements.

When the *Gorgon* sailed out of Port Jackson in December 1791, the spaces occupied on the outward voyage by 'live stock and all kind of necessary provisions' for the colony's survival were now, Parker tells us, 'crowded with Kangaroos, Opposums, and every curiosity which that country produced. The quarter-deck was occupied with shrubs and plants, whilst the cabin was hung around with skins of animals'. There were also many birds, the care of which fell to our author. Parker's contrast between in-coming necessities and out-going curiosities accounts for the somewhat trivializing view of the colony held by the British public. There was already, for instance, a busy commerce in live specimens, the staple of raree-shows for the entertainment of a public eager for displays of the novel, the exotic and the freakish.[94] Governor Phillip also found the colony's specimens and products a valuable means of promoting his own and the settlement's prospects, and a good proportion of the *Gorgon*'s rarer items were ear-marked as gifts for his patrons. But there were also the specimens designed for the royal

Plate 13   Portrait of Bennelong, with his hair dressed in European style, wearing a fashionable frock coat with a high-standing collar (*c.* 1795).
Source: Mitchell Library, State Library of New South Wales.

collections and for learned societies, and for gentlemen like Sir Joseph Banks who subscribed to Mrs Parker's book. Like the clay from Botany Bay which had been sent by Phillip in 1788, scientific analysis of New Holland's productions might possibly yield directions for the colony's future prosperity, including, it was hoped, the colony's eventual financial independence from the mother country. The Parker narrative itself participates in this circular economy of reciprocity and exchange. The very act of writing her narrative, with its naming of all those who had extended their hospitality to her during the long voyage, was to be, in Parker's own pun, the only 'return' she, as a widow, could ever now make.

NOTES

1. For Sierra Leone as a possible destination for convicts, see Ellen Gibson Wilson, *The Loyal Blacks* (New York: Putnam, 1976), pp. 141–42.
2. Mollie Gillen gives a very persuasive account of Government's muddled policy and lack of foresight at this time in 'The Botany Bay Decision, 1786: Convicts, not Empire', *English Historical Review*, vol. 47, no. 385 (October, 1982), pp. 740–66; and see also G. J. Abbott, 'The Botany Bay Decision', *Journal of Australian Studies*, 16 (May, 1985), pp. 21–45.
3. In both Houses of Parliament the choice of Botany Bay was defended as 'a measure of absolute necessity, arising from the crowded state of the jails ... the only remedy for an evil, which required immediate redress' (Gillen, 'The Botany Bay Decision, 1786', pp. 755–56).
4. In London, a small and learned band of Swedenborgians published their utopian *Plan for a Free Community upon the Coast of Africa, under the Protection of Great Britain; but intirely independent of all European Laws and Governments* (London: R. Hindmarsh, 1789). Its authors included two Swedes, Carl Wadstrom (see notes 7, 41) and August Nordenskiold, who died in Sierra Leone after a botched expedition into the interior looking for gold.
5. Granville Sharp (1735–1813). Although I disagree with many of its conclusions, the most detailed account of London's black poor, and the formation of the Sierra Leone colony, is Stephen Braidwood's *Black Poor and White Philanthropists: London's Blacks and the Foundation of the Sierra Leone Settlement, 1786–1791* (Liverpool: Liverpool University Press, 1994). Braidwood's study is unusual in arguing that the Committee and the Government acted at all times with the very best of intentions. Some consideration of the colony's development after 1791 might have led to a rather different reading of the available evidence.
6. Most commentators agree that coercion was used, especially when the time for sailing came round and Government grew impatient with the high number of defections (Wilson, *Loyal Blacks*, pp. 144–51; and Peter Fryer, *Staying Power: The History of Black People in Britain* (London: Pluto Press, 1984), pp. 196–203). Even Braidwood concedes that the Government lost patience and planned some harsh measures (*Black Poor and White Philanthropists*, pp. 139–40).
7. Sierra Leone Company, *Substance of the Report of the Court of Directors of the Sierra Leone Company to the General Court, held at London on Wednesday the 19th of October, 1791* (London: James Phillips, 1792), p. 2 (hereafter *Substance of the Report, 1791*). Carl Wadstrom (see note 41) described these white women as 'chiefly strumpets'; of the 'indigent, unemployed, despised and forlorn' black males he wrote: 'it was necessary they should be sent somewhere, and be no longer suffered to infest the streets of London' in his *An Essay on Colonization, particularly applied to the Western Coast of Africa, with some free thoughts on Cultivation and Commerce; also Brief Descriptions of the colonies already formed, or attempted, in Africa, including those of Sierra Leona and Bulama* (London: Darton and Harvey, 1794–1795), p. 220. It was Anna Maria

Falconbridge's account of an interview with one of the surviving seven of these women that started the controversy over how they came to be included amongst the original settlers. Braidwood devotes an appendix to the issue, but gives no credibility to Falconbridge's version, or to Olaudah Equiano's complaint about 'unauthorised' persons being taken on board (Braidwood, *Black Poor and White Philanthropists*, pp. 280–88).

8. William Dawes (1762–1836), officer of marines, scientist, astronomer and administrator.

9. Watkin Tench, *A Complete Account of the Settlement at Port Jackson, in New South Wales* (London: G. Nicol, 1793), p. 139 (hereafter *Complete Account*). Tench (1758?–1833) was an officer of marines and author of two important books on the Port Jackson colony.

10. Prince Hoare, *Memoirs of Granville Sharp* (London: Henry Colburn, 1820), p. 313 (hereafter *Memoirs*). The letter in which this expression appears is dated 31 October, 1787.

11. Hoare, *Memoirs*, p. 313.

12. Everyone who met Falconbridge commented on his extreme, even violent, temperament. He referred to the slave trade as that 'lump of deformity' (Wilson, *Loyal Blacks*, p. 185).

13. For the history of these black loyalists, see James W. St. G. Walker, 'The Establishment of a Free Black Community in Nova Scotia', in *The African Diaspora: Interpretive Essays*, ed. M. Kilson and R. Rotberg (Cambridge, MA: Harvard University Press, 1976), pp. 205–36; also Wilson, *Loyal Blacks*, passim.

14. *The Voyage of Governor Phillip to Botany Bay; with an account of the establishment of the colonies of Port Jackson & Norfolk Island; compiled from authentic papers* (London: John Stockdale, 1789). Where Stockdale had 458 subscribers, Parker had 400; interestingly, 65 of Parker's subscribers were women compared to Stockdale's 12.

15. For these biographical speculations I am indebted to Gavin Fry's introduction to the Australian National Maritime Museum's limited facsimile edition of Parker's *Voyage Round the World* (Potts Point: Hordern House, 1991).

16. Peter Fryer gives a lively account of the controversy in *Staying Power*, pp. 196–203. See also Wilson, *Loyal Blacks*, pp. 144–53, and Braidwood's *Black Poor and White Philanthropists*, pp. 129–61.

17. Ellen Gibson Wilson, *John Clarkson and the African Adventure* (London: Macmillan, 1980), pp. 58, 79.

18. Stung by the Company's dismissal of him in April 1793, Clarkson admitted to Falconbridge's second husband, Isaac DuBois, that he had 'almost been ready to expose People who are deserving of blame'. But because the colony had so many enemies, he felt 'obliged to be silent' (British Library, Clarkson Papers, MS Add. 41263, vol. 3).

19. *Substance of the Report delivered by the Court of Directors of the Sierra Leone Company, to the General Court of Proprietors, on Thursday the 27th March, 1794* (London: James Phillips, 1794), pp. 10, 18, 25–27 (hereafter *Substance of the Report, 1794*).

20. *The British Critic, a New Review*, vol. 4 (July–August, 1794), p. 555.

21. The same reviewer started his second paragraph: 'If the letters deserve that credit which their internal evidence seems to demand ...', *The Monthly Review; or, Literary Journal*, vol. 16 (January–April, 1795), pp. 102–3.

22. Some clues are the two slips in dating 1794 for 1791 (see *Plate* 2). For the Journal section of her narrative, beginning Jan. 1793, Falconbridge dipped into the journal Isaac DuBois began writing the day after Clarkson left the colony. The addressee of this journal is Clarkson, who had asked DuBois to keep a record (British Library, Clarkson Papers, MS Add. 41263, vol. 3).

23. Anna Laetitia Barbauld, *The Correspondence of Samuel Richardson*, 6 vols (London: Richard Phillips, 1804), vol. 1, p. xxvii.

24. For an excellent study of public and private spheres, and the notion of the 'citizen–critic', see Elizabeth Cook, *Epistolary Bodies: Gender and Genre in the Eighteenth-Century Republic of Letters* (Stanford: Stanford University Press, 1996).

25. Mary Louise Pratt suggests that Falconbridge's book may have been 'sponsored' by a pro-slavery faction, but the cheap production somewhat counts against this theory; see Pratt's *Imperial Eyes: Travel Writing and Transculturation* (London: Routledge, 1992), p. 238. For further discussion of Falconbridge's *Two Voyages*, see my 'Sierra Leone, Slavery, and Sexual Politics: Anna Maria Falconbridge and the "Swarthy Daughter" of Late 18th Century Abolitionism', in *Women's Writing*, vol. 2, no. 1 (1995), pp. 3–23. Other recent commentators on Falconbridge include Moira Ferguson, *Subject to Others: British Women Writers and Colonial Slavery, 1670–1834* (London: Routledge, 1992) and Felicity Nussbaum, 'The Other Woman: Polygamy, *Pamela*, and the Prerogative of Empire', in *Women, 'Race', and Writing in the Early Modern Period*, ed. M. Hendricks and P. Parker (London: Routledge, 1994).

26. John Matthews, *A Voyage to the River Sierra-Leone, on the Coast of Africa; containing an Account of the Trade and Productions of the Country, and of the Civil and Religious Customs and Manners of the People; in a series of Letters to a Friend in England, during his Residence in that Country in the Years 1785, 1786 and 1787. With an additional letter on the African Slave Trade* (London: B. White and Son, 1788), p. 157 (hereafter *Voyage*).

27. Edited by the radical George Dyer, the book is a plea on behalf of the Scottish martyrs. Two editions appeared in 1794, with a slightly different title-page for the second edition.

28. Matthews, *Voyage*, p. 157.

29. Of course, the equivalence was not just rhetorical. The heavy iron shackles and collars of the convicts at Botany Bay prompted one of the soldiers to say, 'thay are the Same as Slaves all the time thay are in this country', quoted by Alan Atkinson, *The Europeans in Australia: A History* (Melbourne: Oxford University Press, 1997), vol. 1, p. 98.

30. Samuel Taylor Coleridge, *Lectures 1795: On Politics and Religion*, ed. L. Patton and P. Mann (Princeton: Princeton University Press, 1971), pp. 250–51. For an analysis of Coleridge and the rhetoric of abolitionism, see my 'Conspicuous

Consumption: White Abolitionism and English Women's Protest Writing in the 1790s', *English Literary History*, 61 (Summer, 1994), pp. 341–62.

31. One of the best accounts of Granville Sharp's abolitionist philosophy and politics is to be found in David Brion Davis, *The Problem of Slavery in the Age of Revolution, 1770–1823* (Ithaca: Cornell University Press, 1975), pp. 386–406.

32. According to Sharp, the blacks were 'deterred by a jealousy which prevailed among them that Government intended to send them to Botany Bay' (Hoare, *Memoirs*, pp. 315–16).

33. Ottobah Cugoano (born *c.* 1757) and Olaudah Equiano (*c.* 1745–1797), prominent abolitionist activists in the 1780s and 1790s. Cugoano is named as the author of *Thoughts and Sentiments on the Evil and Wicked Traffic of the Slavery and Commerce of the Human Species* (London, 1787), but Equiano, best known for his *Interesting Narrative of the Life of Olaudah Equiano, or Gustavus Vassa, the African* (1789), was almost certainly Cugoano's co-author. Paul Edwards outlines the evidence for this in 'Three West African Writers of the 1780s' in *The Slave's Narrative*, ed. C. T. Davis and H. L. Gates (Oxford: Oxford University Press, 1985), pp. 183–87. The Navy Board appointed Equiano 'Commissary on the part of Government' to Sierra Leone, a senior position which would have involved him in land negotiations with the local chiefs. He was dismissed before the ships sailed; for his account of this episode, see the excerpts and editor's notes in *Unchained Voices: An Anthology of Black Authors in the English-speaking World of the 18th Century*, ed. Vincent Carretta (Lexington: University Press of Kentucky, 1996), pp. 283–86, 313–17.

34. See Wilson, *Loyal Blacks*, pp. 164–65.

35. In the infamous 1781 case of the slave ship *Zong*, sick slaves were thrown overboard so that the shipping company could claim their loss as insurance. See James Walvin, *Black Ivory: A History of British Slavery* (London: Harper-Collins, 1992), pp. 16–22.

36. Erasmus Darwin, *The Botanic Garden; A Poem, in Two Parts. Part I. Containing The Economy of Vegetation. Part II. The Loves of the Plants. With Philosophical Notes* (London: J. Johnson, 1791). The first edition was published in June 1792, its 1791 title-page notwithstanding.

37. See Stockdale's *The Voyage of Governor Phillip to Botany Bay* (1789), p. v.

38. Daniel Defoe, *A New Voyage round the World by a Course never sailed before* (London: A. Bettesworth, 1725), Part 1, p. 178.

39. Tench, *Complete Account*, p. 78.

40. Darwin, *The Botanic Garden*, Part I, Canto II, ll. 315–16.

41. Wadstrom was a Swedenborgian and abolitionist who, together with some like-minded colleagues, had dreamt of founding the Church of New Jerusalem on the west coast of Africa.

42. For a revolutionary inflection given to this cameo by a French manufactory at Sevres *c.* 1796, see Bernard Smith, *European Vision and the South Pacific* (Melbourne: Oxford University Press, 2nd edn, 1989), pp. 178–79.

43. This was an economic argument widely used by abolitionists, both English and African. Olaudah Equiano appealed for his fellow Africans to be treated as

customers rather than merchandise in his letter to the Privy Council, 1788, reprinted in *Sierra Leone Inheritance*, ed. C. Fyfe (London: Oxford University Press, 1964), pp. 109–111.

44. *The Botanic Garden*, note to l. 315, p. 87.

45. This was how John Clarkson described them in his journal; see *Sierra Leone after a Hundred Years*, ed. E. G. Ingham (London: Frank Cass & Co, 1968), p. 85 (hereafter Ingham, *Sierra Leone*). When the dispersed colonists sought refuge in Freetown, Clarkson thought so badly of them that he remarked 'the progress of the Colony is put back at least one week for every day they remain amongst us'; see 'Diary of Lieutenant Clarkson, R. N.', *Sierra Leone Studies*, n. s., vol. 8 (March 1927), p. 13.

46. *Monthly Review*, vol. 16 (January–April, 1795), p. 102.

47. W. H. Smyth, *The Life and Services of Captain Philip Beaver* (London: John Murray, 1829), pp. 59–60.

48. *Monthly Review*, vol. 16 (January–April, 1795), p. 102.

49. The phrase comes from the Sierra Leone Company, *Substance of the Report, 1791*, p. 28.

50. A feudal relic, quit-rent was originally levied as a payment from peasant to lord in lieu of services.

51. After a quarrel with Governor Phillip, Dawes had returned to England at the end of 1791 on the *Gorgon*. Macaulay went to Jamaica in 1784 as a sixteen-year-old. From 1793 until its dissolution in 1808, he was closely associated with the Sierra Leone Company. For an account of these two men, see Wilson, *Loyal Blacks*, passim.

52. *'Our Children Free and Happy': Letters from Black Settlers in Africa in the 1790s*, ed. C. Fyfe (Edinburgh: Edinburgh University Press, 1991), pp. 43–44.

53. Wilson, *Loyal Blacks*, pp. 330, 395.

54. In the latter half of the eighteenth century, three-fifths of Bristol's commerce was represented by the African and West Indian trades.

55. Thomas Peters, ex-slave and spokesman for the Nova Scotians, resented Clarkson's governorship. Had he not died suddenly in the colony, he might have led a rebellion against the whites (Clarkson's journal in Ingham, *Sierra Leone*, pp. 38–44, and Wilson, *Loyal Blacks*, pp. 248–56). An overview of the documents relating to his life is given by C. Fyfe in 'Thomas Peters: History and Legend', *Sierra Leone Studies*, vol. 9 (1953), pp. 4–13.

56. 'Great dissatisfaction appears amongst the settlers, and many of them begin to be very troublesome. The bad example set them by the Europeans when they first landed, the unfeeling manner in which they are often addressed ... may in a great degree account for the irritability of temper, and peevish disposition which it is painful for me to observe amongst them ...' (Ingham, *Sierra Leone*, pp. 26–27). He also noted new habits, like their consumption of rum; see 'Diary', *Sierra Leone Studies* (1927), p. 98.

57. This phrase occurs in the settlers' petition to the Directors (Fyfe, *'Our Children Free and Happy'*, p. 36).

58. Ingham, *Sierra Leone*, p. 144, and 'Diary', *Sierra Leone Studies* (1927), p. 31.

Clarkson's view of Dawes hardened; in July 1793 he wrote to Isaac DuBois that 'his manners are disgusting' and that he was not 'a fit or proper Person to be at the Head of a Colony founded upon the Principles of the Constitution of Free Town' (British Library, Clarkson Papers, MS Add. 41263, vol. 3).

59. Clarkson described him as 'extremely unkind & violent' to his wife (Wilson, *John Clarkson*, p. 126).
60. For information about DuBois, see his journal (Clarkson Papers, MS Add. 41263, vol. 3). John Clarkson was astonished at the Company's dismissal of DuBois in Sept. 1793, protesting to Thornton, Chairman of the Directors: 'His behaviour was so exemplary, his Manners so engaging, and his Zeal and Industry to promote the Happiness and Comfort of the Colony so conspicuous that I ... attribute the first foundation of the Colony in a great part to him' (Clarkson Papers, MS Add. 41263, vol. 3).
61. Alexander Falconbridge, *An Account of the Slave Trade on the Coast of Africa* (London: J. Phillips, 1788). The book was often quoted by abolitionists; see *An Abstract of the Evidence delivered before a Select Committee of the House of Commons in the years 1790, and 1791; on the part of the Petitioners for the Abolition of the Slave-Trade* (London: J. Phillips, 1791).
62. See *Monthly Review*, vol. 16 (January–April, 1795), p. 103.
63. Falconbridge's story appears to bear out a certain strand of contemporary feminist complaint: that anti-slavery enthusiasts were often the greatest slavers when it came to their own domestic relations. See, for instance, Hannah More's essay 'The White Slave Trade', *The Works of Hannah More*, 11 vols (London: T. Cadell, 1830), vol. 3, pp. 384ff. For the view that slave trading was 'a genteel employment' see John Newton's *An Authentic Narrative of some Remarkable and Interesting Particulars in the Life of ******** Communicated in a Series of Letters to the Reverend Mr Haweis* (London: J. Johnson, 5th edn, 1782), p. 148.
64. 'The Nassau Captn. Morley arrived from the Isles De loss—he seems to be a good honest fellow & I am rather gratifyed by his being highly pleased at his sisters Marriage' (Isaac DuBois's Journal, Jan. 20, 1793; British Library, Clarkson Papers, MS Add. 41263, vol. 3).
65. Cf. Letter XIII of *Two Voyages*, pp. 133–34 below, with her husband's *Account of the Slave Trade*, pp. 19–32.
66. 'It is my constant practice, when I visit any of the native chiefs, or go into their villages, for myself and those who attend me, to be unarmed' (Ingham, *Sierra Leone*, p. 98).
67. Ingham, *Sierra Leone*, p. 132.
68. Similarly, in Botany Bay in 1788, during the first contact period with the aboriginals, Watkin Tench wrote of how the colonists' first object was 'to win their affections', the second, 'to convince them of the superiority we possessed' (Tench, *A Narrative of the Expedition to Botany Bay* (London: J. Debrett, 1789), p. 57).
69. See Ingham, *Sierra Leone*, p. 24. Writing of the influence of Portuguese Roman Catholicism on the coastal Africans, Matthews claimed: 'Their religion

principally consists in repeating a *Pater Noster*, or an *Ave Maria*, and in wearing a large string of beads round their neck, with a cross, or crucifix, suspended' (Matthews, *Voyage*, p. 14).

70. Ingham, *Sierra Leone*, pp. 23–26.

71. A spotted negro boy was one of the freaks on display at Bartholomew Fair in the late eighteenth century; see P. Edwards and J. Walvin, *Black Personalities in the Era of the Slave Trade* Macmillan, 1983, and R. D Altick, *The Shows of London* (Cambridge, MA: Belknap Press of Harvard University Press, 1978).

72. Harlequin was the name of a 'white-negro' woman displayed at travelling shows in the late eighteenth century; see Paul Edwards and James Walvin, 'Africans in Britain' in *The African Diaspora*, p. 193.

73. See Mikhail Bakhtin, *Rabelais and his World*, trans. Helene Iswolsky (Bloomington: Indiana University Press, 1984), pp. 29, 43.

74. For instance, Matthews, *Voyage*, pp. 23–24, 96, 159. Matthews was influenced by Edward Long's racist theories in his *History of Jamaica*, 3 vols (London, 1774).

75. Hostage taking, or pawning, was central to slavery transactions on the coast, operating as security between payment and receipt of slaves from the interior. Matthews gives a full account of how the system worked; see Matthews, *Voyage*, pp. 155–56. This form of bartering was well documented by other travellers too; see Thomas Winterbottom, *An Account of the Native Africans in the Neighbourhood of Sierra Leone to which is added An Account of the Present State of Medicine among them*, 2 vols (London, 1803), p. 126, and John Newton, in Fyfe (ed.), *Sierra Leone Inheritance*, p. 75.

76. The term 'courtly encounter' is taken from Mary Louise Pratt's 'Scratches on the Face of the Country; or, What Mr Barrow Saw in the Land of the Bushmen', *Critical Inquiry*, 12 (Autumn, 1985), pp. 131–32.

77. For thought-provoking analysis of the concept of curiosity in travel literature, see Harriet Guest, 'The Great Distinction: Figures of the Exotic in the work of William Hodges', in *New Feminist Discourses: Critical Essays on Theories and Texts*, ed. I. Armstrong (London: Routledge, 1992), pp. 296–41, esp. pp. 320–22; more recently, see her essay 'Looking at Women: Forster's Observations in the South Pacific', in *J. R. Forster, Observations made during a Voyage round the World*, ed. N. Thomas, H. Guest and M. Dettelbach (Honolulu: University of Hawai'i Press, 1996), pp. xli–liv.

78. Tench, *Complete Account*, p. 108.

79. To name only the best known: John White, *Journal of a Voyage to New South Wales* (London: J. Debrett, 1790), John Hunter, *An Historical Journal of the Transactions at Port Jackson and Norfolk Island* (London: John Stockdale, 1793), and Tench's two books, *Narrative of the Expedition* (1789) and *Complete Account* (1793).

80. *Monthly Review*, vol. 20 (May–August, 1796), p. 112.

81. *The Journal and Letters of Lt. Ralph Clark, 1787–1792* (Sydney: Australian Documents Library, 1981), p. 234. See also James Scott, *Remarks on a Passage to Botany Bay, 1787–1792* (Sydney: Angus and Robertson, 1963).

82. Lieutenant Gardner, quoted by Gavin Fry in his introduction to Parker's *Voyage Round the World*, n. p.

83. One reviewer pounced with delight on this detail; see *Gentleman's Magazine*, 65 (1795), p. 941.

84. The reconstruction of the Crown within Phillip's Government has recently been described by Alan Atkinson as one of the most remarkable and complex features of his benevolent paternalism; see Atkinson, *Europeans in Australia*, pp. 108–10.

85. Elizabeth Macarthur, *The Journal and Letters of Elizabeth Macarthur, 1789–1798*, ed. Joy N. Hughes (Glebe: Historic Houses Trust of New South Wales, 1984), p. 24 (hereafter *Journal and Letters*).

86. Macarthur, *Journal and Letters*, pp. 34, 31.

87. Tench, *Narrative of the Expedition*, p. 79; *Complete Account*, p. 163.

88. David Collins, *An Account of the English Colony in New South Wales: with remarks on the dispositions, customs, manners &c. of the native inhabitants of that country* (London: T. Cadell, 1798), p. 103.

89. Macarthur, *Journal and Letters*, p. 22.

90. Such as the description of the natives' huts in Chapter 8; for other debts, see my notes to the text.

91. Bennelong (*c.* 1764–1813) is the most common form of his name. Kidnapped by Governor Phillip in 1789 in order to interrogate him about the new land, Bennelong travelled to England in 1792 and was presented to King George III.

92. Tench, *Complete Account*, p. 188.

93. One of Tench's reviewers in 1793 castigated him for excessive pessimism about the colony, citing Bennelong's presence in the metropolis as counter-argument. Instead of displaying the 'ferocious and intractable manners' described by Tench, Banalong was 'delighted with every thing he sees, and courteous to those who know him' (*British Critic*, vol. 2 (1793), pp. 62–67).

94. A live kangaroo in 1791 was worth £500, but only £30 by the end of the decade.

NOTE ON TEXTS

ANNA MARIA FALCONBRIDGE, *TWO VOYAGES TO SIERRA LEONE* (1794)

The copy-text reproduced here is the first edition of Falconbridge's *Two Voyages to Sierra Leone*, published in 1794, probably around August. Apart from silently incorporating the errata listed at the end of that edition, I have reproduced faithfully the first edition's orthography, and its (many) typographical errors. I have also preserved the paragraphing of the original, but not the large spaces between paragraphs; nor have I attempted to reproduce the text's invariable practice of inserting spaces before and after colons, semi-colons, exclamation marks and question marks.

Falconbridge's book was reprinted twice, once almost immediately in 1794, the second time in 1795 (described, respectively, as second and third 'editions' on the title-pages). All three of these early 'editions' are described as 'printed for the author' in London. Longman and J. Parsons are named as booksellers on two 1795 title-pages I have seen. The second edition (rather than reprint) of 1802 is a much more correct and tidy work, but in most other respects it follows closely the first edition of 1794; any significant changes have been noted in the explanatory notes. The chief difference between the two editions of 1794 and 1802 lies, perhaps, in their title-pages (see Bibliography, 'Writings by Anna Maria Falconbridge').

In 1967, Cass & Co. published a facsimile of the 1802 edition.

MARY ANN PARKER, *A VOYAGE ROUND THE WORLD* (1795)

The copy-text reproduced here is the first (and only) edition of *A Voyage Round the World*, published in 1795. The only subsequent edition has been a facsimile edition, with an introduction by Gavin Fry (see Bibliography, 'Writings by Mary Ann Parker').

Once again, I have reproduced the text faithfully, but have not preserved the spacing between paragraphs.

TWO VOYAGES

TO

SIERRA LEONE,

DURING THE

YEARS 1791—2—3,

In a Series of Letters,

BY

ANNA MARIA FALCONBRIDGE.

To which is added

A LETTER FROM THE AUTHOR,

Henry Thornton, Esq. M. P.

And CHAIRMAN of the COURT of DIRECTORS

OF THE

SIERRA LEONE COMPANY.

If I can hold a Torch to others,
'Tis all I want———.

London:

PRINTED FOR THE AUTHOR, AND SOLD BY
DIFFERENT BOOKSELLERS THROUGHOUT
THE KINGDOM.

———

1794.

Plate 14 Title-page of Anna Maria Falconbridge's *Two Voyages to Sierra Leone* (1794).
Source: State Library of Victoria.

Inhabitants of Bristol.

After revolving in my mind a length of time, whose protection I might solicit for the subsequent pages, it strikes me, I may look up with more confidence to the City I proudly boast to be a native of, than to any other quarter.

Permit me, therefore, to trespass on your patience for a short space, by entreating your Countenance, and Patronage, to a faithful and just account of two voyages to the inhospitable Coast of Africa.—Chequered throughout with such a complication of disasters as I may venture to affirm have never yet attended any of my *dear Country Women*, and such as I sincerely hope they never may experience.

I will not undertake to promise you either elegant or modish diction; and all I shall advance in my favour, is a rigid adherence to truth, which (without embellishment) I am persuaded will meet its just reward from the Inhabitants of Bristol; whom I trust, will have the goodness to keep in mind the infancy of my pen, that the recollection may serve for an apology, should they at any time catch me giving too much scope to its reins.

May every description of happiness attend the Inhabitants of Bristol, is the earnest prayer

Of their Townswoman,
and most devoted,
and obedient humble Servant,
ANNA MARIA ——.

BRISTOL, *June* 1794.[1]

PREFACE.

The Authoress will not imitate a threadbare prevailing custom, viz. assure the Public, the following letters were written without any design or intention of sending them into the world; on the contrary, she candidly confesses having some idea of the kind when writing them, tho' her mind was not fully made up on the business 'till towards the beginning of April,—nay, for some time before then (from a consciousness of the inability of her pen) she had actually relinquished all thoughts of publishing them, which determination she certainly would have adhered to, if her will had not been overruled by the importunities of her friends.

In her first voyage, she has given her reasons for going to Africa, described the incidents and occurrences she met with and (from occular observations) the manners, customs, &c. of the people inhabiting those places she visited,—she has also made an humble attempt to delineate their situations and qualities, with a superficial History, of the peninsula of Sierra Leone and its environs, which she certainly would have enlarged upon during her second voyage, had not Lieutenant Matthews previous to her returning to England in 1791, taken the start of her, by publishing his voyage to that Country;—as that was the case, it would not only have been superfluous, but discovering more vanity than she could wish the World to suppose her possessed of, had she offered to tread in a path already travelled over by such an ingenious and masterly pen, to which she begs to refer the inquisitive reader.[2]

This consideration, and this alone, induced the Authoress to confine the letters of her last voyage principally to the transactions and progress of a Colony, whose success, or downfall she is persuaded the Inhabitants, at least the thinking part, of almost every civilized Country, must feel more or less interested about, and she is sorely afflicted to warn the readers of an unpromising account which could not be otherwise, unless she had done violence to veracity;—she is well aware that truth is often unwelcome, and foresees many facts produced to the World in the course of those letters will not be acceptable to the ears of numbers;—therefore in vindication of herself, *she refers the Public to the whole* Court of Directors of the Sierra Leone Company, *and hopes, if it be in their power, either severally, or collectively, to contradict* one tittle *she has advanced, they will do so in the most candid manner;—for the Authoress is open to conviction, and if convicted on this occasion, she will with all due deference* kiss the rod of correction.

LETTER I.

LONDON, *Jan.* 5, 1791.

My dear Friend,

The time draws nigh when I must bid adieu to my native land, perhaps for ever! the thoughts of it damps my spirits more than you can imagine, but I am resolved to summon all the fortitude I can, being conscious of meriting the reproach of my friends and relations, for having hastily married as I did, contrary to their wishes, and am determined rather than be an incumbrance on them, to accompany my husband even to the wilds of *Africa,* whither he is now bound, and meet such fate as awaits me, in preference to any possible comfort I could receive from them.

Mr. Falconbridge is employed by the St. George's Bay Company,[3] to carry out some relief for a number of unfortunate people, (blacks and whites,) whom Government sent to the river Sierra Leone, a few years since, and who in consequence of some dispute with the natives, are scattered through the country, and are just now, as I have been told, in the most deplorable condition.

He (Mr. Falconbridge,) is likewise to make some arrangements for collecting those poor creatures again, and forming a settlement which the company have in contemplation to establish, not only to serve them, but to be generally useful to the natives.

Mr. Falconbridge, his brother Mr. W. Falconbridge and myself, are to embark on board the Duke of Bucleugh, Captain McLean, a ship belonging to Messrs. John and Alexander Anderson, of Philpot Lane; these gentlemen I understand, have a considerable factory at a place called Bance Island, some distance up the river Sierra Leone, to which island the ship is bound.[4]

The company have either sent, or are to send out a small cutter called the Lapwing, to meet Mr. F——, on the coast, she carries the stores for relieving the people, &c.

This is all the information I can give you at present, respecting my intended voyage, but as it is an unusual enterprize for an English woman to visit the coast of Africa; and as I have ever flattered myself with possessing your friendship, you will no doubt like to hear from me, and I therefore intend giving you a full and circumstantial account of every thing that does not escape my notice, 'till I return to this bless'd land, if it pleases him who determines all things, that shall be the case again.

I have this instant learnt that we set off to-morrow for Gravesend, where the ship is laying ready to sail; should we put into any port in the channel, I may probably write you if I am able, but must now bid you adieu.

LETTER II.

SPITHEAD, *Jan.* 12, 1794.[5]

My dear Friend,

Contrary winds prevented us from proceding directly out of the channel, and made it necessary to put into this place. We have been here two days, but I am told there is an appearance of the wind changing, and that it is probable we shall make the attempt to get away some time this day; therefore I think it best not to defer performing my promise of writing to you, least we sail, and I am disappointed.

We embarked at Gravesend between eleven and twelve o'clock, the night after I wrote you: every thing seemed in dreadful confusion; but this I understand is commonly the case on board ships when on the eve of sailing: besides the captain had several friends who came from London to bid him farewell.

You may guess my mind, in spite of all the resolution a young girl is capable of mustering, could not be undisturbed; but I would not give way to any melancholy reflections, and endeavoured to smother them as often as they intruded; although I must confess they sometimes caught me off my guard, and my heart, for the moment, was ready to burst with the thoughts of what I had to encounter, which was pictured to me by almost every one in the worst of colours.

However I went to bed, and being much fatigued, was in hopes every care would be buried for the night in delightful sleep; but in this I was disappointed, for although my eyes were closed as soon as I got my head on the pillow, yet it was not of long continuance.

I had slept perhaps two hours, when the shocking cries of murder awoke me! I did not at the instant recollect where I was, but the first thoughts which occurred upon remembering myself on ship-board, were, that a gang of pirates had attacked the ship, and would put us all to death.

All the cabin was by this time alarmed; the cries of murder still continuing while the captain and others were loudly calling for lights; and so great was the confusion, that it was a long while before any could be procured: at length the light came, when I found myself some what collected, and had courage enough to ask what was the matter.

My fears were removed, by being informed it was a Mr. B——, a passenger, whose intellects were a little deranged: he continued his disagreeable hideous cries the whole night, and prevented everyone from sleeping; for my part I scarcely closed my eyes again.

At breakfast Mr. B—— apologized, by telling us that his wife had murdered his only child, for which reason he had left her. "And," said he, "the horrid act! has made such an impression on my mind, that I frequently think I see her all besmeared with blood, with a dagger in her hand, determined to take away my life also: it preys upon my spirits, for I want strength of mind to conquer the weakness."*

Mr. Alexander Anderson came on board, and dined: he politely enquired if I was comfortable; assured me, that every thing had been put on board to render us as much so as possible.

In the evening he returned to town, and we got under weigh.

Nothing occurred on our passage here, except such frequent returns of Mr. B's delirium, as has induced Captain McLean to put him on shore, from the opinion of his being an unfit subject to go to the coast of Africa.

I did not experience any of those fears peculiar to my sex upon the water; and the only inconvenience I found was a little sea sickness, which I had a right to expect, for you know this is my first voyage.

There is one circumstance, which I forbode will make the remainder of our voyage unpleasant.

The gentlemen whom Mr. Falconbridge is employed by are for abolishing the slave trade: the owners of this vessel are of that trade, and consequently the captain and Mr. Falconbridge must be very opposite in their sentiments.

They are always arguing, and both are warm in their tempers,[6] which makes me uneasy, and induces me to form this conjecture; but perhaps that may not be the case.

I have not been on shore at Portsmouth, indeed it is not a desirable place to visit: I was once there, and few people have a desire to see it a second time.

The only thing that has attracted my notice in the harbour, is the fleet with convicts for Botany Bay, which are wind bound, as well as ourselves.

The destiny of such numbers of my fellow creatures has made what I expect to encounter, set lighter upon my mind than it ever did before; nay, nothing could have operated a reconciliation so effectually: for as the human heart is more susceptible of distress conveyed by the eye, than when represented by language however ingenously[7] pictured with misery, so the sight of those unfortunate beings, and the thoughts of what they are to endure, have worked more forcibly on my feelings, than all the accounts I ever read or heard of wretchedness before.

I must close this which is the last, in all probability you will receive from me, 'till my arrival in Africa; when, if an opportunity offers, I shall make a point of writing to you.

Pray do not let distance or absence blot out the recollection of her,

Who is truly your's.

---

* I am inclined to think this was only the imagination of a frantic brain, for we were not able to learn any thing more of the story.

LETTER III.

BANCE ISLAND, *Feb.* 10, 1791

My dear Friend,

We sailed the very day I wrote you from Portsmouth, and our passage was unusually quick, being only eighteen days from thence to this place.

The novelty of a ship ploughing the trackless ocean, in a few days became quite familiar to me; there was such a sameness in every thing (for some birds were all we saw the whole way) that I found the voyage tiresome, notwithstanding the shortness of it.

You will readily believe my heart was gladdened at the sight of the mountains of Sierra Leone, which was the land we first made.

Those mountains appear to rise gradually from the sea to a stupendious height, richly wooded and beautifully ornamented by the hand of nature, with a variety of delightful prospects.

I was vastly pleased while sailing up the river, for the rapidity of the ship through the water afforded a course of new scenery almost every moment, till we cast anchor here: [*Plate 15*] Now and then I saw the glimpse of a native town, but from the distance, and new objects hastily catching my eye, was not able to form a judgment or idea of any of them; but this will be no loss, as I may have frequent opportunities of visiting some of them hereafter.

As soon as our anchor was dropped, Captain McLean saluted Bance Island with seven guns, which not being returned, I enquired the cause, and was told, the last time the Duke of Bucleugh came out, she, as is customary, saluted, and on the fort returning the compliment, a wad was drove by the force of the sea breeze upon the roof of one of the houses, (which was then of thatch) set fire to the building, and consumed not only the house but goods to a large amount.

When the ceremony of saluting was over, Captain McLean and Mr. W. Falconbridge went on shore; but being late in the evening, I continued on board 'till next day.

Here we met the Lapwing cutter. She sailed some time before us from Europe, and had been arrived two or three weeks.

The master of her, and several of the people to whose assistance Mr. Falconbridge is come, and who had taken refuge here, came to visit us.

They represented their sufferings to have been very great; that they had been treacherously dealt with by one *King* Jemmy, who had drove them away from the ground they occupied, burnt their houses, and otherwise devested them of every comfort and necessary of life:[8] they also threw out some reflections against the Agent of this island; said he had sold several of their fellow sufferers to a Frenchman, who had taken them to the West Indies.

Mr. Falconbridge, however, was not inclined[9] to give entire confidence to what they told us; but prudently suspended his opinion until he had made further enquiries.

A View of the entrance into Sierra-leone River

Plate 15 'A View of the entrance into Sierra-leone River', from John Matthews, *A Voyage to the River Sierra-Leone* (2nd edn, 1791). Matthews wrote that 'few prospects can exceed the entrance', with the 'high land of Sierra-Leone rising from the Cape with the most apparent gentle ascent' (p. 22).
Source: Cambridge University Library; by permission of the Syndics of Cambridge University Library.

Those visitors being gone, we retired to bed—I cannot say to rest; the heat was so excessive that I scarcely slept at all.

The following day we received a polite invitation to dine on shore, which I did not object to, although harassed for want of sleep the night before.

At dinner the conversation turned upon the slave trade: Mr. Falconbridge, zealous for the cause in which he is engaged, strenuously opposed every argument his opponents advanced in favour of the *abominable* trade: the glass went briskly round, and the gentlemen growing warm, I retired immediately as the cloath was removed.

The people on the island crowded to see me; they gazed with apparent astonishment—I suppose at my dress, for white women could not be a novelty to them, as there were several among the unhappy people sent out here by government, one of whom is now upon the island.

Seeing so many of my own sex, though of different complexions from myself, attired in their native garbs, was a scene equally new to me, and my delicacy, I confess, was not a little hurt at times.

Many among them appeared of superior rank, at least I concluded so from the preferable way in which they were clad; nor was I wrong in my conjecture, for upon enquiring who they were, was informed one was the *woman* or *mistress* of Mr.——, another of Mr. B——, and so on: I then understood that every gentleman on the island had his *lady*.

While I was thus entertaining myself with my new acquaintances, two or three of the gentlemen left their wine and joined me: among them was Mr. Ballingall the Agent,[10] who, in a very friendly manner, begged I would take a bed on shore.

I thanked him, and said, if agreeable to Mr. Falconbridge, I would have no objection: however, Falconbridge objected, and gave me for reason, that he had been unhandsomely treated, and was determined to go on board the Lapwing, for he would not subject himself to any obligation to men possessing such *diabolical* sentiments.

It was not proper for me to contradict him at that moment, as the heat of argument and the influence of an over portion of wine had *quickened* and *disconcerted* his temper; I therefore submitted without making any objection to come on board this tub of a vessel, which in point of size and cleanliness, comes nigher a hog-trough than any thing else you can imagine.[11]

Though I resolved to remonstrate the first seasonable opportunity, and to point out the likelihood of endangering my health, should he persist to keep me in so confined a place.

This remonstrance I made the next morning, after passing a night of torment, but to no purpose; the only consolation I got, was,—as soon as the settlers could be collected, he would have a house built on shore, where they were to be fixed.

I honestly own my original resolution of firmness was now warped, at what I foresaw I was doomed to suffer, by being imprisoned, God knows how long, in a place so disgusting as this was, in my opinion, at that time.

Conceive yourself pent up in a floating cage, without room, to walk about, stand erect, or even to lay at length; exposed to the inclemency of the weather, having your eyes and ears momently offended by acts of indecency, and language too horrible to relate—add to this, a complication of filth, the stench from which was continually assailing your nose, and then you will have a faint notion of the Lapwing Cutter.

However, upon collecting myself, and recollecting there was no remedy but to make the best of my situation, I begged the master (who slept upon deck in consequence of my coming on board) to have the cabin thoroughly cleaned and washed with vinegar; intreated Falconbridge to let me go on shore while it was doing—hinted at the indecencies I saw and heard, and was promised they would be prevented in future.

With this assurance I went on shore, not a little elated at the reprieve I was to enjoy for a few hours.

The gentlemen received me with every mark of attention and civility; indeed, I must be wanting in sensibility, if my heart did not warm with gratitude to Messrs. Ballingall and Tilly, for their kindnesses to me: the latter gentleman I am informed will succeed to the agency of the island; he is a genteel young man, and I am told very deservedly a favourite with his employers.[12]

Mr. Falconbridge this day sent a message to Elliotte Griffiths, the secretary of Naimbana, who is the King of Sierra Leone, acquainting him with the purport of his mission, and begging to know when he may be honoured with an audience of his *Majesty*.[13]

In the evening he received an answer, of which the following is a copy:

ROBANA TOWN.

King Naimbana's compliments to Mr. Falconbridge, and will be glad to see him to morrow.

(Signed)
A.E. GRIFFITHS, Sec.

Such an immediate answer from a *King*, I considered a favorable omen, and a mark of condescension in his *Majesty*, but the result you shall hear by and by, in the mean while, I must tell you what passed the remainder of the day at Bance Island, and give as far as my ideas allow me, a description of this factory. [*Plate 16*]

We sat down to dinner with the same party as the first day, consisting of about fifteen in number; this necessary ceremony ended, and towards the cool of the afternoon, I proposed walking for a while: Mr. Tilly and a Mr. Barber offered to accompany and show me the island, which not being objected to, we set out.

Adam's Town was the first place they took me to; it is so called from a

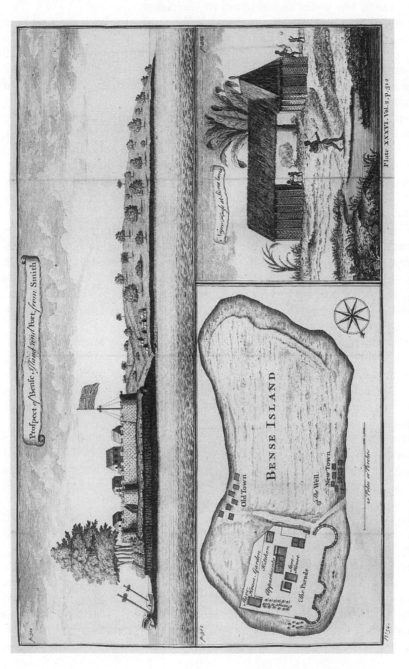

Plate 16 'Prospect of Bense Island and Fort', showing the 'Slave-House' on the left; on the right is depicted a 'Negro House at Sierra Leone', from Thomas Astley, *A New General Collection of Voyages and Travels*, vol. 2 (1745), opp. p. 313.
Source: Cambridge University Library; by permission of the Syndics of Cambridge University Library.

native of that name, who has the management of all the gramattos, or free black servants, but under the controul of the Agent.

The whole town consists of a street with about twenty-five houses on each side:—on the right of all is Adam's house.

This building does not differ from the rest, except in size, being much more spacious than any other, and being barracaded with a mud wall;—all of them are composed of thatch, wood, and clay, something resembling our poor cottages, in many parts of England. [*Plate 16*]

I went into several of them—saw nothing that did not discover the occupiers to be very clean and neat; in some was a block or two of wood, which served for chairs,—a few wooden bowls or trenchers, and perhaps a pewter bason and an iron pot compleated the whole of their furniture.

In every house I was accosted by whoever we found at home, in the Timmany language *Currea Yaa* which signifies—How do you do mother?— the most respectful way they can address any person.

Leaving the town, we proceeded first to the burying ground for Europeans, and then to that for blacks;—the only distinction between them was a few orange trees, that shaded two grave stones at the former,—one in memory of a Mr. Knight, who had died here after residing fifteen years as Agent;—the other was on the supposed grave of a Captain Tittle, who was murdered by one Signor Domingo, a native chief, for (as Domingo asserts) being the cause of his son's death.

The circumstance leading to the murder, as well as the murder itself, has been represented to me nearly in the following words:

"One day while the son of Domingo was employed by Captain Tittle, as a gramatto, or pull-away boy,* Tittle's hat by accident blew overboard, and he insisted that the boy should jump into the water and swim after it, as the only means of saving his hat.

"The boy obstinately refused, saying, he could not swim, and he should either be drowned, or the sharks would catch him; upon which Tittle pushed him into the water, and the poor boy was lost; but whether devoured by sharks, or suffocated by water, is immaterial, he was never heard of, or seen after.

"The father, though sorely grieved for his son's death, was willing to consider it accidental, and requested Tittle would supply him with a small quantity of rum to make a cry[14] or lamentation in their country custom.

"The Captain, by promise, acquiesced to the demand, and sent him a cask; but instead of spirits filled with emptyings from the *tubs* of his slaves.

"As soon as Domingo discovered this insult and imposition, he informed Tittle he must either submit to the decision of a Palaver,[15] or he would put him to death if ever an opportunity offered; but Tittle laughed at these threats, and disregarding them, vauntingly threw himself into the way of

* African term for an oar-man.

Domingo—while the trick played upon him, and the loss of his son were fresh in his memory.

"The African, however, instead of being daunted at the sight of this head strong man, soon convinced him he was serious: he had Tittle seized, and after confining him some time in irons, without food, ordered him to be broken to death, which was executed under the inspection of the injured father, and to the great joy and satisfaction of a multitude of spectators."

Not a sentence or hint of the affair is mentioned on the tombstone; the reason assigned for the omission, was a wish to obliterate the melancholy catastrophe, and a fear least the record might be the means of kindling animosities at a future day.

Now, although I cannot without horror contemplate on the untimely end of this man, yet he assuredly in some degree merited it, if the account I have heard and just now related to you, be true, which I have no reason to question; for he who unprovoked can wantonly rob a fellow creature of his life, deserves not life himself![16]

From the catacombs which lay at the south-east end, we walked to the opposite point of the island; it is no great distance, for the whole island is very little more than a fourth of a mile in length, and scarcely a mile and a half in circumference.

Several rocks lay at a small distance from the shore at this end; they are by the natives called the Devil's Rocks,—from the superstitious opinion that the *old Gentleman* resides either there or in the neighbourhood.

Sammo, King of the Bulloms, comes to this place once a year to make a sacrifice and peace-offering to his infernal Majesty.

From this King Messrs. Anderson's hold all their possessions here, and I understand they pay him an annual tribute—but to what amount I cannot say.[17]

The King comes in person to receive his dues, which are paid him in his canoe, for he never ventures to put his foot on shore, as his *Gree Greemen* or fortune-tellers have persuaded him the island will sink under him, if ever he lands.

I am told at one time he suffered himself to be dragged up to the Factory House in his boat, but no argument was strong enough to seduce him to disembark, for he did not consider he incurred the penalty his prophets denounced while he continued in his canoe; though he could not avoid shewing evident tokens of uneasiness, 'till he was safe afloat again.

We now returned to the Factory, or as it is otherwise called Bance Island house.

This building at a distance has a respectable and formidable appearance; nor is it much less so upon a nearer investigation: I suppose it is about one hundred feet in length, and thirty in breadth, and contains nine rooms, all on one floor, under which are commodious large cellars and store rooms; to the right is the kitchen, forge, &c. and to the left other necessary buildings, all of country stone, and surrounded with a prodigious thick lofty wall.

There was formerly a fortification in front of those houses, which was destroyed by a French frigate during the last war; at present several pieces of cannon are planted in the same place, but without embrassures or breast-work; behind the great house is the slave yard, and houses for accommodating the slaves.

Delicacy, perhaps, prevented the gentlemen from taking me to see them; but the room where we dined looks directly into the yard.

Involuntarily I stroled to one of the windows a little before dinner, without the smallest suspicion of what I was to see;—judge then what my astonishment and feelings were at the sight of between two and three hundred wretched victims, chained and parcelled out in circles, just satisfying the cravings of nature from a trough of rice placed in the centre of each circle.

Offended modesty rebuked me with a blush for not hurrying my eyes from such disgusting scenes; but whether fascinated by female curiosity, or whatever else, I could not withdraw myself for several minutes—while I remarked some whose hair was withering with age, reluctantly tasting their food—and others thoughtless from youth, greedily devouring all before them: be assured I avoided the prospects from this side of the house ever after.

Having prolonged the time 'till nine at night, we returned to our floating prison, and what with the assiduity of the master in removing many inconveniencies, my mind being more at ease, want of rest for two nights, and somewhat fatigued with the exercise of the day, I, thank God, slept charmingly, and the next morning we set sail for Robana, where we arrived about ten o'clock: I think it is called nine miles from Bance Island.[18]

We went on shore, and rather caught his *Majesty* by surprize, for he was quite in *dishabille*; and at our approach retired in great haste.

I observed a person pass me in a loose white frock and trowsers, *whom I would not have suspected for a King!* if he had not been pointed out to me.

Mr. Elliotte and the *Queen* met us; and after introducing her Majesty and himself, we were then conducted to her house.

She behaved with much indifference,—told me in broken English that the *King* would come presently—he was gone to *peginninee* woman house to dress himself.[19]

After setting nigh half an hour, Naimbana made his appearance, and received us with seeming good will: he was dressed in a purple embroidered coat, white sattin waistcoat and breeches, *thread stockings,* and his left side emblazoned with a flaming star; his legs to be sure were *harliquined,* by a number of holes in the stockings, through which his black skin appeared.[20]

Compliments ended, Mr. Falconbridge acquainted him with his errand, by a repetition of what he wrote the day before: and complained much of King Jemmy's injustice in driving the settlers away, and burning their town.

The King answered through Elliotte, (for he speaks but little English) that Jemmy was partly right—the people had brought it on themselves; they had taken part with some Americans, with whom Jemmy had a dispute, and through that means drew the ill will of this man upon them, who had behaved, considering their conduct as well as they merited; for he gave them three days notice before he burned their town, that they might remove themselves and all their effects away; that he (Naimbana) could not prudently re-establish them, except by consent of all the Chiefs—for which purpose he must call a court or palaver; but it would be seven or eight days before they could be collected; however he would send a summons to the different parties directly, and give Falconbridge timely advice when they were to meet.

Falconbridge perceived clearly nothing was to be effected without a palaver, and unless the King's interest was secured his views would be frustrated, and his endeavours ineffectual; but how this was to be done, or what expedient to adopt, he was at a loss for.

He considered it impolitic to purchase his patronage by heavy presents, least the other *great men* might expect the same; and he had it not in his power to purchase them all in the same way, as the scanty cargo of the Lapwing would not admit of it.

At length, trusting that the praise-worthy purposes he was aiming at, insured him the assistance of the King of Kings, he resolved to try what good words would do.

Having prefaced his arguments with a small donation of some rum, wine, a cheese, and a gold laced hat, which Naimbana seemed much pleased with.

Falconbridge began, by explaining what advantages would accrue to his *Majesty,* and all the inhabitants round about, by such an establishment as the St. George's Bay Company were desirous of making;—the good they wished to do—*their disinterestednes in point of obtaining wealth,* and concluded by expostulating on the injustice and imposition of dispossessing the late settlers of the grounds and houses they occupied, which had been honestly and honorably purchased by Captain Thompson of the Navy, in the name of our gracious Sovereign, his Britannic Majesty.[21]

That it was unusual for Englishmen to forego fulfilling any engagements they made; and they held in detestation every person so disposed.

He then entreated the King would use all his might to prevent any unfavourable prejudices which a refusal to reinstate the Settlers, or to confirm the bargain made with Captain Thompson, might operate against him in the minds of his good friends the King of England and the St. George's Bay Company.

The King said he liked the English in preference to all white men, tho' he considered every white man as a *rogue,* and consequently saw them with a jealous eye; yet, he believed the English were by far the honestest, and for that reason, notwithstanding he had received more favors from the French than the English, he liked the latter much best.[22]

He was decidedly of opinion, that all contracts or agreements between man and man however disadvantageous to either party should be binding; but observed, he was *hastily drawn in* to dispose of land to Captain

Thompson, *which in fact he had not a right to sell*, because says he, "this is a great country, and belongs to many people—where I live belongs to myself—and I can live where I like; nay, can appropriate any unhabited land within my dominions to what use I please; but it is necessary for me to obtain the consent of my people, or rather the head man of every town, before I sell any land to a white man, or allow strangers to come and live among us."

"I should have done this you will say at first—Granted—but as I disobliged my subjects by suffering your people to take possession of the land without their approbation, from which cause I was not able to protect them, unless I hazarded civil commotions in my country; and as they have been *turned away*—it is best now—they should be replaced by the unanimous voice of all interested.

"I am bound from what I have heretofore done, to give my utmost support; and if my people do not acquiesce, it shall not be my fault."

Here Falconbridge, interrupting the King, said—"The King of the English will not blame your people, but load yourself with the stigma; it is King *Naimbana* who is ostensible to King *George*—and I hope King, you will not fall out with your good friend."

This being explained by *Mr. Secretary Elliotte,* his Majesty was some moments silent—when clasping Falconbridge in his arms, told him—*"I believe you and King George* are my good friends—do not fear, have a good heart, I will do as much as I can for you."

They then shook hands heartily, and Naimbana retired, I suppose to his *Pegininee woman's house*, but presently returned dressed in a suit of black velvet, except the stockings, which were the same as before.

I often had an inclination to offer my services to close the holes: but was fearful least my needle might blunder into his *Majesty*'s leg, and start the blood, for drawing the blood of an African King, I am informed, whether occasioned by accident or otherwise, is punished with death: the dread of this only prevented me.

We were now invited to walk and see the town, while dinner was preparing.

It consists of about twenty houses irregularly placed, built of the same materials, but in a superior way to those of Adam's town;—the whole of them are either occupied by the King's wives and servants, or appropriated as warehouses.

I saw several of his wives, but his *Pegininee* woman is a most beautiful young girl of about fourteen.

None of them are titled with the appellation of *Queen,* but the oldest, who I was introduced to, and by whom the King has several children; one of the daughter's, named Clara, is wife to Elliotte, and a son named Bartholomew, is now in France for his education.

In different parts of the town I observed some rags stuck on poles, at the foot of each were placed—perhaps a rusty cutlass, some pieces of broken glass, and a pewter bason, containing a liquid of some sort; these are called

Gree Grees, and considered as antidotes against the Devil's vengeance. [*Plate 17*]

I was thoughtlessly offering to examine one of them, when Mr. Elliotte requested me to desist, or I should give offence, they being held in a very sacred point of view.[23]

We were now led to the garden, which was only furnished with African plants, such as pines, melons, pumpkins, cucumbers, &c. &c.

The King cut two beautiful pines and presented to me: he then shewed us a large new house, at present building for him, which is after the same form, and of the same materials with the rest of his town, but much larger.

In our walk we saw many of the King's slaves employed in preparing the palm-nut, to make oil from them: It may not be amiss here to give you some description of the tree which produce these nuts.

It is remarkable strait and of a gigantic height; the trunk is quite naked, having neither limb or bark, for the only branches grow immediately from the top, and incline their points somewhat towards the ground.

This is a valuable tree, the nut not only produces a quantity of oil, but is esteemed excellent food by the natives, who also extract a liquor from the tree, which they call palm wine.[24]

This I am told is done by means of an incision in the upper part of the trunk, in which a pipe is entered to convey the liquor into bottles placed beneath.

I have tasted some of this wine, and do not think it unpleasant when fresh made; it has a sweetish taste, and much the look of whey, but foments in a few days, and grows sour—however I really think this liquor distilled would make a decent kind of spirit.

Having seen all the raree-shows of Robana town,[25] we returned to the Queens house to dinner, which was shortly after put on a table covered with a plain calico cloth, and consisted of boiled and broiled fowls, rice, and some greens resembling our spinage.

But I should tell you, before dinner Naimbana again changed his dress for a scarlet robe embroidered with gold.

Naimbana, Elliotte, Falconbridge, and myself, only set down; the Queen stood behind the King eating an onion I gave her, a bite of which she now and then indulged her *Royal Consort* with: silver forks were placed on the King's plate, and mine, but no where else.[26]

The King is rather above common height, but meagre withal; the features of his face resemble a European more than any black I have seen; his teeth are mostly decayed, and his hair, or rather wool, bespeaks old age, which I judge to be about eighty; he was seldom without a smile on his countenance, but I think his smiles were suspicious.

He gave great attention while Falconbridge was speaking, for though he does not speak our language, he understands a good deal of it; his answers were slow, and on the whole tolerably reasonable.

The Queen is of a middle stature, plump and jolly; her temper seems

A View of YA, MA, COOBA'S Town in White Mans Bay, Sierra Leone.

Plate 17 'A View of Ya, Ma, Cooba's Town in White Man's Bay, Sierra-Leone', from John Matthews, *A Voyage to the River Sierra-Leone* (2nd edn, 1791). Ya Ma Cooba was the queen, or head woman, of this area. In this plate, Matthews draws our attention to the gree grees, or native fetishes (such as the white flag flying from the end of the upright pole, the axe in the stump of a tree), the native drum, and the mortars and pestles for beating rice. *Source:* Cambridge University Library; by permission of the Syndics of Cambridge University Library.

placid and accommodating; her teeth are bad, but I dare say she has otherwise been a good looking woman in her youthful days.

I suppose her now to be about forty-five or six, at which age women are considered old here.

She sat on the King's right hand, while he and Falconbridge were in conversation; and now and then would clap her hands, and cry out *Ya hoo*, which signifies, that's well or proper.

She was dressed in the country manner, but in a dignified stile, having several yards of striped taffety wrapped round her waist, which served as a petticoat; another piece of the same was carelessly thrown over her shoulders in form of a scarf; her head was decorated with two silk handkerchiefs; her ears with rich gold ear-rings, and her neck with gaudy necklaces; *but she had neither shoes nor stockings on.*

Clara was dressed much after the same way, but her apparel was not quite of such good materials as the Queen's: Mr. Elliotte apologized after dinner, that for want of *sugar* they could not offer tea or coffee.

The tide serving, and approaching night obliged us to re-embark and return to this place.

On the whole I was much pleased with the occurrences of the day; indeed, methinks, I hear you saying, "Why the week mind of this giddy girl will be quite intoxicated with the courtesy and attention paid her by such great folks;" but believe me, to whatever height of self-consequence I may have been lifted by aerial fancies, overpowering sleep prevailed, and clouding all my greatness—I awoke next morning without the slightest remains of fancied importance.

The news of our arrival having by this time circulated through different parts of the country, we found several, who either excited by curiosity or some other cause, had come here to pay their obeisance, or as the Africans term it, *make service* to us; but there was none of note or quality worth naming among those visitors, except an elderly man called *Pa, or Father Boson*,[27] who is the head man of a considerable town about fifty miles up the river, and who, guided by the impulse of a good heart, invited the wretched exiles in the hour of distress to refuge at his place, which was excepted by the greater part, who have been fostered and protected ever since by the almsdeeds of this good old man; he was habited in a white linen surplice, and a cap of the same, and made, I assure you a reverential appearance.

I am told this is the dress of a nation in the interior country, called Mundingoes; but Pa Boson is not a Mundingo himself.

He respectfully accosted me in broken English, and bending his knee, offered me his right hand supported under the elbow by his left.

I held out my hand which he slightly touched, and then repeated the same to Falconbridge: he was now invited to be seated under the awning we had erected over the Lapwing's deck—when he detailed a most pitiable account of sufferings and hardships which the unfortunate people had undergone;

but he said there were many bad people among them, who had abused his kindness by ingratitude.

Falconbridge and myself endeavoured what we could to convince him we were highly pleased with his behaviour; but as words are not sufficient to convey thankful acknowledgments in this country, Falconbridge confirmed the assurances we made by a present of a quantity of rum, and some hard ware, and a promise to represent his conduct to the St. George's Bay Company, in a proper light, which he was certain would induce them to make a more ample recompence at a future time.

Well pleased with his reception, and somewhat inebriated with the effects of repeated glasses of spirits he had taken, Pa Boson left us; but first promising faithfully he would befriend us all in his power at the Palaver.

He travelled with much seeming consequence: his canoe was longer than our cutter, and manned with fourteen people, viz. ten oarsmen, a cockswain, two poignard bearers, and another who beat time on a flat sounding drum to a song given out by the cockswain, and re-echoed by the oarsmen; the song I am told was expressive of praises to their Chief, and of their satisfaction for the treatment they had received from us.

The following day we visited a small island named Tasso, opposite to Bance island, at about one mile and a half distance.

This is a well wooded island and I should suppose if cultivated would be a fruitful one.*[28]

It supplies Bance island with water, which is remarkable fine, and the present holders of the latter claim a right to this also, but upon what grounds I cannot say.

Approaching the shore I saw many monkies playing on the beach and catching small fish at the edge of the water, but they all ran away as we drew near; being informed there was no danger to be apprehended from wild beasts of prey, we penetrated some distance into the woods.

In our walk we saw many pine apples and lime trees, the spontaneous production of the country, and a variety of birds beautifully plumed, but none that sung.

We were also treated with the perfumes of fragrant aromatic plants, and indeed were vastly delighted and entertained, though I felt fatigued, with our perambulation.

The next day we went up the river, about twelve miles, to see a secret or reserved factory belonging to Bance Island at a place called Marre Bump,[29] but our curiosity had nearly led us into a serious scrape.

Falconbridge neglected to obtain permission, and consequently had no sanction, from the proprietors.

After landing we walked, at least half a mile on a narrow path, through

---

* A small part of this island is now planted with cotton, coffee and sugar cane, for account of Messrs. Andersons.

amazing thick woods before we reached the houses; as soon as the inhabitants perceived us, the women took to their heels and ran to the woods, the men flew to arms, and in a moment we were met by more than twenty huge fellows armed with guns, pistols and cutlasses.

We were four in number, viz. Falconbridge, the master of the cutter, a black man and myself; our black spoke to them in their own language—they would not listen to him; but said, if we did not return immediately the way we came, they would put us all to death.

It is easier for you to imagine what horrors those threats occasioned, than for me to point them out.

Finding argument fruitless, we put to the right about, and hastened to our boat, they, following, flanked us on each side of the road, watchfully observing our motions till they saw us clear off, when, as a mark of exultation, they discharged their muskets over our heads, and made the woods ring with peals of triumphant clamours.

Recovering from my fright a little, I could not help, you may suppose, exulting (though in a different way) as well as the savages.

My heart overflow'd with gratitude, to the Author of its animation, for our providential escape.

Returning down the river, we observed numbers of orange trees, a cluster of them, overloaded with fruit, invited us on shore, and after gathering what we chose, made the best of our way, and arrived here before night.

Three days are now elapsed since our expedition to Marre Bump, during which time I have confined myself mostly on board, occupied in writing this letter.

It has been, really, a fatiguing job, being obliged to sit in bed with a book placed on my knee, which serves for a writing desk; but I was determined whatever the inconveniencies might be, not to let slip an opportunity, as I find they but seldom offer.

I lament the Palaver is not over, that I might give you my account of an African Court, but my next will remedy this loss.

Mr. Elliotte has informed us the Chiefs will be at Robana the day after to-morrow, when Falconbridge is desired to attend; I shall accompany him, and long to know the result.

Adieu, Heaven bless you, &c. &c.

LETTER III.[30]

GRANVILLE TOWN, SIERRA LEONE
May 13, 1794.

My dear Friend,

Occasional visits to Bance Island, unattended by any important Occurrence worth troubling you with, and a continual concourse of strangers, making their African compliments, engrossed two days interval, between the date of my last letter, and our second expedition to Robana; when we set out in a boat and four hands, taking with us plenty of spirits for the common people, and a little wine for the King and his associates.

When we came in sight of the Town, Multitudes of people thronged to the Beach.

Mr. Elliotte met us at the boat, and the croud formed an avenue, through which he conducted us to the Queen's house, amidst such thundering acclamations, that it was almost impossible to hear one or other speak.

The King and Queen met us at the door, and seemed to give us a hearty welcome.

We were then ushered in, and introduced in general terms to the company, consisting of the parties who were to compose the Court, (and a multiplicity of women,) their wives, daughters, and attendants: having seated ourselves, and wasted almost an hour in receiving the civilities of shaking hands with every individual in the room.

The members of the Court then took their seats, round the large table we dined off, when first there; which was now covered with a green cloth.

The King sat at the head of the table in an old arm chair: on his right was his secretary, and on his left his Palavar man; or, as the office is termed in England, his Attorney general: the other Chiefs appeared to seat themselves by seniority; the oldest next to the *Throne*, if I may so term the *old chair*.

The King wore his hat, which was the gold laced one Falconbridge gave him.

On the table was placed wine and rum, of which every one helped himself plentifully.

I was astonished to see, not only the men, but women, drink rum in half pints at a time, as deliberately as I would water.

After amusing themselves some time in this way, Mr. Palaver Man got up, bending his right knee, presented his *Majesty* with some Cola*[31] from the crown of his hat, then retired to the opposite end of the table, when he

---

*   A fruit much esteemed in Africa, not unlike a chestnut, but somewhat larger. It is an excellent bitter.

opened the business of the day, by a speech of at least an hour and an half long; it being in their own language, I of course did not understand a word, but during the time he spoke, there was the greatest silence and attention observed.

The next spokesman, was King Jemmy, who previously went through the same ceremony his predecessor had done: whether this man's language was eloquent or not, I cannot be a judge, but his vociferation was enough to deafen one; though I had reason to think what he said gave great satisfaction to the by-standers, who frequently interrupted him by clapping of hands and shouts of, *Ya Hoo! Ya Hoo! Ya Hoo!* and other tokens of applause.

My heart quivered with fear least they might be forming some treacherous contrivance: I could not conceal the uneasiness it felt: My countenance betrayed me, a shower of tears burst from my eyes, and I swooned into hystericks.[32]

Recovering in a short time, I observed every one around, treating me with the utmost kindness, and endeavouring to convince me that neither insult or injury would be offered us: but my fears were not to be removed, or even checked hastily, for I had scarcely got the better of my fright at Marre Bump; however I struggled to awaken my resolution, and collected enough, after awhile, to affect composure; but believe me, it was mere affectation: Night was drawing nigh, and I solicited Falconbridge to return as soon as possible: He argued, the Court had been impeded by the awkward situation my fears had thrown me into: but he would set out time enough to reach *Bance Island* before dark.

The Assembly now resumed their business.

One or two members offered Cola to the King, which he refused; a grey headed old man then made the offer, and it being accepted, he took the foot of the table, and a few words compleating what he had to say: Mr. Elliotte intimated that King Naimbana intended to give his sentiments; upon which every member rose up, and the King continuing in his chair, covered, delivered his speech in a concise, clear, and respectable manner.

After this Mr. Elliotte acquainted Falconbridge the Court could not come to one mind that night, but it was generally understood, if he would give fifteen hundred Bars,* they would confirm King Naimbana's engagement with Captain Thompson, and re-establish his people.

Falconbridge, whom you know is naturally of an irritable disposition, quickened at Elliotte's information; but had prudence enough only to say, he should consider such a demand very extravagant, and his small cargo, which he was desired to appropriate another way, would not permit him to pay so much, if he had the inclination.

---

*   A Bar is the nominal price of a certain quantity of goods, which the natives formerly considered of equal value with a bar of iron; but at present they do not appear to have any criterion: two pounds of tobacco is a bar, and two yards of fine India cotton, or a yard of rich silk is no more.

We then made our congees,[33] and took leave of those African *gentry*; indeed it was high time, for the liquor they had drank began to operate powerfully: Mr. Elliotte and several others accompanied us to the boat: in our walk thither, he much admired a handsome fowling piece of Mr. Falconbridge's, which Falconbridge without hesitation requested he would accept, thinking such an immediate shew of generosity might have a favourable tendency.

Both of us promised to be down again the following day, when it was expected the Palavar would be finished: but I must be honest and tell you, I was resolved not to visit Robana again, while this mock judicatory lasted.

About seven o'clock we reached the Cutter; I was almost famished with want of food, for I had not eat a morsel the whole day: there was not a thing on board, but salt beef, so hard, we were obliged to chop it with an axe, and some mouldy, rotten biscuits; however, so great was my hunger, that I could not help satisfying it with some of this beef and bread, uncouth as it was.

In the morning I feigned sickness, and begged to be excused from attending Falconbridge; he therefore set out, reluctantly leaving me behind: when he was gone, I went on shore, and spent the day in comfort and pleasantry, under the hospitable roof of Bance Island house; where I related the adventures of the preceeding day, which afforded much mirth and glee to the company.[34]

I met one Rennieu (a Frenchman) there; he has a factory at a small Island, called Gambia, up another branch of this River, named Bunch River, whither he politely invited me, and made a tender of any thing in his power to serve us.[35]

Before Falconbridge returned, which was not till between eight and nine o'clock at night, I had not only got on board, but in bed, and as he did not ask how I had spent the day, I did not inform him: he was vexed and out of humour, said he thought the wretches were only *bamboozling* him, he believed they would do nothing but drink the liquor, while he had a drop to carry them, for he was no forwarder than the day before.

In this manner he was obliged to repeat his visits for five successive days, before he got their final decision, which however, was at last tolerably favorable on our side.

They consented to re-establish the people, and to grant to the St. George's Bay Company, all the land King Naimbana had formerly sold Captain Thompson; for a paltry consideration, of about thirty pounds; and for the good faith and true performance of the contract, the King said he would pledge his second son John Frederic, whom Falconbridge might take with him to England: In answer to this offer, Falconbridge told Naimbana, he would be very glad to take his son to England, where he was sure the Company would have him educated and treated kindly without considering him as a hostage.

This pleased the old man vastly, and it was agreed, John Frediric shall accompany us, when we leave Africa.[36]

The following or sixth day, Falconbridge had engaged to carry down to Robana the stipulated goods for repurchacing the land, and by his importunities, I was prevailed on to accompany him. We arrived early in the morning, and having soon made a delivery of the goods, which was all the business for the day, I was just about expressing a desire to see some salt works, I learned were upon the Island, when the King, as though he had anticipated my wishes, enquired if we liked to see them? if so, he would walk their with us: We accordingly went, passing in our way a hamlet or two, inhabited by Kings slaves.

These works lay near a mile from the town, and are a parcel of small holes, or basons formed in a low, muddy place; they are supplied with sea water, which the burning sun quickly exhales, leaving the saline particles, and by frequent repetition, a quantity of salt is thus accumulated, which the King conveys into, and disposes of in the interior country, for slaves.

Making this salt is attended with a very trifling expence, for none but *old, refuse, female* slaves, are employed in the work, and the profit is considerable.[37]

Early in the afternoon we returned to Bance Island, taking Clara, the wife of Elliotte, with us: She remained with me several days, during which I had opportunities (for I made a point of it) to try her disposition; I found it impetuous, litigious, and implacable: I endeavoured to persuade her to dress in the European way, but to no purpose; she would tear the clothes off her back immediately after I put them on.

Finding no credit could be gained by trying to new fashion this *Ethiopian* Princess, I got rid of her as soon as possible.

Falconbridge now had effected the grand object; he was next to collect and settle the miserable refugees: no time was to be lost in accomplishing this; the month of February was nearly spent, only three months of dry weather remained for them to clear their land, build their houses, and prepare their ground for a crop to support them the ensuing year; he therefore dispatched a Greek, who came out in the Lapwing, with some of the blacks, up to Pa Boson's, to gather and bring down the people, while we went in the Cutter, taking a few who were at Bance Island, to locate an eligible place, for the settlement.

The spot they were driven from, was to be preferred to any other part; but by treaty it was agreed they should not settle there: There were other situations nearly as good, and better considerably than the one fixed on; but immediate convenience was a powerful inducement.

Here was a small village, with seventeen pretty good huts, which the natives had evacuated from a persuasion they were infested by some evil spirits; but as they made no objection to our occupying them, we gladly took possession, considering it a fortunate circumstance to have such temporary shelter for the whole of our people.

When those from Pa Bosons had joined us, Falconbridge called them all together, making forty-six, including men and women; and after representing the charitable intentions of his coming to Africa, and issuing to them such cloathing as were sent out in the Lapwing; he exhorted in the most pathetic language, that they might merit by their industry and good behaviour the notice now taken of them, endeavour to remove the unfavourable prejudices that had gone abroad, and thereby deserve further favours from their friends in England; who, besides the cloaths they had already received, had sent them, tools of all kinds, for cultivating their land, also arms and ammunition to defend themselves, if necessary; that these articles would be brought on shore when they got a storehouse built; where they would be lodged for their common good and occasional use; he then concluded this harangue by saying he now named the place, GRANVILLE TOWN, after their friend and benefactor, GRANVILLE SHARP, Esq, at whose instance they were provided with the relief now afforded them.

I never did, and God grant I never may again, witness so much misery as I was forced to be a spectator off here: Among the outcasts were seven of our country women, decrepid with disease, and so disguised with filth and dirt, that I should never have supposed they were born white; add to this, almost naked from head to foot; in short, their appearance was such as I think would extort compassion from the most callous heart; but I declare they seemed insensible to shame, or the wretchedness of their situation themselves; I begged they would get washed, and gave them what cloaths I could conveniently spare: Falconbridge had a hut appropriated as a hospital, where they were kept separate from the other settlers, and by his attention and care, they recovered in a few weeks.

I always supposed these people had been transported as convicts, but some conversation I lately had with one of the women has partly undeceived me: She said, the women were mostly of that description of persons who walk the streets of London, and support themselves by the earnings of prostitution; that men were employed to collect and conduct them to Wapping, where they were intoxicated with liquor, then inveigled on board of ship, and married to *black men,* whom they had never seen before; that the morning after she was married, she really did not remember a syllable of what had happened over night, and when informed, was obliged to inquire, *who was her husband?* After this to the time of their sailing, they were amused and buoyed up by a prodigality of fair promises, and great expectations which awaited them in the country they were going to: "Thus," in her own words, "to the disgrace of my mother country, upwards of one hundred unfortunate women, were seduced from England to practice their iniquities more brutishly in this horrid country."

Good heavens! how the relation of this tale made me shudder; I questioned its veracity, and enquired of the other women who exactly corroborated what I had heard; nevertheless, I cannot altogether reconcile myself to believe it; for it is scarcely possible that the British Government at this advanced and enlightened age, envied and admired as it is by the universe, could be capable of exercising or countenancing such a Gothic infringement on human Liberty.[38]

Immediately after we had fixed on this Place for the settlement, I singled out one of the best huts for my own residence; where I remained nigh a month, though I did not sleep on shore the whole time: About a fortnight I continued to go on board the Cutter at night, when it was necessary to send her to Bance Island; I then had a kind of bedstead, not unlike an hospital cradle, erected in my hovel; but the want of a door was some inconvenience, and as no deal, or other boards could be procured for the purpose, I made a country mat supply the place—for I now find 'tis necessary to accommodate myself to whatever I meet with, there being but few conveniencies or accommodating things to be met with in this part of Africa.

The river abounds with fine fish, and we get abundance of them; which, with rice, wild deer, and some poultry, forms my common food since I came to Granville-Town.

In something less than four weeks we got a large store-house and several additional huts for the settlers, built, and had the goods landed from the Lapwing—they consist chiefly of ironmongery, such as blacksmiths and plantation tools, a prodigious number of children's trifling *halfpenny knives*, and some few dozen scissars of the same *description*.

I am *charitable enough* to think the *benevolent gentleman,* who purchased those goods, had a double purpose in view, viz. to serve his sister, from whom he bought them—and the persons to whom they are sent; but certainly he was unacquainted with the quality of the latter articles, or he must have known they were very improper gifts of charity.

A part of the store-house being partitioned off for us, we took up our abode there whenever it was ready for our reception—it is rather larger, and consequently more cool, which is the only preference I can give it to the last habitation.

The men all do duty as militia, and we have a constant guard kept during the night;[39] but the natives seem to dread this spot so much, that we see very few, and I really think have less to fear from them than our own people, who are extremely turbulent, and so unruly at times, that 'tis with difficulty Falconbridge can assuage them, or preserve the least decorum.

He was desired by the Company to build a fort, and they sent out six pieces of cannon, which are now on board the Lapwing—but omitted to *send carriages,* and consequently the guns are useless; though if they were compleat, Falconbridge thinks it would not be prudent to trust them with the present settlers, from a belief that they might apply them improperly.

He is also requested by his instructions to collect as many samples of country productions as he can, and he wished to employ some of the people in that way, but none would give their services for less than half a guinea per day, which price he has been forced to pay them; this is the greatest instance of ingratitude I ever met with.

We were alarmed a little while since by dreadful shouts, in the vicinity of our town, and supposed the natives meant to attack us; immediately Falconbridge armed his militia, and marched out towards where the noise was heard,—they had not gone far when they met three or four *Panyarers*, or man thieves, just in the act of ironing a poor victim they had caught hunting, and the shouts we heard proved to be rejoicings of the banditti.

Falconbridge did not think it advisable to rescue the prisoner by force, or to interfere further than what words would do; and as some of the *Panyarers* spoke English, he remonstrated against the devilish deed they were committing, but to little effect.

They said somebody belonging to the prisoner's town had injured them, and it was the custom of their country to retaliate on any person living in the same place with an offender, if they could not get himself, which the present case was an example of.

They then carried him away, and in all probability this man will be deprived of his liberty while he lives, by the barbarous customs of his country, for the imaginary offences of another.

I omitted mentioning in my last letter, that the day after we arrived at Bance Island, Mr. William Falconbridge, in consequence of a trifling dispute with his brother, separated from us, and went into the service of Messrs. Anderson's, but his constitution was not adapted for this unhospitable climate.

He went down the coast to York Island, in the river Sherbro, about twenty leagues distance, where he was unavoidably exposed to the severity of the weather, from which he got a fever; and although he immediately returned to Bance Island, and had every assistance administered; yet, I am sorry to say, the irresistible conqueror, *Death,* made all endeavours fruitless, and hurried him to eternity yesterday, after a short illness of four days.

The tornados, or thunder squalls, which set in at this season of the year, preceding the continued rains, have commenced some time, the vivid intense lightning from dismal black clouds, make them awfully beautiful; they are accompanied with violent winds and heavy rains, succeeded by an abominable stench from the earth, and disagreeable hissings and noises from frogs, crickets, and many other insects which the rains draw out.

Musquettos also are growing so troublesome, as to oblige us to keep continued smokes in and about the house.

I have not seen any serpents, but am told there are abundance, and some very venomous.

Here are a vast variety of beautiful lizards constantly about the door catching flies: and I have often seen the changable camelion.

We have not yet been troubled by any of the ferocious wild beasts which inhabit the mountains of Sierra Leone; but I understand there are numbers, both tygers and lions, besides divers other kinds.[40]

I have now in spirits an uncommon insect, which was caught here a day or two ago, in the act of stinging a *Lascar,* (one of the settlers);[41] it is rather larger than a locust, covered with a tortoise coloured shell, has forceps like a lobster, and thin transparent wings like a fly; the bite has thrown the poor Lascar into a dreadful fever, which I fear will carry him off.

I have three monkies, one a very handsome Capuchin, with a sulphur coloured beard of great length.

Nature seems to have been astonishingly sportive in taste and prodigality here, both of vegetable and animal productions, for I cannot stir out without admiring the beauties or deformities of her creation.

Every thing I see is entirely new to me, and notwithstanding the eye quickly becomes familiarized, and even satiated with views which we are daily accustomed to; yet there is such a variety here as to afford a continual zest to the sight.

To be frank, if I had a little agreeable society, a few comforts, and could insure the same good health I have hitherto enjoyed, I should not be against spending some years of my life in Africa; but wanting those sweeteners of life, I certainly wish to return to where they may be had.

When that will be, is not in my power at present to tell; but if I have a chance of writing to you again, I then may be able; in the interim accept an honest farewel from

Your affectionate, &c.

LETTER IV.

GRANVILLE TOWN, *June* 8, 1791.

My dear Madam,

Since my last I have been to the French Factory, visited several neighbouring towns, and made myself a little intimate with the history, manners, customs, &c. of the inhabitants of this part of Africa, which, it seems, was first discovered by the Portugueze, who named it *Sierra de Leone,* or *Mountain of Lions.*[42]

The tract of country now called Sierra Leone is a Peninsula one half the year, and an island the other—that is, during the rains the isthmus is overflowed.

The river, which was formerly called *Tagrin,* now takes its name from the country; at its entrance it is about ten miles from one Promontory to the other, but here, it is scarcely half that distance across, and a few miles higher up it becomes very narrow indeed.

It is not navigable for large vessels any higher than Bance Island, but small craft may go a great distance up.

Besides the islands I have mentioned, there are several others, uninhabited, between this and Bance Island.

Granville town is situated in a pretty deep bay on the south-side of the river, about nine miles above Cape Sierra Leone,* fifteen below Bance Island, and six from Robana.

* The Cape lies in 8. 28. N. Lat. ... 12. 30. W. Lon.

Half a mile below us is the town of one *Pa Duffee;* two miles lower down is *King Jemmy's*; and beyond him is *Queen Yamacubba's*, [*Plate 17*] and two or three small places; a mile above us *Signor Domingo* lives, and a little higher one *Pa Will.*

I have been at all these places, and find a great similitude in the appearance of the people, their behaviour, mode of living, building, amusements, &c.

The men are tall and stout, and was it not that their legs are generally small in proportion to their bodies, and somewhat crooked, I should call them well limbed.

The mode of treating infants 'till they are able to walk, accounts for their being bandy legged.

A few days after a woman is delivered, she takes her child on her back to wherever her vocation leads her, with both its legs buckled round her waist, and the calves pressed to her sides, by which means the tender bones are forced from their natural shape, and get a curve that never after grows out;[43] and thus, the infant is exposed either to the scorching sun, or any change of weather that happens.

The women are not nigh so well shaped as the men, being employed in all hard labour, makes them robust and clumsy; they are very prolific, and keep their breasts always suspended, which, after bearing a child or two, stretches out to an enormous length; disgusting to Europeans; though considered *beautiful* and ornamental here.

They are not only obliged to till the ground, and do all laborious work, but are kept at a great distance by the men, who seldom suffer a woman to sit down or eat with them.

The day I dined at King Naimbana's, he told me I was the first woman that ever eat at the same table with him.

Great respect and reverence is shewn to old age, by all ranks of people.

Polygamy likewise is considered honorable, and creates consequence.

When an African speaks of a great man, he or she will say, "Oh! he be fine man, rich too much, he got too much woman."

The higher class of people hereabout, mostly speak broken English, which they have acquired from frequent intercourse with vessels that come to purchase slaves.

They seem desirous to give education to their children, or in their own way of expressing it, "Read book, and learn to be *rogue* so well as white man;" for they say, if white men could not read, or wanted education, they would be no better rogues than *black gentlemen.*

I was treated with the utmost hospitality at every town I visited.[44]

Their common food is rice, pepper pot, or palaver sauce,[45] palm nuts, and palm oil; with the latter both sexes anoint their bodies and limbs daily, tho' it does not prevent them from smelling vastly strong.[46]

Wherever I went, there was commonly a fowl boiled, or broiled for me: I liked the pepper pot, it is a kind of soup made with a mixture of vegetables highly seasoned with salt and red pepper.[47]

Their houses are much like those I have heretofore described, but very low, they are irregularly placed, and built either in a square or circular form; and as this part of the country is thinly inhabited, each town contains a very few houses.

The inhabitants are chiefly Pagans, though they believe the existence of a God, but consider him so good that he cannot do them an injury; they therefore pay homage to the *Devil,* from a belief that he is the only supernatural being they have to fear; and I am informed they have consecrated places, in different parts of the woods, where they make annual sacrifices to him.

Cleanliness is universally observed; their simple furniture, consisting generally of a few mats, wooden trenchers and spoons, made by themselves, are always tidy, and their homely habitations constantly clean swept, and free from filth of any kind: nor do I think nature has been so unkind to endow those people with capacities less susceptible of improvement and cultivation than any other part of the human race.

I am led to form this conjecture, from the quickness with which even those who cannot understand English, comprehend my meaning by gestures or signs, and the aptness they have imitated many things after me.

Their time is calculated by plantations, moons, and days; the reason of the first is, they clear a new field once a year, and if asked the age of a child, or any thing else, they will answer, so many plantations, in place of years: they register their moons by notches on a piece of wood, which is carefully hanged up in some particular part of the house.

Their chief amusement is dancing: in the evening, men and women assemble in the most open part of the town, where they form a circle, which one at a time enters, and shews his skill and agility, by a number of wild comical motions.

Their music is made by clapping of hands, and a harsh sounding drum or two, made out of hollowed wood covered with the skin of a goat.

Sometimes I have seen an instrument resembling our guitar, the country name of which is *bangeon.* [*Plate 18*]

The company frequently applaud or upbraid the performer, with bursts of laughter, or some odd disagreeable noise; if it is moonshine, and they have spirits to drink, these dances probably continue 'till the moon goes down, or 'till day light.

The *Timmany* dialect is commonly spoke here, though the nation so called is some distance to the northward.

The natives account for this in the following way.

Many years ago the Burees, a tribe of people formerly living upon the banks of the river, Sierra Leone, were conquered and drove away to other parts of the country by the Timmany's, who, having possessed themselves of the land, invited many strangers to come and live among them.

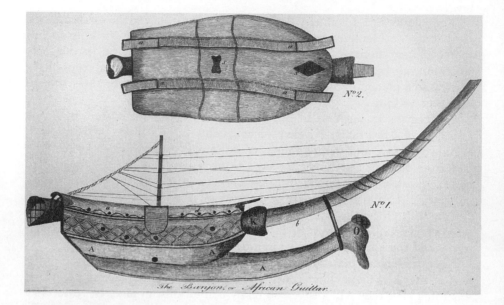

Plate 18 'The Banjon, or African Guitar', from John Matthews, *A Voyage to the River Sierra-Leone* (2nd edn, 1791). Of this instrument Matthews writes: 'It is played upon with the fingers, and the sounds proceeding from it are soft and sweet, though they have no kind of notes or variation of tune.'
Source: Cambridge University Library; by permission of the Syndics of Cambridge University Library.

The Timmanys being again engaged in war, which the inhabitants of Sierra Leone did not chuse to join in, they therefore alienated the connection, and declared themselves a distinct nation, and have been considered as such ever since.

Every chief or head man of a town is authorized from the King to settle local disputes—but when disagreements of consequence arise between people of separate places, then a Palaver is summoned to the residence of the complainant, when the King attends or not as suits him; but if inconvenient to go in person, he sends his Palaver-man, who carries the King's sword, cane, or hat, as a signal of inauguration, to his office.

When all the parties are met, they enquire into the business of their meeting, and a majority of voices determine who has *reason* of his or her side.

If the crime is fornication, the punishment is slavery, unless the offender can ransom him or herself, by paying another slave, or the value in goods.

It is customary when the *Judges* cannot procure sufficient proof, to oblige the party accused to take a poisonous draught, called Red Water—this potion is prepared by the *Judges* themselves, who make it strong or weak as they are inclined by circumstances—if strong, and the stomach does not reject it instantaneously, death soon ensues—but if weak, it seldom has any other effect than a common emetic.[48]

At the last town I visited, the head man's favorite woman had a beautiful *mulatto* child, and seeing me take much notice of it, he said, "God amity, sen, me dat peginine, true, suppose he no black like me, nutting for that, my woman drinkee red water, and suppose peginine no for me, he dead."

I could not help smiling at the old fool's credulity, and thinking how happy many of my own countrywomen would be to rid themselves of a similar stigma, so easily.[49] [*Plate 19*]

Crimes of larger magnitude, such as *witchcraft*, murder, &c. are punished in the same way, i.e. the criminal is obliged to drink of this liquor, unless there be evidence sufficiently strong to acquit or condemn him: when that is the case, if convicted, he either suffers death, or is sold as a slave.

On the opposite shore lives a populous nation called the Bullams, whose King I had occasion to mention in a former letter. I have been at only one of their settlements, a place directly over against us, belonging to a man named Dean.

The people appear more inclined to industry than the Sierra Leonians, which a stranger may readily discern, by the superior way their houses are furnished in.

I am told it is a fertile country, and the inhabitants make so much rice, that they are able to sell a quantity annually.

In the neighbourhood of Dean's Town, at a place called Tagrin Point, was formerly an English factory, belonging to one Marshall; but he unluckily got into a dispute with the natives, who drove him away, and pillaged his goods; they are a barbarous implacable set of people.

This is all the history I have learnt of the Bullams, therefore shall return to my own side of the water.

We have had heavy tornadoes and falls of rain for several weeks, and I yet enjoy my health as well, if not better, than I did for several years past in Europe.

Deaths are not frequent among the natives; indeed I have not heard of one since we arrived.

Their national diseases are few; probably anointing themselves as they do with palm oil, makes them less liable to evil consequences from the unhealthy putrid vapour that almost constantly hovers about these mountains; the poisonous effects of which carries off numbers of foreigners.

About ten days ago the master of the cutter went to Bance Island, where

A method whereby
the MEN of GUINEA oblige
their Wives to purge themselves
from the accusation of
ADULTERY

Published by Alex.r Hogg May 24. 1794.

Plate 19 'A method whereby the Men of Guinea oblige their Wives to purge themselves from the accusation of Adultery', from William Portlock's *A New Collection of Modern Voyages and Travels* (1794), opp. p. 164.
Source: State Library of Victoria.

he drank too freely, and returning a little indisposed, signified a wish of going to the French factory for medical assistance.

Falconbridge having had some difference with this man, therefore, lest he might wrong construe any offers to serve him, without hesitation complied with his desire, and he immediately set out in the cutter to Gambia, Falconbridge and myself accompanying him.

The distance being but six miles, and a fresh sea breeze, we soon ran up.

Mr. Rennieu not only received us with the politeness of a Frenchman, but with kindness and friendship.

When he saw the master of the Lapwing, he said to me, "Madam, Captain Kennedy (for that was his name) will never leave Africa, but in two or three days time he will come under my *big tree*."

I did not instantly comprehend him, which the Frenchman perceived, and explained himself by saying, "under the large tree I saw a little distance off, was the burying ground, and" added he, "there is something in the countenance of Kennedy denoting his dissolution to be near at hand; and I am persuaded the man cannot live more than two or three days."

I took care not to mention or hint to Kennedy what Mr. Rennieu said to me, lest the force of imagination might kill him—however, in spite of all our endeavours, the prophecy was fulfilled; a severe fever came on the same night, and the second day he was a corpse.

There was no accommodation for sleeping on shore at the Factory, which Mr. Rennieu could offer us—we were, consequently, obliged to sleep on board.

I could not think of allowing the poor sick man to be exposed to the inclemency of night air, and insisted on his taking a birth in the cabin—nor could I think of continuing in the cabin while he was ill, lest his disorder might be infectious; and the only alternative was to lay upon deck, or in the hold.

The former being most preferable, our mattresses were spread at night under the awning, where we lay; but I took the precaution to wrap myself up in a flannel gown, and cover'd my head with a cap of the same—was it not for that, in all probability, I must have added to the number under Mr. Rennieu's big tree.

For two nights we lay on deck, and each of them, we were unlucky enough to have violent tornadoes; during the storm I threw two large blankets over me, and though the rain penetrated through both, yet my flannel gown and cap intercepted it, and prevented me from getting wet, except my feet, which I bathed in spirits when the tornado was over, and thus, I believe, escaped any bad consequences; but being under the necessity of staying another night at Gambia, I did not chuse to experience the good effects of my blankets a third time, and accepted an invitation which the Captain of an American had made us—to take a bed on board his ship.

Immediately after the corpse was removed, we had the Lapwing scowered, washed with vinegar, and smoaked with tobacco and brimstone, to free her from every suspicion of dangerous infection.

I must avail myself of the present moment to give you some description of Gambia Island.

It is small and low, not two miles in circumference, situated in the midst of swamps and marshes, from whence a continued stench comes sufficient to choak a carrion crow—'tis wonderful how any human beings could pitch on such a place to live in.[50]

The Europeans there have all complexions as if they were fed on madder and saffron.

Their manner of living is slovenly and hoggish, though they seem to have plenty of fresh stock, and provisions of almost every kind—they are very inactive and indolent, which I am not astonished at, for such must ensue from the lassitude produced by the unhealthiness of the place.

The buildings are of mean and disrespectable appearance, being a pile of grass and sticks clumsily put together.

They have a factory ship, and few goods are kept on shore, from a fear of being surprised and robbed by the natives.

Formerly the island was protected by a company of French soldiers, but the vast and rapid mortality, deterred their government from sending fresh supplies.

Rennieu, however, preserves a kind of consequence, and keeps his neighbours in awe by a number of strange legerdemain tricks he has learnt, some of which he shews when ever he has visitors.

After seeing Gambia, I consider Granville Town a delightful spot, where we have none of those swampy low grounds; but a reviving sea breeze that cheers us every day, which is almost spent before it reaches them; I suppose, this must be owing to the heavy dense atmosphere that opposes its progress, for distance cannot be the cause.

Since the rains commenced, the nights grew alternately cooler, indeed I find a blanket very comfortable; even during the dry weather (when I had room to breathe), I found night many degrees colder than day; but it is now, at times, cold, that I am glad to find a fire.

This sudden transition from heat to cold, and from cold to heat, I am rather disposed to think, accounts for the turpitude of the climate, at all events it certainly is one of the most considerable causes.

From a fear that my inadequateness to give historical delineations, will expose me to your criticism, I have to beg you will look over any rhapsodies with lenity; *this* is all I can hope for,—*that* all I dread.

Falconbridge thinks of leaving Africa the middle of this month; the loss of Kennedy, want of provisions fit for taking to sea, and the late Mate (now Master of the cutter), and several of our people being sick, disconcerts us a good deal: but we are told the rains will be considerably worse, and every day will render it more dangerous and difficult to get off the coast: Falconbridge is determined to do his best, and get away as quick as possible.

Oh my friend! what happiness shall I feel on seeing Old England again; and, if it pleases God for us to arrive safe, the difficulties, dangers, and inconveniences I have surmounted, and have yet to encounter, will only serve me to laugh at.

Your's, &c. &c.

LETTER V.

LONDON, *Sept.* 30, 1791.

My dear Friend,

I have many apologies to make for not giving you earlier intelligence of our arrival; but my excuses are good ones, and no doubt will convince you my silence cannot be attributed to the slightest shadow of negligence or forgetfulness.

We arrived at Penzance, in Cornwall, the 2d instant, when (not being able to walk), I was carried in an arm chair, by two men, to the house of *Mrs. Dennis,* who friendly invited us to shelter under her hospitable roof, while we remained there.

The hurry and fatigue of moving, with the restraint one customarily feels, more or less of, upon going to a strange house, prevented me writing you the first day; but the day subsequent I wrote as follows:

My dearest Madam,

"I am returned to this blessed land; join with me in fervent prayer and thanksgiving to the Author of all good works, for his miraculous protection and goodness, during a circuitous passage of nigh three months, replete with hardships unprecedented, I believe, in any voyages heretofore related, the particulars of which I must take some other opportunity to furnish you with."

Here I made a full pause; and, after thinking and re-thinking for near half an hour, whether I should subscribe my name and send it to the post, a thought struck me,—"Why! I shall be in London in eight or ten days, when it will be in my power to send a narration of what has happened since I last wrote Mrs —— ; and if I write now, I shall only excite curiosity, and keep her in unpleasant suspence for some time; so, it is best to postpone writing till I can do it fully."

Now, in place of eight or ten days, it was almost three weeks before we reached this metropolis; and since I arrived, my time has been wholly occupied in received inquisitive visitors, and answering a few pertinent, and a number of ridiculous questions.

I could make many other reasonable pleas, in behalf of my silence, but trust what is already said will be amply satisfactory; shall therefore forbear making any further apologies, and proceed with an account of myself since I last wrote to you.

The 16th of June we went to Robana to take leave of the *Royal Family*, and to receive the young Prince John Frederic on board; all this we accomplished, and sailed the same day.

Naimbana seemed unconcerned at parting with his son, but the old Queen cried, and appeared much affected.

The Prince was decorated in an old blue cloak, bound with broad gold lace; which, with a black velvet coat, pair of white satin breeches, a couple of shirts, and two or three pair of trowsers, form a compleat inventory of his stock of cloaths, when he left Africa.

The old man gave John all the cash he had, amounting to the *enormous sum* of eight Spanish dollars (about thirty-five shillings); and just when we were getting under way, saluted us with twelve guns, from some rusty pieces of cannon, lying on the beach, without carriages.

The Lapwing was badly equipped for sea; the crew and passengers amounted to nine: four of the former were confined with fevers, consequently there were only four, (and but one a sailor) to do the ship's duty.

Mr. Rennieu gave me a goat and half a dozen of fowls: King Naimbana put a couple of goats, and a dozen of fowls on board for his son.

Besides these, I purchased some poultry, and when we sailed, considered ourselves possessed of a pretty good stock, consisting of three goats, four dozen of fowls, a barrel of flour, half a barrel of pork, and a barrel of beef.

We had not been at sea a week, when all our live stock were washed or blown overboard, by repeated and impetuous tornadoes—so that we had not a thing left but the flower and salt provisions; however, we were in hopes of getting in a few days to Saint Jago, one of the Cape De Verd Islands, where the loss of our stock might be replaced.[51]

In this we were disappointed, for instead of a few days, a continued interruption of calms and boisterous weather, made it six weeks before we reached that island; during the whole of which time I was confined to my cabin, and mostly to my bed, for it rained incessantly.

After being about three weeks at sea, our sick got clear of their fevers, but were so emaciated as to be unfit for any duty, *except eating*, and though there was no food fit for convalescent persons on board, yet the coarse victuals we had stood no chance with them, and made it necessary to put all hands to an allowance.

Upon enquiring into the state of our provisions, we found they had been lavishly dealt with; there was not more than one week's full allowance of meat, and scarcely four days of flour remaining.

These were alarming circumstances, for we had two thirds further to go, than we had then come, towards Saint Jago.

I did not selfishly care for the want of beef or pork, as I had not tasted either since we sailed from Sierra Leone; but I lamented it for others.

All hands were restricted to a quarter of a pound of beaf or pork, and a small tea-cup full (rather better than a gill) of flower per day.

What would have been more dreadful, we should have wanted water, was it not for the rains; the worms having imperceptibly penetrated our water casks, all the water leaked out, except a small cask, which would not allow us more than a pint each, for three weeks.

My tea cup of flower, mixed with a little rain water and salt, boiled to a kind of pap, when the weather would admit a fire, otherwise raw, was, believe me, all my nourishment for ten days, except once or twice, when some cruel unconscionable wretch robbed me of the homely morsel, I was forced to taste the beef.

The week before we arrived at St. Jago, our Carpenter, who had been ill, and was on the recovery, relapsed, and died in twenty-four hours; which circumstance terrified me exceedingly, least our afflictions were to be increased with some pestilential disease; however, no similar misfortunes attended us afterwards.

We arrived at Porta Praya in St. Jago, I think, the 25th of July, when Falconbridge immediately went on shore to obtain sufferance to remain there a few days, while he re-victualled and watered.

An officer met him as he landed, and conducted him to the chief magistrate of the port, who lives in a Fort on top of a hill which commands the harbour.

Falconbridge was well received, his request granted, and he and myself were invited to dine at the Fort next day—but he was informed that no provisions were to be had for almost any price—a fleet of European ships had just sailed from thence, and drained the country of almost every kind of eatable.

After being six weeks confined in the narrow bounds of the Lapwing's cabin, and most of the time in bed, fed as I was upon scanty wretched food, notwithstanding the benignity of heaven had preserved me from disease of any kind, you will not question my energy of mind and body being considerably enervated; indeed, so enfeebled did I feel myself, that it was with much difficulty I accompanied Falconbridge to dinner at the Consul's, for so the Chief Officer of Porto Praya is termed; but the distance I had to walk was short, and with the help of a Portuguese Officer on one side, and my husband on the other, I accomplished it tolerable well.

The company consisted of the Portuguese and French Consuls, five Portuguese and two French gentlemen, two Portuguese ladies, Falconbridge, and myself.

None of the foreigners spoke English, so you will readily guess we but poorly amused or entertained each other; through the medium of a linguist, who attended, any compliments, questions, or answers, &c. &c. were conveyed to and fro.

Our dinner was very good, and I had prudence enough to be temperate, having often heard of fatal consequences from indulgencies in similar cases.

During dinner we had excellent claret and madeira, but no wine was drank after; directly as the cloth was removed, tea was introduced in the most uncommon way I ever saw or heard of, before; it was brought in china mugs, containing three pints each, and every person was presented with one of those huge goblets.

I had not tasted tea for several weeks, nevertheless, one third of this quantity was more than I chose to swallow—but with astonishment I beheld others make a rapid finish of their allowance.

Having thus inundated their stomachs, every one arose, and our host desired the linguist to acquaint me they were going to repose themselves for a while, and if I was inclined to follow their example, a sofa, or bed was at my service; being bed sickened, I declined the offer, and chose, in preference, to stretch my feeble limbs with gentle walking in a pleasant portico, fronting the sea; for I had gathered strength enough, in the few hours I was on shore, to walk alone.

The company having indulged about an hour in their habitual slothfulness, re-assembled; we were invited to take a bed on shore, but Falconbridge learnt, the generality of people were thievishly disposed, and for that reason did not chuse to sleep from the cutter; and you know it would have been very uncomfortable for me to remain without him, among a parcel of strangers, when we could not understand what one or other said; besides, I had other prudential objections for not remaining without Falconbridge, which the horror of our loathsome bark could not conquer.[52]

After this, we remained four days in Porto Praya Road, during which, I went on shore frequently.

The town is situated on the same height with the fort.

They have a Romish chapel, (for the inhabitants are all Roman Catholics) market-place, and jail, built of stone, and covered with slate in the European way—the other buildings are mostly of wood and thatch, after the African manner.

The French Consul has his house within the fort, which is a decent good looking building, as is the Portuguese Consul's; but this is of stone, and that of wood.

The people of most countries have their peculiar modes of habiting themselves, but surely the custom of Port Praya is more odious than any other;—in meeting a hundred men, two are not to be seen dressed alike—perhaps one will have a coat thrown over his shoulders without occupying the sleeves; another, a woman's petticoat drawn round his neck, with his arms through the pocket holes, and so on, except the higher ranks.

The women dress rather more uniformly; they wear very short petticoats, and tight jackets, of a coarse linen, like Osnaburg,[53] but no *shifts*; I mean the lower class, or natives, who are mostly black, or of mix'd complexions; for the few European ladies there, are genteely habited with fine India muslins, and their hair neatly plaited, and put up in silk nets.

A narrow, handsome kind of cotton cloth is manufactured at St. Jago; I went to one of the manufactories, and purchased several pieces; they are in great estimation, and sell for a high price—I paid five and six dollars a piece, (about two yards and a half) for those I bought.—The loom they are wove in resembles our garter loom.

I understood the inhabitants raise their own cotton, and have several small sugar works, which makes a sufficiency of sugar for the consumption of those islands, but no quantity for exportation.

The Governor resides at a town named St. Jago, a considerable distance from Porto Praya, and on the opposite side of the island, which put it out of our power to visit it.

The Consul at Porto Praya is his Vicegerent, but has his authority from Portugal; there appeared to me a great want of government among the people, notwithstanding a strong military force is kept there.

We got a superabundance of fine fish while we remained at St. Jago, which was a fortunate circumstance—for our intelligence respecting the scarcity of provisions was perfectly true.

With our utmost endeavours we could not procure but two goats and two dozen of fowls, to take with us to sea; and those I was obliged to purchase with some of my wearing apparel, which was preferred to money; or, I should say, they were not to be had for money.

Bread and salt provisions were not to be had in the smallest quantity, for any price; however, we purchased a number of cocoa nuts, which they have in plenty, as a substitute for bread.

With these trifling and ordinary sea-stores we departed from Porto Praya, the 30th of July, trusting by oeconomical management, to make them serve till we reached some other port.

I recovered my strength and spirits considerably during the short time we were at that place, as did all our sick; indeed it was necessary, and lucky, for it enabled us to contend against misfortune, and conquer the hardships, and inconveniencies, which afterwards attended us.

We had fine moderate weather the first twenty-four hours, and got the length of St. Vincent, one of the same islands,[54]—where, falling calm, we came to anchor.

Some of the people went on shore, thinking to kill a few birds; and supposing the island uninhabited, it being a small barren place, without a tree or shrub of any sort, a kind of fern excepted, so that no houses could be there, and escape our notice.

The boat's crew had scarcely landed, when we were greatly astonished and alarmed to behold from the cutter (for we lay no distance off the shore) five *naked human beings*, who had just started up from behind a hilloc, running towards them—however, our fears were quickly abated, by seeing the boat returning.

The master was one that went on shore, and he understood a little Portuguese, in which language these victims to barbarity addressed, and told him, they had, several months past, been banished from an adjacent island, called Mayo,[55] and landed where they then were in the deplorable condition he beheld them.

The Lapwing was the first vessel that had anchored there since their exilement, and they begged and prayed we would take them off—they did not care where!

This we could not do with any kind of discreetness, from the danger of starving them and ourselves.

They consisted of three men and two women, and we mustered two petticoats and three pair of trowsers for them.

I was curious to know something more of the poor wretches, and went with Falconbridge and the Master on shore.

Before we landed, they had retired behind the hilloc, and we sent forward their cloathing that they might be dressed by the time we came up.

We found them in the act of broiling fish over a fire made of dry fern, which was the only fuel they could possibly have.

Our Skipper asked, if they had any houses? but was answered in the negative; and pointing to the heaven and the earth, signifying *this* was their bed, and *that* their covering; he then enquired, how they subsisted? and for what they were banished?

To the first they replied,—When put on the Island, fishing lines, hooks, and implements for striking fire, were given them, through which means they supported themselves; there was plenty of fish, and a good spring of water; but said they, "we have not tasted bread since we left Mayo."

To the second, no further answer could be obtained, than their having offended the Governor of Mayo, who was a *black man*.

They were miserably emaciated, and a hapless melancholy overhang'd their countenances.—When we first came up, joyful smiles beamed through the cloud, which soon darkened when they learnt there was no prospect of being relieved.

They followed us to the boat, and I really believe, if they had been armed, would have taken her from us: as it was, our men were obliged to use violence, and turn them out, for all hands had jumped in, and attempted to get off.

We offered to take any one of them, but not one would consent to separate or share any good fortune the whole could not partake off.

When we got clear from the shore, they pursued us up to their necks in water, crying and howling so hideously, that I would have given the world! (were it at my disposal) if it was either in our power to bring them away, or that I had not seen them.

Here we remained all night, and till three o'clock the day following, when a light favourable breeze enabled us to sail; before our departure, we sent the convicts an iron pot, for cooking, and a few fishing utensils, which was all we could possibly spare them.

To the northward of St. Vincent's, about eight or nine miles, is St. Anthony, another of the Cape de Verd Islands, which we had to pass close by.

The wind was very week, but every one imagined there was enough of it to take us clear off that Island before morning; whether that was not the case, or whether things were badly managed, I shall not decidedly say, though I have a decided opinion on the subject; for towards four o'clock in the morning, being uncommonly restless, I thought, as the vessel appeared very quiet, and the moon shone beautifully bright, I would get up and set upon deck for awhile.

Perhaps merciful Providence directed this,—for the like I never did before or since; and had I not, in all probability we must have been driven against the rude rocks of St. Anthony, and God only knows what would have been the consequence, as I was the only person awake.

The first thing I saw, upon lifting my head out of the cabin, was those lofty perpendicular rocks pending almost directly over us, and not a man upon deck but King Naimbana's son, and him fast asleep.

"Good God!" cried I, "Falconbridge, we are on shore!"

He instantly sprung up, and called all hands, who got the boat out, and with the utmost exertion towed us off a small distance.

When day light came on, our danger appeared more forcibly, for, notwithstanding the oars had been diligently employed an hour and an half, we were not two hundred yards from the Island.

Some said it was a current; others, it was the land which influenced or attracted us; but what the real reasons were I know not; this only I can tell you,—after trying every possible means to no purpose, 'till four o'clock in the afternoon, when the men complaining their strength was exhausted, and they could do no more, it was agreed to abandon the Lapwing, and look out for a place where we might land before night, and thereby secure safety for our lives, if the vessel could not be preserved.

Accordingly every one was desired to get into the boat, but we found she was too small to carry us all at once; and two of the sailors agreed to stay 'till she could make a second trip.

Falconbridge and myself got in, taking with us a few shiftings of cloaths and our bedding; we then rowed to the land, and after pulling too and fro for near two hours, could not discover a single spot where there was a possibility of landing; during which time, we observed the Cutter drifting fast toward the shore, and expected every moment to see her strike.

Despondency was visibly pictured in every face!—"What shall we do, or what is best to be done?" was the universal cry.

Conscious of a woman's insignificance in such matters, I was silent till then; when finding a general vacancy of opinion among the men, I ventured to say—"Let us return to the Lapwing, and put our trust in him who is all sufficient, and whose dispensations are always unquestionably just."

To this forlorn proposition every one assented; but said it was only deferring the evil moment a few hours, for we should certainly have to trust to our boat very shortly again, unless a breeze came off the land.

After getting on board it was settled—one person should watch while the rest refreshed themselves with sleep, that they might be somewhat able to encounter the looked-for fatigues of the night.

For my part, I did not in the least incline to sleep, but with watchful eyes and aching heart, awaited the expected moment when eight of us were to commit ourselves, in a small open boat, to the mercy of the ungovernable ocean.

Many reflections pressed upon me, but one more powerful than any—"that our dilemma was probably a mark of divine vengeance, for not relieving the distressed people at St. Vincent's."

I often asked the watch, if we neared the rocks; sometimes he answered in the affirmative, and sometimes doubtfully—but said we seemed to drift coastways withall; and he believed there was a strong current setting to the southward.

About twelve o'clock Falconbridge came on deck; and I mentioned this information to him: he then took notice himself, and found it really so.

All hands were immediately turned out, and the boat again manned to tow our bark with the current, for though it had not been observed, we were doubtless working against it all the preceding day.

This proved a propitious speculation; in about four hours we could see the south-west end of the Island, and at the same time had got near a mile off the land.

What a change of countenance was now on board: I felt my bosom fill with gratitude at hearing the glad tidings!

General tokens of joy and congratulations passed from one ship-mate to another; and when daylight appeared, instead of gloom and sorrow, every cheek blush'd cheerfulness.

We then found ourselves clear of the Island, and having a fine moderate breeze, bid adieu to the African coast; nevertheless our troubles did not end here.

After running to the Westwarn eight and forty hours, a tremendous storm came on, and continued to increase in violence for five days.

This had scarcely abated, when it was succeeded by another, nearly as bad—which however ran us as far as Fyal, one of the Azores, or Western Islands, where we arrived the 18th of August.

I do not mean to take up your time with a description of those storms, or a detail of our sufferings, since we left St. Anthony, 'till our arrival at Fyal, though I must not pass over them wholly unnoticed.

Every horror, the most fertile ideas can picture a sea storm with, aggravated the former; and, consequently augmenting the miseries of the latter, rendered them almost unbearable and past representation.

God knows they would have been bad enough without; for the day we reached Fyal, about two pounds of salt beef and half a dozen cocoa nuts, were all the provisions we had left.

We remained there a week, and were hospitably entertained by Mr. Graham, the English Consul, who had the goodness to insist on our taking a bed at his house, directly as our arrival was announced to him.

Being much bruised and indisposed by our boisterous rough passage, and eating food I had not been accustomed to, prevented me from walking abroad for two or three days; while thus confined, I was highly delighted and amused with admiring Mr. Graham's beautiful garden adjoining his house, where are almost all the fruits of the torrid, frigid, and temperate zones, in the greatest perfection; peaches, apples, pears, oranges, pine apples, limes, lemons, citron, grapes, &c. &c. the finest I ever saw.

Mrs. Graham treated me with motherly kindness: by her attention, and the wholesomeness of the climate, I gained so much fresh strength and spirits, that before I came away, I was able frequently to walk about the town, and once took an excursion into the country, with her and a party of her friends, to the seat of a Mr. Perkins, an English gentleman.

We all rode on asses, for carriages (if they have any) could not pass the way we went.

I was pleased with the reception this gentleman gave us, as well as his polite and generous behaviour.

In our way thither we passed a number of vineyards; and, as far as I could judge, the country seemed fruitful.

Besides this excursion, Mr. and Mrs. Perkins persuaded me to take one with them, to the Island of Pico, about eight miles from Fyal, where they have a valuable vineyard; and where they assured me, I should see the most wonderful natural curiosity, in the Azore Islands; viz. two springs of water within eighteen feet of each other—one nearly as cold as ice, the other boiling with heat.

When we arrived there, several washerwomen were employed in their vocation; they told me the water was soft, and well adapted for washing; that they made it of what temperature they pleased, by mixing a proportion of each, and declared they had frequently boiled fish in the hot well: I had a mind to try the heat by putting my finger in, but found the steam powerful enough to convince me I should be *scalded.*

There are public Baths at those Wells, well attended by the inhabitants of Fayal, and the adjacent Islands; they lay somewhat to the eastward, at the foot of the mountain, which gives its name to this Island.

This is the highest mountain I ever saw, very thickly wooded towards its base, but picturesque, with many gentleman's seats, and on the whole vastly gratifying to the eye.

It produces a particular and favourite kind of wood, called *Teixa,* or *Teixo,*[56] which, from its valuable qualities, no one is allowed to sell for private use, it being reserved by the Queen of Portugal, after the custom of her predecessors, solely for the service of the Portugueze government.

I was but a few hours at Pico, and this was all the information I collected.

There are two nunneries, and a magnificent Romish church at Fyal, which I visited.

The former were crouded with nuns, and many of them beautiful women.

I saw two who spoke English, with whom I conversed for some time, and purchased several artificial flowers, and a few sweatmeats from them.

One of them had all the traces of beauty yet unblemished, but to a certainty somewhat tinged by ruinous time; for by her own account she must be far advanced in years.

Upon asking her opinion of a monastic life, she said, "Madam, I have been within the walls of this convent forty-three years, and had I to travel over my life anew, I would prefer the same path to all others."

But a charming buxom young girl thought otherwise.—She said, "Can you suppose an animated creature, like me, full of youthful fire, was designed by nature to spend her days within these dismal walls? No! nor can I figure to myself, that any one (in spite of what many may tell you) can find pleasure in burying herself alive, and thwarting the purposes of her creation, for such is certainly the case with all nuns," and continued she: "My parents placed me here at a time when I was not capable of judging for myself; nor do I scruple to say, that my ideas and fancies are fluttering among the amusements and gaieties of the world, and had I my will, my person would be there also."

I attended the church at mass time; after service was ended, I observed several men bringing in a large sail of a ship, which had a curious appearance to a stranger, as I was; but a gentleman present said, "Those people have been in the same storm with yourselves, and they are giving that sail to the church as a thanks offering for their deliverance:"—he then shewed me part of the boat which Captain Inglefield had been saved in, and which was kept here as a record of divine favour to that gentleman.[57]

This circumstance refreshed my memory with the notorious sufferings and wonderful escape of Capt. Inglefield and his boat's crew; and after mentally weighing our misfortunes with his, I summ'd them both up as follows.

"Captain Inglefield experienced all the miseries of hunger, fatigue, and oppression of spirits, which sixteen days in an open boat, exposed to the furious, untameable wind and sea, without provision, in momentary expectation of being hurried to eternity, could inflict, besides the additional horrors produced by ruminating on the hapless condition of such numbers of his fellow-creatures, in the same situation with himself."

"We have been fifty-eight days in a deck'd boat, not twice the size of Captain Inglefield's—continued rains almost all the while—three weeks a quarter of a pound of beef, and about half the quantity of flour our allowance—eighteen days more baffled by calms, and contrary winds, or beat about by merciless storms, fed upon mean disagreeable food, and scarcely enough of that to keep soul and body together; and, what was worse than all, the apprehension of being left morseless of any kind of nourishment; which certainly must have been the case, had we not arrived at Fayal when we did."

Having done this, I compared them with one another—and though it is unfair to give my decision, we being too often apt to magnify our own misfortunes, and always supposing them greater than those of others; yet I shall hazard making you acquainted with the conclusion I drew, which, however, was very laconic.

I said to myself, "Captain Inglefield's sufferings are matchless, and were it not for the duration, and repetition of mine, they could have but little semblance to one another."

The small pox was committing prodigious ravages among all ranks of people when we left Fyal; and, I suppose, continues still so to do.

A child of the French Consul's lay dangerously ill with that disease, and he requested Falconbridge would visit it;—he did so, and found the infant confined in a small close room, where every means were taken to shut out the least breath of air.

Falconbridge directly recommended the child to be brought into a large open hall, which was done against the absurd remonstrances of the Portuguese Physician, who pronounced immediate death to it; however, before our departure we had the pleasure of seeing this innocent babe (who would in all probability, have otherwise fallen a victim to those ridiculous notions of treating the small pox) quite out of danger; and I trust the precedent will be generally attended to, and may prove equally efficacious.

Many of our countrymen reside there, who are Roman Catholics, and married to Portuguese ladies, with few exceptions.

I saw two or three English women—perhaps all on the Island; they seem to have preserved their native manners and customs in high perfection, which the Portuguese ladies emulously try to copy; more especially in the article of dress, than any thing else; but in this they are much hindred by the jealousy and narrow ideas of their husbands, who never suffer their wives to go abroad, or appear in company with other men, whether single or married, without a deep black or white sattin veil that hides not only the face but the body.

In a conversation with one of those ladies, she said to me "the women of your country must surely be very happy: they have so much more liberty than we have, or I believe, than the women of any other country, I wish I was an English woman!" I thanked her in behalf of my country women, for her good opinion, but assured her they had their share of thorns and thistles, as well as those of other countries.[58]

How deeply do I regret our short stay at Saint Jago and Fayal, disables me from giving you a more historical and intelligent account of those Islands; but I was long enough at each place to form this summary opinion: The latter is, without exception, the most desirable spot I ever saw; and the former, as far opposite as 'tis possible for you to conceive.

Having repaired such damage as our vessel had received coming from St.

Anthony, and supplied ourselves with abundance of stores to bring us to this country, we set sail from Fayal the 25th of last month, and arrived at the time and place before-mentioned.

Our passage was short and unattended with such boisterous weather as we had experienced, yet it was so stormy that I was obliged to keep my bed the whole time: which circumstance and a cold I caught, threw me into an indisposition that I have not yet recovered from.

The day after landing at Penzance, Falconbridge wrote to Mr. Granville Sharp,[59] and by return of Post received his answer, a copy of which I herewith inclose.

"LEADENHALL-STREET, 7*th Sept.* 1791.

"Dear Sir,

"The agreeable account of the safe arrival of the Lapwing at Penzance, which I received this morning, gives me very particular satisfaction.

"I have communicated your letter to Henry Thornton, Esq. Chairman of the Court of Directors of the *Sierra Leone Company*[60] (for under this title the late St. George's Bay Company is now established, by an Act of the last Session of Parliament) and to some of the Directors, and they desire you to come by land as expeditiously as you can, bringing with you in a post-chaise, Mrs. Falconbridge and the Black Prince, and also, any such specimens of the country as will not be liable to injury by land-carriage.

"I inclose (from the Directors) a note from Mr. Thornton's house, for thirty pounds, for which you may easily procure cash for your journey, and if more should be wanting for use of the people of the Lapwing, I have no doubt but Mrs. Dennis (to whose care I send this Letter) will have the goodness to advance it, as she will be reimbursed by return of the Post, when I receive advice of your draft.

"The Lapwing may be left to the care of any proper person whom you may think capable of taking due care of her, until the Directors give farther orders respecting her.

"I remain with great esteem,
"Dear Sir,
"Your affectionate friend,
"And humble Servant,
"GRANVILLE SHARP."

Mr. Alexander Falconbridge.

In the interim Falconbridge went to Falmouth to procure money for our journey to London.

There he met the Rev. Thomas Clarkson, that unwearied stickler for human liberty, with whom, (or at whose instimulation) the abolition of the Slave Trade originated, and at whose instance Falconbridge quitted his comfortable situation at Ludway, to enlist in the present (though I fear chimerical) cause of freedom and humanity.

Mr. Clarkson is also a Director of the Sierra Leone Company, under which title, you find by Mr. Sharp's letter, the late St. George's Bay Company is now called.

He informed Falconbridge that his brother, Lieutenant Clarkson of the navy, was gone to Nova Scotia, authorised by government to collect several hundred free blacks and take them to Sierra Leone, where they are (under the care and patronage of the Directors of our new company) to form a colony.

It was surely a premature, hair-brained, and ill digested scheme, to think of sending such a number of people all at once, to a rude, barbarous and unhealthy country, before they were certain of possessing an acre of land; and I very much fear will terminate in disappointment, if not disgrace to the authors; though at the same time, I am persuaded the motives sprung from minds unsullied with evil meaning.

We set out from Penzance the 12th, taking with us the Black Prince, and the following day arrived at Plymouth, where by appointment we met Mr. Clarkson; after staying there four days we went on towards London, stopped at Exeter three days, and arrived here the 24th.

As soon as our arrival was known Mr. Thornton, (the chairman) Mr. Sharp, and several others of the directors came to see us, and after many compliments expressive with condolence for our misfortunes, and congratulations for our deliverance and safe arrival, a number of enquiries, &c. &c. Mr. Thornton requested Falconbridge and the Prince would dine with him, at the same time gave the latter to understand he was to consider his (Mr. Thornton) house as his home.

I could not help secretly smiling to see the servile courtesy which those gentlemen paid this young man, merely from his being the son of a nominal king.[61]

It has slip'd my notice till now to describe him to you: His person is rather below the ordinary, inclining to groseness, his skin nearly jet black, eyes keenly intelligent, nose flat, teeth unconnected, and filed sharp after the custom of his country, his legs a little bandied, and his deportment easy, manly, and confident withal. In his disposition he is surly, but has cunning enough to smother it where he thinks his interest is concerned; he is pettish and implacable, but I think grateful and attached to those he considers his friends; nature has been bountiful in giving him sound intelects, very capable of improvement, and he also possesses a great thirst for knowledge.

While with me although it was seldom in my power, yet now and then I amused myself with teaching him the alphabet, which he quickly learned, and before we parted, could read any common print surprisingly well.[62]

He is not wanting in discernment, and has already discovered the weak side of his patrons, which he strives to turn to good account, and I dare say, by his natural subtility, will in time advantage himself considerably by it.*

The Directors seem much pleased with Falconbridge's exertions, have appointed him Commercial Agent to the Company, and he is shortly to return to Sierra Leona.[63] They are very pressing for me to accompany him, but my late misfortunes are yet too fresh in remembrance to consent hastily. Indeed, you may suppose, I cannot but painfully remember them while the bruises and chafes produced by the voyage on different parts of my body, continue unhealed. However, it is probable, whether with or against my will, I must tacitly assent to hazard a repetition of what I have already undergone.

When matters are wholly fixed you will hear from me, and perhaps I may shortly have the happiness of assuring you in person how I am,

Your's, &c.

LETTER VI.

LONDON, 27th Nov. 1791.

My Dear Madam,

The Directors have acted so honorable and handsome it was not possible for me to hold out in refusing to return to Sierra Leona, besides increasing Falconbridge's salary near three times what it was, they have voted us a sum of money as an equivalent for the extraordinary services they consider he has rendered them, and as a compensation for our private losses of cloaths, &c.

But surely mortal never was more harrassed than I have been by their importunities.

They used every flattering and inticing argument, the ingenious brain of man is capable of, to no purpose; however, tho' all their rhetoric could not persuade me to revisit Africa, their *noble, generous* actions have effected it.

Mr. Thornton is a good creature, one of the worthiest men I ever met; he has assured me, should any accident happen Falconbridge I shall be well provided for by the Company; he has also, as well as many others of the Directors, made me a profusion of friendly promises and professions, so extravagant, that if they came from any other set of men I should look upon them, either as chicanery,[64] or without meaning.

The Court has granted 50l. to be laid out in presents for King Naimbana

---

* This young man returned to Sierra Leone in July 1793, and died the day after his arrival.

and his old Queen, and have particularly desired, that I shall purchase those for the latter, and present them as from myself, by way of enhansing my consequence.

They have likewise granted another sum for me to lay out in such private stores as I may chuse to take with me for our use after we get to Africa; besides ordering a very handsome supply for the voyage.

A few days ago I only hinted an inclination to visit my friends at Bristol, before we left England, and Mr. Thornton said I should have a Chaise when I liked, and the expence should be defrayed by the Company. Do you not think these are pretty marks of attention?

We have thoughts of setting out for Bristol in the course of next week, where I figure to myself much of that undescriptionable pleasure which lively affectionate minds involuntarily feel upon meeting the bosom friends and sportive companions of their youthful days, grown to maturity with hearts and countenances neither altered by absence, or rusted by corroding time.

But I lament to say this happiness will be of short duration, being obliged quickly to proceed to Falmouth, where we are to embark on board the Company's ship Amy, for Sierra Leona.

Adieu.

LETTER VII.

FREE TOWN, SIERRA LEONA,
10th April, 1792.

My Dear Madam,

Here I am, once more exposed to the influence of a Torrid Sun, near three thousand miles apart from my dearest friends, experiencing, not only, the inevitable hardships of Colonization, but wallowing in a multiplicity of trouble and confusion, very unnecessarily attached to an infant Colony.

We sailed from Falmouth the 19th of December, and arrived at this place the 16th of February, when we found the Harpy, Wilson, a Company ship, that left England some time after us; but our voyage was prolonged, in consequence of being obliged to stop at Teneriffe for a few pipes of Wine.

Immediately on entering the river we were visited by Captain Wilson, and after the customary civilities, he told us, several Colonial Officers, a few Soldiers, and some independent Settlers came passengers with him, who were greatly rejoiced at seeing the Amy; for being all strangers, they were at a loss what to do, and wholly relied on Falconbridge to make good their landing.

In the course of conversation many sentences escaped Captain Wilson, importing a very unfavourable account of his passengers, but imagining they proceeded from some misunderstanding between them and him, neither

Falconbridge or myself allowed what he said, to bias or prejudice us in any shape.

Captain Wilson having directed the most eligible spot for us to bring up, waited until our anchor was gone, and then returned to his ship; Falconbridge accompanied him to make his obeisance to the Ladies and Gentlemen on board.

In a short time he was confirmed, our surmise, with regard to disagreements subsisting between the parties, was well grounded, for they were constantly snarling at each other; but it required very little penetration to arrive at the true source of their animosities, and before I proceed further I must acquaint you, the Directors have appointed eight persons to represent them, and conduct the management of their Colony, under the *dignified appellation* of *Superintendant* and *Council.*[65]

It is a pity when making those appointments, they had not probed for characters of worth and respectability, as success in any enterprise greatly hinges on skilful, prudent conduct; qualities more especially requisite in an undertaking like this, laboring under a load of enemies, who will, no doubt, take advantage to blow the smallest spark of mal-conduct into a flame of error.

Perhaps the Directors imagine they were particularly circumspect in their choice of representatives, if so, they are grossly deceived, for never were characters worse adapted to manage any purpose of magnitude than some whom they have nominated.

Are men of little worth and much insignificance fit to be guardians and stewards of the immense property required, for erecting the fabric of a new Colony? Are Men, whose heads are too shallow to support a little vicissitude and unexpected *immaginary* aggrandizement, whose weak minds delude them with wrong notions of their nominal rank, and whose whole time is occupied with contemplating their fancied consequence, in place of attending to the real and interesting designs of their mission, calculated for the executors of a theory, which can only be put in practice by wise and judicious method?

Certainly not; yet of this description are the greater part who guide and direct our Colony; a majority of whom came passengers in the Harpy, and who, intoxicated with false ideas of their authority, wished to assume the prerogative of controuling Captain Wilson in managing and governing his ship; but the latter treated their arrogance with contempt, and consequently grew the dissentions alluded to, which have since been the cause of many disagreeable unpleasant occurrences.

Falconbridge soon returned with Captain and Mrs. Wilson, whom we had invited to dine with us; four Honorable Members of the Council, dressed cap-a-pie, in a uniform given them by the Directors to distinguish their rank, came with them, to make their bows to your humble servant, as the wife of their *superior*, Falconbridge being the eldest member of this *supreme* body.

A message was then sent to King Jemmy (opposite to whose town the

Amy lay) to announce our arrival to him and King Naimbana (who was there at the time), requesting they would come on board.

Naimbana, accompanied by Mr. Elliotte and a number of attendants, soon complied with our request, but Jemmy would not be prevailed upon.

The old King was overjoyed at seeing me; being seated, Falconbridge shewed him the portrait of his son,* a present from the directors.

The picture is an admirable likeness, and the poor Father burst into tears when he saw it.[66]

He stayed with us five days; and, notwithstanding every courteous art was used to persuade King Jemmy to honour us with a visit, we could not effect it: He once consented on condition I remained in his town a hostage till he returned; this I agreed to, and went on shore for the intention; but his people dissuaded him just as he was going off.

You may remember I mentioned in a former letter, the ground where the *first settlers* were driven from by King Jemmy, being the most desirable situation hereabouts for a settlement, but by the Palaver it was objected to; however, with coaxing, and the powerful influence[67] of presents, King Naimbana was prevailed upon to remove whatever objections there were, and on the 28th of February, put us in quiet possession of the very spot; which is named *Free Town*, from the *principles* that gave rise to the establishment.** [*Plate 20*]

The second day after our arrival there was a grand council held on board the Amy, when their secretary delivered Mr. Falconbridge new instructions from the Directors, directly counter to those he received in London; subjecting him, in his commercial capacity, to the control of the Superintendant and Council, and acquainting him, Lieutenant Clarkson was appointed Superintendant.

This has disconcerted Falconbridge vastly, and inclines him to construe their conduct to us in England, as juggle and chicane, for the mere purpose of enticing him here, knowing he was the fittest, nay only person, to secure a footing for the Nova Scotia emigrans; but I cannot think so harshly.

After being here a fortnight, Mr. Clarkson arrived, with the blacks from America, a part of whom came some days before him.

When he left Nova Scotia, they amounted to between eleven and twelve hundred, but during the voyage a malignant fever infested the Ships, and carried off great numbers.

---

*   The first of his family transfered on canvas.

**   It is situated on a rising ground, fronting the sea; six miles above Cape Sierra Leone, and eighteen fron Bance island; seperated from King Jemmy's town by a rivulet and thick wood, near half a mile through: before the Town, is pretty good anchorage for shipping, but the landing places are generally bad, in consequence of the shore being bound with iron rocks, and an ugly surge, most commonly breaking on them.

Plate 20 'A View of Sierra-Leone River, from St. George's Hill, where the Free Black settlement was made in the year 1787', from John Matthews, *A Voyage to the River Sierra-Leone* (2nd edn, 1791). This was the first glimpse for the British public of 'The Province of Freedom'. *Source*: Cambridge University Library; by permission of the Syndics of Cambridge University Library.

Mr. Clarkson caught the fever and miraculously escaped death, which would have been an irreparable loss to the colony, being the only man calculated to govern the people who came with him, for by his winning manners, and mild, benign treatment, he has so gained their affections and attachment, that he can, by lifting up his finger (as he expresses it) do what he pleases with them.

They are in general, a religious, temperate, good set of people; at present they are employed in building huts for their temporary residence, till the lands promised them can be surveyed; when that will be, God only knows; the surveyor, being a *Counsellor* and *Captain* of our *veteran host*, is of too much consequence to attend to the servile duty of surveying, notwithstanding he is paid for it.[68]

Few of ths settlers have yet got huts erected, they are mostly encamped under tents made with sails from the different ships, and are very badly of for fresh provisions; indeed such is the case with us all, and what's worse, we have but half allowance of very indifferent salt provision, and bad worm eaten bread.*

Painfully do I say, nothing promises well.—Mr Clarkson, as Superintendant, is so tied up, that he cannot do a thing without the approbation of his Council, and those opinionated upstarts thwart him in all his attempts.

He is an amiable man, void of pomp or ostentation, which his senatorial associates disapprove of exceedingly, from the ridiculous idea that their *dignity* is lessened by his frankness.

How truly contemptible is it to see men stickle in this way after foolish unbecoming consequence, blind to the interest of their employers, whereby, they must, without question, rise or fall.[69]

Their absurd behaviour** make them the laughing stocks of the neighbouring Factories, and such masters of slave ships as have witnessed their conduct, who must certainly be highly gratified with the anarchy and chagrin that prevails through the Colony.

The Blacks are displeased that they have not got their promised lands; and so little do they relish the obnoxious arrogance of their rulers, that I really believe, was it not for the influence of Mr. Clarkson, they would be apt to drive some of them into the sea.

The independant European Settlers are vastly disappointed, and heartily wish themselves safe back in their own country.

---

* The James of Bristol, being unfit to proceed her voyage, was condemned and sold at Bance Island about this time; from her a quantity of beans and other provisions were purchased which was a fortunate circumstance for the colony, then in a starving state.

** Few days escaped without a quarrel, which sometimes came the length of blows: Members of Council were daily ordering goods from the ships, not wanted, and inevitably to be destroyed, merely for the purpose of shewing their authority.

This is not to be wondered at, when in addition to the calamity of being in a new Colony over-run with confusion, jealousy, and discordant sentiments, they are exposed to the oppression of wanting almost every necessary of life, having no shops where they might purchase, or any other medium of procuring them.

I have only one piece of pleasing intelligence to give you:—The Colony just now is tolerable healthy; very few deaths have occurred among the Blacks since their arrival, and but two among the Whites; the latter were Doctor B——, (our physician), and the Harpy's gunner.[70]

The gunner's death was occasioned by that of the former, who brought on his dissolution by inebrity[71] and imprudence; being a member of the Magisterial body, he was buried with all the pomp and ceremony circumstances would admit of.

While the corpse moved on in solemn pace, attended by the Members of Council, and others, in procession, minute guns were fired from the Harpy; in executing this, the gunner lost his arm, of which he died very shortly.

I yet live on ship-board, for though the Directors had the goodness to send out a canvas house purposely for me, I have not the satisfaction of occupying it, our *men of might* having thought proper to appropriate it another way.

Mr. Gilbert, our clergyman,[72] returns to England in the vessel I write by, a fast sailing schooner Mr. Clarkson has purchased for the painful but indispensible intention of sending the Directors information of our distracted, deplorable situation; at the same time exhorting them in their *wisdom* to make some immediate, efficacious change in our government, without which their colony will, irrecoverably be stifled in its infancy.

Mr. Gilbert is a man of mild agreeable manners, truly religious, without the hypocritical shew of it; he is universally liked in the Colony, and I am sure his absence will be greatly regretted; but Mr. Clarkson's indisposition, rendering him unable to write so fully as he wishes, or necessity demands, has prevailed on him (Mr. Gilbert) to return to England, and represent to the Directors, by word of mouth, whatever he may neglect to do in writing.

A party of us will accompany him to the Banana Islands, about ten leagues from hence, where he is in hopes of procuring fresh stock, and other necessary sea stores, which are not to be had here for love or money.

I do not think it will be in my power to write you from the Bananas; shall, therefore, close this letter with sincere hopes my next may give you a more favourable account of things.

Farewell, &c.

LETTER VIII.

My dear Friend,

We accompanied Mr. Gilbert to the Island of Banana, where he succeeded in getting some fresh stock, and after staying there two days, departed for your quarter of the globe, and I hope is safe arrived in London long ere now.

The Island of Bananas derives its name from the fruit so called, which grows there spontaneously, and in great abundance, as do most tropical fruits.

It is a small Island, but a wonderful productive healthful spot, throngly inhabited by clean, tidy, sociable, and obliging people.

They have a town much larger and more regularly built than any other native town I have yet seen: the inhabitants are mostly vassals to one Mr. Cleavland, a black man, who claims the sovereignty of the Island from hereditary right.

The houses are chiefly constructed in a circular form, but of the same kind of stuff with those I formerly noticed.

In the centre of the town is a Palaver, or Court House; here we observed a bed neatly made up, a wash-hand bason, clean napkin, and every apparatus of a bed chamber.

This had a very curious appearance; but we were told that the late Mr. Cleveland used to indulge himself with the luxury of sleeping in this airy place, and the inhabitants superstitiously thinking (though he has been dead more than a year), that he yet invisibly continues the practice, they would not upon any account forego the daily ceremony of making up his bed, placing fresh water, &c. as was the custom in his life time.

The idolatry shewn the memory of this man, I make no doubt is greatly encouraged by his son, as it secures consequence and popularity to him.[73]

He was from home, I therefore did not see him, but understand he is clever, and (being educated in England) rather polished in his manners.

We sailed from the Bananas, in company with Mr. Gilbert, consequently my time was so short, that I am not able to give you but a very superficial account of that Island; but shall refer you to Lieutenant Mathews's Voyage to Sierra Leone, where you will find it amply described.[74] While there, we dined on board an American ship, commanded by an Irishman, who has since then been here entertaining himself at the expence of our *Senators*.

He invited them all to dine with him, which being accepted (by every one but Mr. Clarkson and Falconbridge), they were treated with true Hibernian hospitality, and made beastly drunk.[75]

Our illegitimate son of Mars[76] was of the number who the master of the ship cull'd out for his butt, he not only played upon him during dinner, but afterwards finding him lull'd into the arms of Morpheus, by the sleepy effects of wine,[77] had the ship's cook, a slave, dressed in the noble

Captain's dashing coat, hat, sword, &c. and stationed immediately before him with a *mop stick* on his shoulder, when the master himself fired two pistols, very heavily charged, within an inch of his ear, and having thus roused him from his lethargy, the sable cook was desired to shew with what expertness he could perform the manual exercise, which he went through, our *Hero* giving the word of command, to the ridicule of himself, and great amusement of his colleagues and the ship's crew.

Since this, I have taught a large overgrown female Monkey of mine to go thro' several manoeuvres of the same, and have made her exhibit when the Captain came to see me, who not seeing the diversion I was making of him, would sometimes take the pains of instructing her himself; but, poor fellow! he has been sadly galled lately, by the arrival of a gentleman from England, who supersedes him in his military capacity.

When I last wrote to you I was in hopes my next would atone by a more favourable and pleasing account, for the hapless description I then gave of our new Colony, but alas! alas! in place of growing better, we seem daily advancing towards destruction, which certainly awaits us at no great distance, unless some speedy change takes place.

There is about twelve thousand souls, including all ranks of people, in the Colony, seven hundred or upwards of whom, are at this moment suffering under the affliction of burning fevers, I suppose two hundred scarce able to crawl about, and am certain not more, if so many, able to nurse the sick or attend to domestic and Colonial concerns; five, six, and seven are dying daily,* and buried with as little ceremony as so many dogs or cats.

It is quite customary of a morning to ask "how many died last night?"[78] Death is viewed with the same indifference as if people were only taking a short journey, to return in a few days; those who are well, hourly expect to be laid up, and the sick look momently[79] for the surly Tyrant to finish their afflictions, nay, seem not to care for life!

After reading this, methinks I hear you invectively exclaim against the country, and charging those ravages to its unhealthiness; but suspend your judgement for a moment, and give me time to paint the true state of things, when I am of opinion you will think otherwise, or at least allow the climate has not a fair tryal.

This is the depth of the rainy season, our inhabitants were not covered in before it commenced, and the huts they have been able to make, are neither wind or water tight; few of them have bedsteads, but are obliged to lie on the wet ground; without medical assistance, wanting almost every comfort of life, and exposed to nauceous putrid stenches, produced by stinking provisions, scattered about the town.

Would you, under such circumstances, expect to keep your health, or even

---

* About three-fourths of all the Europeans who went out in 1792, died in the course of the first nine or ten months.

live a month in the healthiest part of the world? I fancy not; then pray do not attribute our mortality altogether, to baseness of climate.

I cannot imagine what kind of stuff I am made of, for though daily in the midst of so much sickness and so many deaths, I feel myself much better than when in England.

I am surprised our boasted Philanthropists, the Directors of the Company, should have subjected themselves to such censure as they must meet, for sporting with the lives of such numbers of their fellow creatures, I mean by sending so many here at once, before houses, materials for building, or other conveniences were prepared to receive them, and for not hurrying a supply after they had been guilty of this oversight.

But I really believe their error has proceeded from want of information, and listening with too much credulity, to a pack of designing, puritanical parasites, whom they employ to transact business; I cannot help thinking so, nay, am convinced of it, from the cargoes they have sent out, composed of goods, no better adapted for an infant Colony than a cargoe of slaves would be for the London market.

Two vessels arrived from England last month, viz. the Sierra Leona Packet, belonging to the Company, and the Trusty of Bristol, a large ship they chartered from that port; several passengers came in each of them, in the former were, a Member of Council, a worthy discreet man; a Botanist, who, I cannot say any thing of, having seen but little of him; a sugar planter, who is since gone to the West Indies in disgust, and the Gentleman who has superseded our *Gallant* Captain, and who, I understand, is also a cotton planter, but it is not likely he will have much to do in either of those departments for some time; his fellow soldiers being mostly dead, and agriculture not thought on.

In the latter came the store-keeper, with his wife, mother-in-law, and a large family of children; a mineralist, and several clerks and tradesmen, in all twenty three.*

Those vessels brought so little provisions, (with which they should have been wholly loaded) that we have not a sufficiency in the Colony to serve us three weeks. The goods brought out in the Trusty and quantities by other ships, amounting to several thousand pounds value, at this moment line the shore, exposed to the destructive weather and *mercy* of our neighbours, who cannot, I am sure, withstand such temptation. Those remaining on ship board, I have heard Falconbridge say, are perishing by heat of the hold, and damage received at sea. Notwithstanding the Company's property is thus suffering, and our people dying from absolute want of nourishment, Mr. Falconbridge has been refused the Sierra Leona packet to go in quest of cattle, and otherwise prosecute the duties of his office as Commercial Agent.

---

*　Six returned to England, one left the Colony and went into the employ of Bance Island, and the remainder died in the course of three or four months.

She is the only vessel fit for the business; but it is thought necessary to send her to England; yet, if things were ordered judiciously, she might have made one serviceable trip in the mean while, and answered three desirable purposes by it: relieve the Colony, bartered away goods that are spoiling, and please the Directors by an early remittance of African productions; in place of this she has only been used as a *Pleasure Boat*, to give a weeks airing at sea, to *Gentlemen* in perfect health.

Mr. Falconbridge has had no other opportunity but this to do any thing in the commercial way; the Directors no doubt, will be displeased, but they should not blame him; he is placed altogether under the control of the Superintendant and Council, who throw cold water on every proposal of the kind he makes.[80] His time is at present employed in attending the sick, particularly those of scrophulous habits, while our military gentleman, who has acquired, by experience, some medical knowledge, attends those afflicted with fevers, &c. This is the only phisical help at present in the Colony, for though we have two Surgeons they are both so ill, as to disable them from helping either themselves, or others; one of them returns to England in the Packet, as does our *mortified soldier.*

I am, &c.

LETTER IX.

SIERRA LEONA, *Aug. 25th*, 1792.

My Dear Friend,

You must not promise yourself either instruction or entertainment from this letter, for my strength of body and mind are so debilitated by a severe fit of illness, that with much ado I could summon resolution enough to take up my pen, or prevail on myself to write you a syllable by this opportunity, but having made a beginning, (which is equal to half the task) I shall now endeavour to spin out what I can.

I was confined three weeks with a violent fever, stoneblind four days, and expecting every moment to be my last; indeed I most miraculously escaped the jaws of death; fortunately just as I was taken sick, a Phisician arrived, to whose attention and skill I consider myself principally indebted for my recovery;[81] I am yet a poor object, and being under the necessity of having my head shaved, tends to increase ghastly figure.[82] You will readily guess it was very humbling and provoking for me to loose my fine head of hair, which I always took so much pride in, but I cannot help it, and must thank God my life is preserved.

A few weeks since, arrived the Calypso from Bulam, with a number of disappointed adventurers who went to that Island; they came here in expectation of finding accommodation for a part of them during the rainy season, who meant afterwards to return to Bulam: but they entertained wrong notions of our Colony, when they supposed we had it in our power to accommodate them, for most of our own gentlemen are obliged to sleep on ship board, for want of houses or lodging on shore.

The adventurers seem vexed at being thus defeated in their expectations, and intend returning to England in the Calypso when she sails, which will be shortly.

Perhaps you have not heard of the Bulam expedition before, and I can give you but a very imperfect account of it, however, I will laconically tell you what I know.

A Mr. Dalrymple was engaged by the Directors of the Sierra Leone Company to come out as governor of this colony; but they disagreed from some trifling circumstance, and Mr. Dalrymple feeling himself offended, set on foot (towards the latter end of last year) a subscription for forming a settlement on the Island I am speaking of, in opposition to the Sierra Leone Company: A number of speculators soon associated, subscribed to Mr. Dalrymple's plan, and I fancy, prematurely set about the completion of its objects, before they had well digested the theory, or accumulated a sufficient fund to ensure success;[83] be that as it may, they purchased a small sloop, chartered the Calypso and another ship, engaged numbers of needy persons, who with many of the subscribers, personally embarked in the enterprize, and placing themselves under the direction of Mr. Dalrymple, and a few others, sailed from England in April last, and arrived at Bulam in June.

I understand they were all novices in the arts and modes requisite for attaining their wished for possession, which was unfortunate, for their ignorance led them into an error that proved fatal to several.

Although the island of Bulam was uninhabited, it was claimed by persons residing in the adjacent Islands, who by some means or other learnt the errand of the adventurers, and to prevent them from getting a footing, without consent of the proprietors, secretly landed a party of men on the Island, where they for several days watched the motions of Mr. Dalrymple's people: between thirty and forty of whom, having disembarked and landed, (without any previous ceremony, according to the custom of the country,) the natives took the first opportunity to catch them of their guard, fell upon them, killed five men and one woman, wounded two men, carried off three or four women and children, and obliged the remainder to return to their ship.

After this Mr. Dalrymple went to the neighbouring Island of Bissao, belonging to the Portuguese, where he, through the medium of a merchant of that country, became acquainted with the measures he should have adopted at first, and having courted the friendship of the native chiefs, and made them sensible of his peaceable and honorable intentions, they restored the women and children uninjured and gave him possession of the Island, for some trifling acknowledgement I have not yet ascertained.

After this Mr. Dalrymple fell sick, and many of the emigrants foreseeing frightful hardships which they were unwilling to encounter during the present rains, he and they resolved to return to England, but first to come hither for the purpose I before mentioned.

The Island is not altogether abandoned; a Lieutenant Beaver of the Navy, with a few people remain upon it.[84]

Since their arrival here many of them have died and the ship is just now very sickly.—So much for Bulam.[85]

Now I must say something of ourselves, which I have the heartfelt satisfaction of telling you before hand will be more cheerful and satisfactory than any thing I have heretofore said.

By the last ship Mr. Clarkson received instructions from the Directors, vesting him with more ample powers than he held before: this was much to be wished for, and its beneficial effects are already visible.[86]

Directly after getting this enlargement of authority, Mr. Clarkson invited all the gentlemen and ladies in the Colony to dine at a mess-house, built for the gentlemen who came out in the Sierra Leone Packet: every one that was well enough, gladly attended to celebrate a meeting which was intended to give birth to pleasantness, unanimity, and perpetual harmony; and to deface every thing to the contrary, that previously existed in the Colony: The day I am told (for being sick at the time, I could not be there) was spent as it should be, with every demonstration of satisfaction, by all parties, and the house was named *Harmony Hall*, by which name it is now, and I suppose ever will be known, while a stick of it stands: This house and the one I have, are all the buildings yet finished, (I mean for the Whites,) but several others are about.[87]

The Colony is growing healthier every day; most of the Blacks are able to turn out to work. The men are employed in the Company's service, and receive two shillings per day wages, out of which they pay four shillings per week for their provisions.

The women are occupied in attending their little gardens, and rearing poultry.

The natives daily grow more intimate with us, and are constantly bringing in fruits of different kinds, but seldom any live stock, unless now and then a few fowls, or perhaps a goat, which they barter away for cloath, soap, or spirits.

Every moon-light night we hear the drums of King Jemmy's town, which is scarcely half a mile from hence. This music of our neighbours, for a long time after we arrived, used frequently to alarm the Colony; but by custom it has become familiar. For several months *King* Jemmy could not be persuaded to come into Free Town; but at last being prevailed upon, and relishing his reception, he now repeats his visits so often, as to be very troublesome. Whenever he comes, a boy attends him with a pair of horseman's pistols, loaded, and I will not be surprised, if he does mischief with them some day or other, for he never returns home until he has drank a sufficient quantity of rum or brandy, to kindle his savage nature for any manner of wickedness.

The last ship brought out a large house of one hundred feet in length, which is to be erected in the vicinity of the town, as an hospital; but the people being mostly on the recovery, I think it would be more advisable to erect it as a store-house, and thereby not only save the Company's valuable property, which is just now perishing for want of shelter; but would serve as a repository for vending many goods that are wasting on board of ships, which would greatly contribute to our comfort, and which we are deprived of from not having a proper place where they might be exposed to sale; and again, I do not think our Blacks will submit to be sent to an hospital, therefore the intention will be frustrated, however, the house is so constructed, that it can be put up or taken down in a few hours, consequently may, at any time hereafter, be removed; and we understand several houses of the same kind are expected in two large ships, which are hourly looked for.

Since the rains we have been sadly infested by a variety of insects, but more particularly cockroaches and ants; the latter come from their nests in such formidable force, as to strike terror wherever they go. You will think it strange, that such an insignificant insect as the ant is in England, should be able, in another country, to storm the habitations of people, and drive out the inhabitants; but I pledge my veracity to you, I have known them in one night, force twelve or fourteen families from their houses, who were obliged to make use of fire and boiling water to destroy them, which are the only weapons we can attack them with, that will effectually check their progress.[88]

Musquetos are not so troublesome here as I have felt them elsewhere; but we have a perpetual croaking of frogs and buzzings of various vermin, very discordant and unpleasant to the ear of a person in perfect health, yet much more so to those who are sick.

There has been several large serpents killed in the Colony, but none of the overgrown size, Lieutenant Mathews and other authors mention,[89] the largest I have heard of, measured nine feet in length.—We have been twice visited by some ferocious wild beast, supposed to be a tyger; the last time it was attacked by two mastiffs of ours, who were beat off and materially injured. One of my poor domestics, a very heavy Newfoundland dog, had his throat terribly lacerated; the other, I imagine, fought shy, as he came off with little damage.

There are many good hunters among our Settlers, through whom we some times get wild deer or pork; the latter is a coarse unpleasant food; I lately had a haunch, the hide of which was full an inch and an half thick; the former is meagre, dry meat, very unlike your English venison, but such as it is, we are glad when it comes in our way.

Some little time ago an accident happened, one of the most expert hunters we have, which has considerably lessened our supply of game; he was laying in ambush near where he knew a deer frequented; another person, in pursuit of the same, passing hard by, and hearing the rustling of leaves, immediately fired into the thicket from whence the noise proceeded, and lodged the greater contents of his gun in the head and right shoulder of his unfortunate rival, but not killing him, he brought him home, two miles through the wood, on his shoulder. Falconbridge extracted several of the shot, and thinks he may recover.

Our Botanist and Mineralist have as yet made little proficiency in those branches of natural philosophy; the confusion of the Colony has retarded them as well as others; they are both Swedes, and considered very eminent in their professions.[90] The Mineralist is about to make an excursion into the interior country, and is very sanguine in his expectations. He has but slightly explored the country here abouts, and been as slightly rewarded; the only fruits of his researches are a few pieces of iron oar, richly impregnated with magnetism, with which the mountains abound.

The Botanist is preparing a garden for experiments, and promises himself much amusement and satisfaction when he can strictly attend to his business. His garden is now very forward, but it is attended with considerable expence; however, a mere nothing, when put into the great scale of Colonial charges, which, including shipping, Officers' salaries, wages of labourers, and provisions, does not amount to less than the enormous sum of one hundred and fifty pounds per day, without naming incidental charges, such as presents to natives, daily waste and destruction of property, &c. Those aggregated from the birth of the Company to the present time, may at least be computed at 25,000l.

This is not a supposition of my own, for I have heard it from those who must certainly be informed on the business; but notwithstanding the Company's purse is so much weakened, by folly and want of circumspection; if the harmony and good understanding, at present existing in the Colony, continues, it is yet sufficiently strong, by being applied with method, and proper exertions, not only to retrieve their losses, and answer their original laudable and magnanimous purposes, but amply requite any pecuniary motives they may have.

Mr. Falconbridge has obtained permission from Mr. Clarkson to commence his commercial career, and had selected goods for the purpose, but was checked by illness, and is dangerously ill at this moment. If he recovers, his first assay will be on the Gold Coast, where he flatters himself with success,[91] and often says he hopes he shall be able to cheer the despondent Directors, by a valuable, unexpected cargo.

Mr. Clarkson thinks it too early to meddle with trade, from the idea that it will procrastinate the regularity and comfort of the Colony, which he is strenuously endeavouring to establish, but from my slender notion of things, I humbly beg leave to differ from him, and rather suppose it would greatly contribute to accelerate his wishes; at least it would not be the smallest hindrance, or by any means interfere with our police, which to be sure will not yet bear a scrupulous investigation,—however it is mending, and I dare say, in time, our able, zealous pilot, will steer us clear of the labyrinth which he found us entangled in.

May it be so, is the earnest wish of,
Your's, &c. &c.

LETTER X.

FREE TOWN, SIERRA LEONE,
28th Dec. 1792.

My dear Friend,

Within ten or twelve days after the date of my last, arrived the two ships that were expected. One is the York, a large vessel of a thousand tons (belonging to the Company), that is intended to end her days here in the character of a storeship, for which purpose she is admirably adapted; the other is the Samuel and Jane, likewise a vessel of great burden, chartered to remain here six months if wanted. This vessel arrived some days before the York; in her came a Mr. Wallis, to supersede Falconbridge; the Directors having thought proper to annul his appointment as Commercial Agent.[92]

That they had a right to do so, I will not question; but methinks it developes treachery; and I now suspect their whole conduct to us in England, was only a complication of hypocritical snares, to answer selfish purposes, which having attained, they cared not any longer to wear the mask.

In their dismission they accuse Falconbridge of not extending their commercial views, and wanting commercial knowledge. The latter charge may be in some measure well founded, for Mr. Falconbridge was bred to physic, and men of perspicuity would have known how unfit such a person must be for a merchant, indeed he was aware of it himself, but it being a place of much expected profit, (a temptation not to be withstood), he was in hopes by application, soon to have improved the little knowledge he had, so as to benefit both his employers and himself; but in this they disappointed him, and were actually the cause of choking the attempts he might have made.

They should recollect the deep deception played upon him. He left England with independant and unlimitted powers, which were restrained immediately on our arrival here. Thus bridled, with the reins in possession of men, who considered commerce only as a secondary view of the Company, and who negatived every proposition of the kind Falconbridge made, till a very short time before his appointment was annulled.—What was he to do?

Two days before his dismission came out, he crawled from his sick bed, and, at the moment it was delivered him, was in the act of arranging and preparing matters for the trading voyage I mentioned in my last. I am certain it proved a mortal stab to him; he was always addicted to drink more than he should; but after this, by way of meliorating his harrowed feelings, he kept himself constantly intoxicated; a poor forlorn remedy you will say, however it answered his wishes, which I am convinced was to operate as poison, and thereby finish his existence; he spun out his life in anguish and misery till the 19th instant, when, without a groan he gasp'd his last.!!!![93]

I will not be guilty of such meanness as to tell a falsehood on this occasion, by saying I regret his death, no! I really do not, his life had become burthensome to himself and all around him, and his conduct to me for more than two years past, was so unkind, (not to give it a harsher term) as, long since to wean every spark of affection or regard I ever had for him. This I am persuaded, was his greatest crime; he possessed many virtues, but an excellent dutiful son, and a truly honest man, were conspicuous traits in his character.

I shall now return to the arrival of the York; in this ship came out the Rev. Mr. Horne and a Mr. Dawes, who is a new appointed member of council.[94] I must not proceed any further till I inform you that the Directors have wholly changed their original system of government, dismounted the old Council, and placed their political reins in the hands of Mr. Clarkson, who is to be assisted by two Counsellors, one of whom is the gentleman I just mentioned, the other is not yet appointed.

This new ministry is titled, "the Governor and Council," and are charged with the management of all civil, military, and commercial affairs, but have no authority whatever to interfere in ecclesiastical matters, which are left to the guidance of Mr. Horne or any other Minister for the time being.

Time will shew whether this alteration of politics proves propitious, as yet things have not fallen of[95] but rather mended.

We are and have been frequently much pestered by renegade seamen, quiting ships employed in the Slave Trade, and refuging here, to the great detriment of their employers and inconvenience of the Colony. The circumstance considerably perplexes Mr. Clarkson, who, on the one hand is not only threatened with lawsuits by the masters and owners of ships detained for want of their sailors, but is well convinced of the injury they sustain; on the other, his orders are to *protect every man*, which leaves him in an aukward situation, and at a loss what to do; however, by way of intimidation to practices of the kind, he had the following notification, (which has not availed any thing) sent to some of the neighbouring factories, and stuck up in the Colony:

FREE TOWN, SIERRA LEONE,

Sept, 3d, 1792.

"This is to give Notice, that I will not on any account, permit Seamen, who may leave their respective Vessels, to take shelter in this Colony; and I shall give orders in future, that the Constables seize every man who cannot give a good account of himself, or whom they may suspect to have deserted from their employ. At the same time I shall be always ready to listen to the complaints of every injured man, and shall transmit their affidavits home to England, provided they make application in a proper manner.

(Signed)

JOHN CLARKSON."

It is much to be lamented, however desirable the abolition of the Slave Trade may be, while it is sanctioned by the English Government, property of individuals in that trade should be harrassed and annoyed by want of order and regularity in this Colony, or by the fanatical prejudices of any set of men. One ship in particular has suffered most essentially, viz. the Fisher, Clark, of Liverpool, whose men deserted from her in July last, and though she has had her cargo engaged ever since, she is not yet able to quit the coast for want of seamen; some of whom died, and others are now here, *employed in the Company's service.*

On the 26th, 27th, and 28th of September, there was an assembly of native Chieftains here, and a Palaver was held for the purpose of ascertaining the limits of the Company's territory. This was attended with considerable more expence than Falconbridge's palaver, and the consequence far less productive. They finished by curtailing the bounds from twenty miles square, (the quantity purchased by Captain Thompson, and afterwards confirmed to the St George's Bay Company) to about two miles and a quarter fronting the sea, and running in a direct line back, as far as the district of Sierra Leone may be, which is generally supposed not to exceed five or six miles, and three fourths of it a barren, rocky, mountaneous country, where it will be impossible, for men who are to earn their bread by agriculture, even to support themselves; but admitting it was all good, there is not more than will enable the Company to comply with one-fifth part of their engagements to the blacks brought from America, which proportion is now surveying for them.

This circumstance, I am persuaded, will hereafter lead to much discontent and uneasiness among the setlers, and, if I do not soothsay wrongly, will shackle those gentlemen, who have been the instruments of removing them, with such disgrace as they will not easily expunge.

When the Palaver was ended, and Naimbana (who presided at it on the part of the natives) was about to return to Robana, Mr. Clarkson, by way of amusing and complimenting the King, took him in a boat with six oarsmen and a cockswain, who rowed them through the fleet in the harbour, consisting of six or seven sail; each vessel, as they past, saluted them with several guns, till they came to the Harpy, when they were not noticed by the smallest token of respect; on the contrary, Captain Wilson called to Mr. Clarkson and told him he had a few words to say to him; Mr. Clarkson replyed, if they were not of much consequence he wish'd to be excused just then:—but upon Wilson's assuring him they were of some importance, the Governor complyed with his request and went on board: Captain Wilson then said, he was much offended that Mr. Clarkson should take a boats crew from his ship and a cockswain from another: Till that moment Mr. Clarkson had not observed such to be the case, and assured Captain Wilson it was done inadvertently, without the slightest intention of giving offence. This acknowledgment was not enough for Captain Wilson, and his temper being irritated, he used some very indiscreet expressions to Mr. Clarkson: such as telling him—"Damn me, Sir, if ever you shall have another boat's crew from my ship, unless you have a cockswain also," &c. &c. The governor was hurt at such language and returned to his boat: King Naimbana enquired of him, why that ship did not fire? he answered "Mrs. Wilson is sick, and the Captain does not like to disturb her with the noise."

The King then embarked on board the Lapwing Cutter, and went home: When he was gone, and the colony clear of all the chiefs, Mr. Clarkson sent a message to Captain Wilson, desiring him to make an apology for his unhandsome behaviour, or he (Mr. Clarkson) would be under the necessity of taking steps very repugnant to his inclination. Wilson positively refused, and continuing obstinate two days, (wholly engrossed with messages and answers, to and fro), Mr. Clarkson, although a man of humility and condescension, unwilling to brook so gross an insult, summoned every gentlemen in the colony to meet him on board the Amy; and, when they were collected, wrote a letter, summoning Captain Wilson: which summons being disobeyed, he appealed to the assembly, who unanimously determined the delinquent should be dismissed from command of the Harpy; in consequence whereof, his dismission, signed by the Governor and Mr. Dawes was sent immediately.

When the boat that carried it, came under the Harpy's stern, (being a little after eight at night,) she was hailed, and asked whither she was bound? "To the Harpy, with a letter for Captain Wilson," answered the bearer; "I am desired to inform you, no boat will be permitted to come alongside, at such an improper hour; and, if you proceed a boat's length further, Captain Wilson's orders are to fire on you" replied a voice from the Harpy: these threats not intimidating the boat's crew, two muskets were actually fired on them, but did no mischief; and reaching the ship before another fire, the undaunted messenger attempted to ascend the gangway, but was prevented by the ship's company, who cut away the gangway ropes, and beat him off with cutlasses, sticks, &c.

Captain Wilson having learnt the purport of this letter, from some person who afterwards went on board, declared he would not be removed from his ship with life, and he would blow out that man's brains, who dared attempt to enforce him!

This boisterous disposition subsided by the following day, when his dismission, with minutes of every gentleman's opinion who had been at the meeting over night, were sent him. He then persisted that he would not *tamely* leave his ship, but if any person, authorised, forcibly attempted to take him out, he would make no unlawful resistance. Mr. Dawes volunteered this duty, went on board, and after in vain persuading Wilson not to put him to the unpleasant task of using violence, he took him by the collar, and gently led him over the ship's side. When descending into the boat, he called to his officers and men, "Observe, I am forced out of my ship." He was then conducted to the York, where he was informed his residence would be until an opportunity offered to send him to England.

This fracas being thus quieted, perfect harmony otherwise subsisting among us, and Mr. Clarkson having some idea of returning to Europe, wished before hand, to furnish Mr. Dawes with a trial of his influence among the blacks, and individual management of the colony; and judging a trip to sea, for a few weeks, would be the best means of affording such an opportunity, he sailed in the Amy on the 2d of October, in company with a small brig of the Sierra Leone Company's, then bound home to England; but in which Mr. and Mrs. Wilson could not take their passage, the accommodations being previously disposed of.

When Mr. Clarkson sailed, he desired Captain Wilson might be informed, he was not to consider himself a prisoner, but at liberty to conduct himself as he pleased, and visit any where he liked, except the *Harpy*, which ship he was strictly prohibited from putting his foot on board.

In about three weeks Mr. Clarkson returned; a multiplicity of complaints were then poured into him by the Settlers, against Mr. Dawes, whose austere, reserved conduct (so reverse to the sweet manners of the other), they could not possibly relish, and, consequently, all hopes or expectations of the latter gaining popularity, proved abortive. It may not be *mal-a-propos* to mention here, that Mr. Dawes is a subaltern of Marines; that the prejudices of a rigid military education has been heightened by his having served some time at Botany Bay, where, no doubt, it is necessary for gentlemen to observe an awful severity in their looks and actions; but such behaviour, however suitable for a Colony formed wholly of Convicts, and governed by the iron rod of despotism, should be scrupulously guarded against in one like this, whose *basis is Liberty and Equality*, and whose Police is dependant, in great measure, if not altogether, on the whimsical disposition of an ignorant populace, which can only be advantageously tempered by placidness and moderation.

The Directors having ordered home the Harpy, when she could be spared from the Colony, Mr. Clarkson, on his return, desired she might be expeditiously fitted for sea, and on the 28th of last month, being Sunday, and most of the Colony piously engaged, Captain Wilson, knowing she was nearly ready, availed himself of the chance, and through the means of her boat, that came under pretence of giving him an airing, replaced himself, by consent of his Officers and crew, in command of his ship, and immediately after divine service, Mr. Clarkson received the following letter from him.

November 18, 1792.

SIR,

I apprehend it is needless to inform you I have taken possession of the Harpy, and mean, in defiance of all opposition, to carry her to England.

As I should be very sorry to be exceeded in politeness, on this occasion,[96] I write this to ask your commands for London, intending to sail immediately; nevertheless, Sir, if within an hour I receive an answer, assuring me of your pacific intentions, signed by *yourself* and *Mr. Dawes*, I will wait your orders.

Take care, Sir, how you attempt any thing like force; if blood is shed, be it upon your head. Wishing you more prudence, and better advisers,

I remain, Sir,
Your most humble Servant,

T. H. WILSON

John Clarkson, Esq. &c. &c.

This was a step so unlooked for, that it puzzled the Governor and Council how to conduct themselves: after some deliberation, they determined not to answer Captain Wilson's letter, and the time he limited having elapsed, we saw the Harpy under the guns of the York, and under the guns of the Battery, get under way, and triumphantly sail off.

Various opinions prevailed respecting the propriety of Captain Wilson's repossessing himself of the Harpy: some said it was an act of piracy, and they were certain he would never take her to England; but others judged less harshly, with whom I join; and, from my knowledge of Captain Wilson, feel myself authorized to say, he possesses too great a share of pride, and too high sense of honor, to shipwreck his character on the rock of infamy—but at the same time I will not aver him inerrable; on the contrary, think his behaviour to Mr. Clarkson monstrous disrespectful and inconsistent, which without doubt he was betrayed into by warmth of temper, and too lofty, but wrong notions of punctilio's.

I have been particularly obliged to Captain Wilson, therefore it would be truly ungenerous, nay, the blackest ingratitude in me, mischievously, to hint at any thing prejudicial to him, and must beg you not to suppose I have touched upon the subject by way of assailing his character; considering it a circumstance of importance, I could not pass it over in silence.*

On the 2d instant arrived the Felicity from England. I mention the arrival of this vessel, because she was expected to bring a number of useful stores for the Colony, in place of which her cargo consisted principally of *garden watering pots.*[97]

In her way out she stopped at Gambia, and took in several head of cattle, whereby we are now and then indulged with roast beef, the first we have had since our arrival, for the inhabitants, here-abouts, are too indolent to attend to rearing domestic quadrupeds of any kind.—King Naimbana has two or three very fat beeves; and I think there may be as many more at Bance Island; but, before the Felicity arrived, I can venture to say, those were all in this part of the country, unless I include a couple of milch cows, and a bull brought out from England by the York, which, from the inimical climate, died in a very short time. These brought from Gambia are thin, the flesh dark and coarse, and only the name of beef as a recommendation. Mutton and goat's flesh are the most preferable in their kinds; indeed, the former, though not overloaded with fat, I think nearly as sweet as our English mutton, but the little we get of them, come chiefly from the interior country.

About the latter end of October, the rains began to diminish; and for a month past have entirely ceased: they are succeeded by dense, disagreeable, and unwholesome fogs, which are supposed will continue near a month longer. These are termed smoaks, and considered more unhealthy than the worst rains, but we cannot say so from experience, for the Colony is healthier just now, than it has been since the beginning of May; yet a few deaths happen now and then: among those who lately died was Mr. Nordenschold, the Mineralist, who was taken ill on the expedition I noticed in my last, he was then about to make, and forced to return without acquiring any satisfaction for his journey, which was attended not only with innumerable disadvantages from the time of year, but with many other impediments he did not foresee or expect.

The loss of him is much to be regreted, for he was an enterprising clever man, and no doubt had he lived, would have procured a vast deal of useful information.[98]

The Governor and Council have at last thought it advisable to embark in Agriculture, and have purchased a small track of land on the opposite (Bullam) shore.—This new undertaking is placed under the management of a man, who was some time an Overseer in Dominica, and who was a *Member of the first Council:*[99] it is called *Clarkson's Plantation*, and from the richness and apparent fertility of the soil, much advantage may be looked

---

* Should this Narrative meet the eye of Captain Wilson, I trust he will do me the justice to say, I have not wandered from the broadway of the truth.

for, provided no disagreement arises with the natives, and a sufficient number of steady labourers can be obtained; but being in its infancy, all we can do at present is to wish it success, which time must determine.

Three or four new houses are now erected, and most of the gentlemen are comfortably lodged; there is a retail shop opened in the Colony, from whence we are furnished with such goods as the Directors have sent out, most of which are not only badly adapted for a warm climate, but wretchedly bad in their kind.

We have little gold or silver among us; that want is substituted by paper notes, from five dollars down to six-pence, signed by the Governor or Mr. Dawes.—The credit of this medium is established by giving bills of exchange, to the holders, upon the Directors, at a trifle more than eleven per cent. discount, which is only the difference between sterling and currency, a guinea being nominally twenty-three shillings and four-pence here; it is taken in payment for goods at the Company's store, and its reputation is now so good, that the neighbouring Factories and casual Traders receive it for what our Settlers purchase for them.

Mr. Clarkson is so convinced the Company have been sadly imposed upon, that a few weeks ago he wrote a circular letter to the gentlemen of the Colony, acquainting them with his intention of sailing for England very quickly,—requesting their opinion of the various goods that came under their notice,—their general ideas as to the wants of the Colony, and their advice how to prevent abuses being practised on the Company in future.

I saw part of a letter from one gentleman in answer, wherein he says— "You have done me the honour of asking my advice how to prevent abuses being practised on the Company in future? In answer to this I shall only say, it would be the height of presumption in me to offer an opinion on the subject, being persuaded your own penetration and discernment is sufficient to discover a remedy, without the assistance of any one; and if the Directors will attend to your advice upon this as well as every other circumstances respecting the Colony, I am sure they will find their advantage in it."

Had my opinion been asked, I should have said, "let the Directors shake off a parcel of hypocritical puritans, they have about them, who, under the cloak of religion, are sucking out the very vitals of the company; let them employ men conversant in trade, acquainted with the coast of Africa, and whose *religious tenets have never been noticed*; under this description they will find persons of sound morals, fit to be intrusted, but they will ever be subject to impositions, while they employ a pack of canting parasites, who have just cunning enough to deceive them."

We are in great tribulation about Mr. Clarkson's going away, for Mr. Dawes is almost universally disliked, and more than probable, anarchy and discord will again return, in full force among us, when the management of things are left to him alone; however, it is wrong to anticipate misfortunes, and our Governor has made every arrangement in his power to prevent intruders of this kind.

The Surveyor has assured him, the blacks shall have the proportion of land now surveying for them, in a fortnight at furthest. Every one has pledged himself to use his utmost efforts to preserve harmony and order, during Mr. Clarkson's absence, which we expect will be five or six months; and to insure Mr. Dawes the good will of King Naimbana, he has been allowed to make the King a very considerable present *out of the Company's Property.*

Adieu,
Your's, &c.

JOURNAL.

FREE TOWN, SIERRA LEONE,
Jan. 1st, 1793.

Two days ago Mr. Clarkson sailed; his departure operated more powerfully and generally upon people's feelings, than all the deaths we have had in the Colony; several gentlemen accompanied him two or three leagues to sea, and returned the same night.

Jan. 2d. The Surveyor has stopped surveying the lots of land for the settlers, although he assured Mr. Clarkson they should have them in a fortnight. His attention is now taken up with fortification, which seems to be the hobby-horse of Mr. Dawes, and a large Fort is planed out upon a hill about a half a mile from the water side.[100]

King Jemmy came to see me this day; he asked what was the reason Mr. Clarkson did not call upon him before he sailed, and said he did not suppose Mr. Clarkson would have left the country without coming to see him; his cheek was furrowed with tears as he spoke; I did not imagine he had so much sensibility.

There was a very heavy tornado last night, an unusual thing at this time of the year; The roof of my house has become so dry, that the rain had free access through, and I got thoroughly wet.

5th. A remarkable fine ox, (sent as a present to the Colony, by King Naimbana) was killed this day, I never saw fatter meat in my life; our acting governor, (notwithstanding it was a present) had it sold at 4d. per pound. I suppose he has done this to shew us he intends being an oeconomist, and thereby reimburse the Company's heavy losses; but that will require more fat oxen than he will be able to procure in this part of Africa for some years. This is not the only instance of his oeconomy, or I should say, parsimony, for a few days after Falconbridge died, he came and demanded of me his uniform coat, sword, gun, pistols, and a few other presents that the Directors had made him, and which I gave up, they being of no use to me; he also engrosses all the *Yams, Pumpkins, Turtle,* and almost every kind of provisions in the neighbourhood, and has them retailed from the Company's store at an enormous advance, when turtle is killed he sends his own servant to take an account of the weight, lest the butcher should embezzle a few pounds; but I doubt, after all, he will verify the trite proverb, "penny wise and pound foolish" for I have heard it remarked by a Gentleman of information, that the new fort, if finished on the plan proposed, will cost 20,000l.

7th. This day another plantation was began at Savoy Point, about half a mile from hence, which is intended for the cultivation of cotton, whether it succeeds or not, clearing the wood about the town will certainly be conducive to health.

The manager of Clarkson's plantation[101] complains that most of his gramattos or labourers have left him to attend the cry or funeral ceremony of one of their brethren, who lately died by the wound of a shark; it is uncertain how long the cry will last.

9th. Came down from Bance Island, the Duke of Buccleugh, bound for Jamaica, with upwards of three hundred slaves.[102] Yesterday arrived two ships, one an American, the other a French man; they have plenty of provisions on board, which the Colony is greatly in want of. Mr. Dawes called on most of the gentlemen to request they would not purchase any, saying he intends buying what is wanting by wholesale, and will retail it to them at a *small advance*; such a proposal would have come better from a jew pedlar, then from the Governor of Sierra Leone, or a Lieutenant of Marines.

11th. The Duke of Buccleugh sailed yesterday, and the French man this day. I understand Mr. Dawes has purchased some articles of provisions from the Frenchman, who would have nothing but slaves in return, and for the sake of accommodation, Mr. Dawes gave him an order on Mr. Rennieu, who pays him in slaves. I think if this is not, it borders on an infringement of the Act of Parliament, for incorporating the Company, which says, "that the Company shall not, through the medium of their servants, or otherwise, directly or indirectly, traffic in slaves".[103] It seems as if Providence frowns on this purchase, for an unusual high tide carried away part of the provisions after they were landed.

A small coasting cutter of the Company's called the Providence, arrived this day from the Turtle islands, about fifteen leagues to leeward; she brought eight goats, four sheep, and twenty-one turtle; sixteen of the latter died since twelve o'clock, which has disconcerted the Governor very much; but I am told he has made a *calculation*, and thinks, if he can sell the other five at *four pence per pound*, it will be yet a *saving voyage*.

Between eleven and twelve o'clock last night, the Colony was alarmed by the report of guns, beating of drums, and shrill shoutings of our neighbours at King Jemmy's town.—Mr. Dawes assembled all the men, and had arms and ammunition given them, from a supposition that the natives meant to attack us—but it turned out to be a groundless alarm, and is suspected to have been a contrivance of some ill-disposed persons to get the settlers armed.[104]

King Jemmy and Signior Domingo being informed of this, came to-day to enquire why their *good faith* was mistrusted; they dined with Mr. Dawes, and after dinner King Jemmy paid me a visit; he seemed much offended, and said it was very foolish to suppose he would make war without a cause—if he had a Palaver with the Colony, he would first come and talk it over, and if it could not be settled in that way, and he was forced to make war, he would give us timely notice, that we might defend ourselves, but it was the custom of his country to compromise disputes amicably, and never to engage in war till there was no other alternative, or words to the same effect.—The former assertion, I believe, is not untrue, and his behaviour to the first settlers is an example; in that dispute, he gave them three days notice of his intention to drive them off, and burn their town;—with regard to the latter, I have frequently heard wars were common among the natives for the purpose of obtaining slaves; such may have been the practice, but I have enquired of several Chiefs, who positively deny it; and I am certain, since my first acquaintance in this part of the world, none of those predatory wars have happened hereabouts, notwithstanding upwards of two thousand slaves have been shipped and sent to the West Indies, from this river, within these last twelve months.

15th. Arrived a Cutter belonging to Bance Island, from the Isle de Loss. A Mr. McAuley, Member of Council, and the Reverend Mr. Gilbert, came passengers in her. These gentlemen came from England to the River Gambia, in the Sierra Leone Packet, where they left her to take in cattle for the Colony. The Settlers are highly pleased at Mr. Gilbert's return; indeed, every one must rejoice in the society of so amiable a man.

I have not heard any thing of Mr. McAuley, except his lately being an overseer upon an estate in Jamaica: Tis not to be questioned that the prejudices of such an education must impress him with sentiments favorable to the slave trade, and consequently I should not suppose him qualified for a member of Administration in a colony, formed mostly of *blacks*, founded on principles of *freedom*, and for the *express purpose* of abolishing the slave Trade.[105]

16th. I heard this morning there was another alarm last night, but as groundless as the last. Seven or eight canoes full of natives, passing the settlement on their way to King Jemmy's, hooping and hallooing as they went, stirred up unnecessary fears in the minds of the settlers, who flocked to Mr. Dawes, requesting he would furnish them with ammunition, which (not thinking requisite) he refused, and they returned home greatly dissatisfied.

I learn those people are come down to make one of their periodical sacrifices to the *devil*—I should like to witness the ceremony, but strangers (particularly whites) are not admissible; it will be performed between Free

Town and King Jemmy's, on the side of a small brook, under a cluster of large trees.

The weather is particularly fine at present—the fogs or smoaks are mostly dispelled, a salubrious sea breeze fans us daily, and agreeably tempers the burning sun.

17th. We are prodigiously distressed to understand King Naimbana is so dangerously ill, that his death is hourly looked for:—Mr. Dawes, Mr. Gilbert, the Physician, and some others, went up to visit him this morning; his death will certainly inconvenience the colony very much.[106]

Last night arrived the Lapwing cutter from the river Carimanca, (twelve or thirteen leagues from hence) with a load of Camwood, ivory, and rice—the Company have a small factory there, under the direction of a free mulatto-man, but the trade is yet very trifling, not nearly equal to the charges attending it.

That river produces the largest and finest oysters I ever eat—not such as are in common hereabouts, generated on the mangrove tree, and rocks, but genuine bed oysters—I have been fortunate enough to get a supply of them several times.

The settlers, having now a number of small boats, are able to furnish the colony with abundance of capital fish, and they have such plenty of fowls, that the gentlemen get what they require; but the propagation of the feathered species, is considerably protracted by the multitude of enemies they have here, viz. snakes, rats, wild cats, armadillas,* ants, &c.—The most formidable of all these are the ants—in the dead hour of night, they come in swarms, and attack the helpless chickens, while roosting under the mother's wing, who is scarcely able to defend herself.—I have had four or five killed in a night by them; and so prying and assiduous are they after their prey, that I have known them discover two doves, which were hanging in a cage up one pair of stairs, whom they not only killed, but carried off every morsel, except the feathers, before morning.

19th. Mr. Dawes and two or three other gentlemen went to Bunch river this morning to visit Pa Bunkie, who some people imagine will succeed King Naimbana; they took a present, or as it is termed, Dash, for this chieftain, by far richer than any yet made, King Naimbana, or any other chief.

Returning in the evening, they stoped at Signior Domingo's, where they expected to have seen a late favourite woman of King Jemmy's drink the red water, for suspicion of witchcraft, but their curiosity was disappointed by the ceremony being performed in an inland town;[107] however they were informed the woman had drank the water, and recovered, and that in consequence, Jemmy, by the customs of his country, is obliged either to pay the woman's parents, a slave, or the value of one in goods.

At half past twelve o'clock P.M. a spark from the kitchen fire, kindled in

---

* A kind of scaly lizzard.

the roof of my house, and before water could be procured, communicated itself in all directions: In a few moments the roof fell in, and in less than fifteen minutes, the whole building was consumed; but by the extraordinary exertions of some labourers who were working hard by, most of my cloaths and furniture were saved, so that my loss is trifling. I suppose (from a cursory view of what has escaped), not above 50l. As luck would have it, I moved my lodgings some days ago, and only stayed in the thatched house during the day, intending to leave it entirely, when another room was finished in the house where I now am, which will be the case shortly; indeed, it is already so forward, that I have asked a party of two and twenty to dine with me the day after tomorrow, on an *extraordinary occasion*, therefore I cannot complain of *wanting shelter*.

20th. I have been informed, that Pa Bunkie was advised by his Palaver-Man, not to accept the great *dash*, which, Mr. Dawes carried him yesterday; and that this Palaver *Gentleman* made use of the following, or similar language, to dissuade him from taking it:

"Father—these people have been here twelve moons now, have they ever taken the slightest notice of you, by inviting you to their camp,* or making you the smallest present heretofore?—No, Father!—And what makes them thus suddenly over generous to you?—Because they think your services will soon be requisite for them. Do not you know white men well enough, to be convinced that they never give away their money without expecting it returned many fold?—Cannot you see the drift of this profuse, unlooked for, and unasked for present? Let me warn you against taking it—for be assured, however disinterested and friendly they appear at this moment, they are aiming at some selfish purposes, and although they may not discover what their wishes are immediately—before twelve moons more you will know them." Bunkie replied, "I know they want something, nevertheless I'll take the *dash*—it rest with me, whether to comply with any request they make or not. I shall not consider the present, by any means binding on me."

Mr. Gilbert and Mr. Horne went up this afternoon to Signor Domingo's, where Mr. Horne preached a sermon to a congregation of natives. How preposterous! Is it possible that a sensible man, like Mr. Horne, can suppose it in his power to imprint notions of Christianity, or any sort of instruction, upon the minds of people, through the bare medium of a language they do not understand? He might as well expect, that holding a candle to the eyes of a blind man, or exposing him to the sun, would reclaim his sight! The desire of spreading Christian knowledge through this ignorant land, is questionless, most praise worthy, but it will require patience and time to effect it.[108]

21st. Last night arrived the Nassau, (Morley) from Bristol, but last from the Isles de Loss; Captain Morley this day added to the number at our convivial gala:[109] I was highly complimented for the elegance, variety, and

---

*   The name given *Free Town* by the Natives.

richness of my dinner, which, without doubt, was superb, considering where we are; we had three removes, from six and twenty, to thirty dishes, each; besides an admirable desert, consisting of a variety of European and tropical fruit, the whole of which was garnished with comfort and pleasantry.[110]

24th. On Sunday last, notice was given that Mr. Horne, or Mr. Gilbert, would perform divine service, in future, every morning and evening; and every one is desired to attend. I am of opinion the morning service is superfluous.—Why? For many reasons, and I will here enumerate three or four.

Among the Black Setlers are seven religious sects, and each sect has one or more preachers attached to it, who alternately preach throughout the whole night; indeed, I never met with, heard, or read of, any set of people observing the same appearance of godliness; for I do not remember, since they first landed here, my ever awaking (and I have awoke at every hour of the night), without hearing preachings from some quarter or other.[111]

Now, those people being so religiously bent, I think it unnecessary, or, as I first said, superfluous, that they should be convened every morning; because the primest part of the day, for exercising their worldly vocations, is occupied thereby; the vicious and lazy (and some such will creep into every society), are furnished with the plea of being at church; an excuse, I am told, many already make, after skulking an hour or two beyond the customary and proper time, when they have not been within a church door; and it detains the mass of labourers an hour every day, which, lost time, costs the Company at the rate of 1300l. per annum.

Vice and laziness surely ought not to be protected by Religion any where;[112] but they should be more especially discountenanced in a new Colony, where success greatly depends on industry.

This day I dined on board the Nassau, in company with Mr. Rennieu, and some gentlemen of the Colony.

Rennieu says, an old man named *Congo Bolokelly*, is on his way from the interior country to succeed King Naimba; and that such great pains has been taken to impress him with an unfavourable opinion of our Colony, that he is determined the Company shall re-purchase their land, or he will do every thing in his power to perplex and annoy us.

Mr. Dawes met with a circumstance very galling to him this forenoon. He had in contemplation to palisade a piece of ground, for an immediate asylum, in case the natives should take it in their heads to attack us.

The spot fixed upon, unfortunately took in part of a lot occupied by one of the Settlers, which, Mr. Dawes, conscious of his unpopularity, did not wish to encroach upon, without obtaining permission, although the Settlers only hold their present Town lots as a temporary accommodation, until their permanent ones are surveyed.

He called on the tenant, and took him out to explain what he wanted; many people in the neighbourhood, having previously heard of Mr. Dawes's intentions, assembled about him, who declared they would not suffer an inch more ground to be enclosed upon any pretence whatever, before their town and country lots were given them, and most solemnly protested they would destroy every fence which might be erected till such time.

Mr. Dawes endeavoured to persuade them by argument, that what he wanted to do, was for their protection; but they were deaf to every thing he said, and gave him language in return which he could not stomach: He told them, if he had imagined they would have treated him with so much indignity, he should not have come among them; and if they continued to behave in the same way, he would certainly leave them as early as he could. To this, with one voice, they exclaimed, "Go! go! go! we do not want you here, we cannot get a worse after you." He was so disgusted at this, that he turned his back, and walked off. It was directly before my door, therefore I witnessed the whole, and could not help feeling for the *Governor*, who seemed dreadfully mortified and out of temper.

Feb. 3. Nothing worth recording for these ten days past; yesterday the manager of Clarkson plantation came over from Bulam; he has had a serious quarrel with the natives, but *reason* was determined on his side. His advances in cultivation, I understand are very slow; for he is not able to keep any number of labourers together, more than a month at a time; it is customary to pay them every moon, and when they get their wages, like our English tars, they quit work while they have money.

The Sierra Leone packet arrived from Gambia this day, with thirty head of cattle; I have not learnt what her European cargo consists of, but it is said to be very trifling.

7th. Since the departure of Mr. Clarkson a number of subtle ungentlemanlike attempts have been made, to singe his reputation, in the opinion of the people, and to warp away their affections from him; which as yet have proved unsuccessful; but I never heard of so unmanly, unprincipled, and diabolical an assault on any one's character, as was last night made on his. The Settlers were summoned to meet Mr. Dawes and the Surveyor in the evening; and being collected, they were informed that their permanent *Town Lots* were surveyed and ready for them, and that they must relinquish those they at present occupy, immediately; to this they replied, "when placed on the lots we at present occupy, we were informed, they were merely for our temporary accommodation, and we promised, when the plan of the town was fixed upon and surveyed we would remove, but we were assured no public or other buildings would be erected between our lots and the sea; now, in place of this, the sea shore is lined with buildings, therefore, your promise being broken, we consider ours cancelled, and will not remove unless the new lots are run from the water's edge, and we indiscriminately, partake of them. Mr. Clarkson promised in Nova Scotia that no distinction should be made here between us and white men; we now claim this promise, we are free British subjects, and expect to be treated as such; we will not tamely submit to be trampled on any longer. Why are not our country alotments of land surveyed? Why are not all the Company's promises to us fulfilled? We have a high regard and respect for Mr. Clarkson, and firmly believe he would not have left us, without seeing every promise he made performed; if gentlemen here had not given him the strongest assurances they should be complied with immediately." In answer, they were told, "that it was not uncommon for Mr. Clarkson to make prodigal and extraordinary promises without thinking of them afterwards, that the great advantages he held out to them in Nova Scotia he was in no shape authorised by the Sierra Leone Company to make; they all came from himself merely to seduce them here; and he never had an idea of fulfilling of them, nay, he had it not in his power, and more than probable *was drunk* when he made them."[113] Here they groaned and murmured, but said "they believed Mr. Clarkson to be a man of honor, and that he never made any promise to them but such as he was authorised by the Company to make." The altercation now ended; I have had it nearly in the same language from more than a dozen people who were at the meeting.

The blacks seem vastly alarmed and uneasy, nothing else is spoken of all this day, and I understand they have determined to send two deputies to the Court of Directors to know from them what footing they are on, and what were the promises Mr. Clarkson was authorised to make them; indeed, it is not to be wondered at, for no other conclusion can be formed from such base insinuations, but that a wish exists *somewhere* to do them injustice.

12th. We had reason to think, for some days past, that King Naimbana was dead, but had no certainty of it until this morning; nor do we exactly know, when he died, but it is supposed several days ago. The country custom is to keep a great man's death secret some time; his coffin (the first in all probability any of his family ever had) is making here, and will be sent up to Robana this evening.[114]

14th. Yesterday being the anniversary of the Harpy's arrival, a few celebrated it by dining at the house of a late member of council, who came out in her; I think it would have been more a *propos* to have fasted and mourned on the occasion. The day was cloudy accompanied with a rumbling thunder and spitting rain,* as if the heavens *were groaning and weeping at the recollection*. It was intended to have fired minute guns in compliment to the remains of Naimbana, which would have been very timely, but that ceremony was postponed until this day, when it was performed.

---

*   A circumstance rarely known at this season.

LETTER XI.

February 15th, 1793.

My dear Madam,

The Good Intent, Captain Buckle, affords me an opportunity of sending you the foregoing journal, which I fear you will think very insipid, but every day produces such a sameness that really there is not subject for high seasoning, even a common epistle, and you will allow journalizing still more difficult; however, to avoid tautological writing, as much as possible, I skiped over several days at a time, which of course you will have observed, but after all, it is so dry, that I am almost ashamed to send it you, and am determined in future to have recourse to my old epistolary mode.

My dinner on the 21st of January will somewhat puzzle you at first, and least you may not at once hit upon what occasioned it, I must not keep you in suspence, but acquaint you that I have changed the name of Falconbridge for one a little *shorter,* under which I beg to subscribe myself,

Your's sincerely, &c. &c.[115]

LETTER XII.

FREE TOWN, SIERRA LEONA,
June 5th, 1793.

My Dear Madam,

I finished my last by hinting that I had once more enlisted under the banners of Hymen, but made no apology for my hastiness; or in other words for deviating from the usual custom of twelve months *widowhood.* To be plain, I did not make any, because I thought it unnecessary. Narrow minds may censure me, and perhaps the powerful influence of habit might operate against me in your opinion, before you reflected upon my situation, or well digested the many circumstances which plead in my favour; but having done this, I am mistaken indeed, if your heart is not too expanded to sully me with reproach afterwards. My own conscience acquits me from having acted wrong; next to that, I wish for the approbation of my friends, and after them, the charitable construction of the world. I know you wish me happy, and no woman can be more so than I am at present, with every expectation of a continuance.

I must now proceed to give you a summary view of occurrences since the fifteenth of February.

The first thing I shall mention is the universal discontent which has prevailed among the Settlers ever since the altercation they had with Mr. Dawes and the Surveyor on the 7th of February, and it must be confessed by every candid person, their murmurs are not excited without cause.

To give you an idea of what their complaints are, I shall state the outlines of a petition which they intend sending to the Court of Directors by two Deputies elected about the middle of March, who, for want of an opportunity, have not yet sailed, but are just on the eve of embarking in the Amy, for England. I have not only seen the petition, but have a copy of it verbatim.[116]

It first of all states, "That the Petitioners are sensible of, and thankful for the good intended by sending them from Nova Scotia to this country, and in return assure the Directors, they are well inclined to assist the Company's views, all in their power.

"That they are grieved beyond expression to be forced to complain of hardships and oppressions loaded on them by the managers of the Colony, which they are persuaded the Directors are ignorant of.

"That the promises made by the Company's Agents, in Nova Scotia, were preferable to any ever held out to them before, and trusting the performance of them, with the Almighty's assistance and their own industry, would better their condition, induced them to emigrate here. That none of those promises have been fulfilled, and it has been insinuated to them that Mr. Clarkson had not authority for making any, they therefore beg to be informed, whether such is the case or not, and that the Directors will point out on what footing they are considered.

"That health and life is valuable and uncertain; that notwithstanding they labour under the misfortune of wanting education, their feelings are equally *acute* with those of *white men,* and they have as great an anxiety to lay a foundation for their children's freedom and happiness, as any human being can possess. That they believe the Directors wish to make them happy, and that they think their sufferings are principally due to the conduct of the Company's Agents here, which they suppose, has been partially represented to the Directors.

"That Mr. Clarkson had promised in Nova Scotia, among other things, they should be supplied with every necessary of life from the Company's stores, at a moderate advance, of ten per cent. on the prime cost and charges. That while Mr. Clarkson remained in the Colony they paid no more; but since then they have been charged upwards of 100 per cent. That they would not grumble even at that, if the worst of goods were not sold, and paltry advantages taken of them, particularly in the article of rum. That they had known, by Mr. Dawes's order, several puncheons filled up with thirty gallons of water each, and even, though thus reduced, sold to them at a more extravagant price than they had ever paid before.*

---

*   This is perfectly true, but upon investigation, it appeared to proceed from *religious* motives; Mr. Dawes said, he ordered a *little* water to be put into each puncheon, from a fear the consumers would neglect to dilute the spirit sufficiently. Had such a trick been played at a *Slave Factory,* how would it be construed?

"That the only means they have of acquiring those goods, is by labouring in the Company's service, and even this they are deprived of, at the whim of Mr. Dawes, or any other Gentleman in office, which they consider a prodigious hardship, as it is the only resource whereby they can provide bread for their families; that out of mere pique several have been discharged from service, and not permitted, even with their little savings, to purchase provisions from the Company's store-house, the only one here.

"That Mr. Clarkson informed them before he sailed for England, the Company had been mistaken in the quantity of land they supposed themselves possessed of, and in consequence only one fifth part of what was originally promised them (the petitioners) could be at present performed; which quantity the Surveyor would deliver them in a fortnight at furthest, but they should have the remainder at a future time."

"That they should have been satisfied had they got one fifth part of their proportion (*in good land*) time enough to have prepared a crop for the ensuing year, but the rains are now commenced, and the Surveyor has not finished laying out the small allotments, which he might have done, had he not relinquished the work as soon as Mr. Clarkson sailed; and the greater part of those he has surveyed, are so mountainous, barren and rocky, that it will be impossible ever to obtain a living from them."

After mentioning many more trifling complaints, and dwelling greatly on the happiness and prosperity of their children, they conclude with words to this effect.

"We will wait patiently till we hear from you, because we are persuaded you will do us justice; and; and if your Honors will enquire into our sufferings, compassionate us, and grant us the priviledges we feel entitled to, from Mr. Clarkson's promises, we will continually offer up our prayers for you, and endeavour to impress upon the minds of our children, the most lasting sense of gratitude, &c. &c."

This petition is signed by thirty one of the most respectable Settlers in behalf of the whole; and they have raised a small subscription for supporting their representatives while in England: 'tis to be hoped the Directors will pay attention to them, and not suffer themselves to be biassed by the misrepresentations of one or two plausible individuals, who must of course say all they are able in vindication of their conduct, and who, we have reason to believe, from their hipocritical pretensions to religion, have acquired a great ascendency over a few of the leading Directors;—but surely they will not be so forgetful of their own characters and interests, as to allow that ascendency to operate against honesty, truth and justice, and ruin the quiet and happiness of a thousand souls:—no! they must be strangely altered indeed, laying aside their partiality for Ethiopians, if they do not possess too much probity to hesitate a moment when it comes before them.

Besides displeasing the blacks, and rendering them uneasy, Mr. Dawes is at constant variance with some one, or other of the officers, and since I wrote you last, few days have pass'd over without some fresh feud; one in particular is of so extraordinary a nature I must relate it, that you may have a peep into the disposition of our Governor.

Mr. S—— a surgeon, who came out in the Sierra Leone Packet, was two months here without a room to lodge in on shore, which was attended with great inconvenience to him, and interfered considerably with his duty; he, after some time, interceded with Mr. Dawes to let him have a small room fitted up in our house, which he soon got finished, and removed into; the apartment being very comfortable and snug, Mr. Dawes took a fancy to it, and the day after Mr. S—— had taken possession, without any apology or preface, sent his servant to demand the key; Mr. S—— was surprised at so uncouth and arbitrary a proceeding, and did not feel inclined to treat it with passive obedience, but gave a positive refusal, as such rudeness merited; in consequence, he was immediately dismissed from the service, and here follows an accurate copy of his dismission.

Council, FREE TOWN, 26th *April,* 1793.

Sir,

I am desired to transmit the enclosed resolution of Council to you, and am Sir,
your obedient humble Servant,

(signed) J. STRAND, Secretary.

Resolved, that Mr. S——, who came out to this Colony as surgeon in the Hon. the Sierra Leone Company's service, has pointedly refused obedience to the commands of the Superintendant, he be dismissed from the service, and that from this day he is no longer considered as a servant of the said company.

entered

JAMES STRAND, Secretary.
(signed)

Did you ever hear of any thing more ridiculously despotic? but mark the sequel; the day following, Mr. Dawes attended by the Secretary and his (Mr. Dawes's) servant, came to the Hummums, for by this name I must tell you our house is known,[117] I was sitting in the piazza reading; they took no notice of me, but Mr. S—— being present, the Governor address'd him, and demanded the key of his room, which of course was not complied with; he then desired his servant to break open the door, who immediately got to work, and would have done it, but was slily check'd by Mr. Dawes, who with as little ceremony or preface as he had offended, went up to Mr. S—— and said "I am much concerned sir for what has passed, if you feel offended, I beg your pardon I've been unwell, or would not have acted so rudely; I wanted your room, because it was retired, that I might be a little quiet, pray sir return my papers, and forget what has passed, you will greatly oblige and make me happy by doing so."

Mr. S—— heard this penitential confession with amazement, and replied, "Had you asked me in a gentlemanlike manner for my room at first, it would have been much at your service as it is now, I bear no malice—here are your papers."

I could fill up twenty pages was I to acquaint you with all the private quarrels of this sort: but as they can neither afford amusement or instruction, it is best to pass them over in silence.[118]

On the 25th of April we heard of the French King being massacred, and that England had declared war, against the blood thirsty banditti, who have usurped the reins of government in France. This account came by the Swift Privateer Cutter of Bristol, to the Isles de Loss, where she destroyed a French Factory, and made some valuable reprisals.

His Majesty's frigate Orpheus, Captain Newcomb, Sea-flower Cutter, Lieutenant Webber, and the African Queen, a ship chartered by the Company, arrived here the beginning of last month. Captain Newcomb, in his way out, touched at Senegal and Goree, and captured six French ships, four of which arrived safe at this port, and have since been condemned and sold at Bance Island; the other two were lost on the shoals of Grandee.

The Orpheus came out to protect the British Trade on this part of the coast of Africa, as did the Sea-flower, in some measure; but she is only to run down the Coast, and proceed to the West Indies. After remaining here a few days, they both went to leeward, unfortunately three or four days too late, or they would have intercepted a French Corsair that has scowered the coast from Cape Mount (about fifty leagues from hence) downwards, considerably annoyed our trade, and taken eight valuable ships clear away, it is supposed to Cayenne; she had captured many more, which have been retaken by the Sea-flower and Robust (a Privateer from Liverpool); these two vessels, we hear, have consorted and gone to Old Calabar, where they expect to fall in with and take a large French Guineaman, that has twelve hundred slaves on board, and is just ready to sail. One of the ships they re-captured was sent in here. I have seen the master of her, who says he never saw such a savage looking set in his life, as were on board the Frenchman. They all had on horsemen's caps (having a tin plate in front, with the emblem of *Death's head and marrow bones,* and underneath inscribed, "Liberty, or Death)," a leather belt round their waist, with a brace of pistols, and a sabre; and they looked so dreadfully ferocious, that one would suppose them capable of eating every Englishman they met with, *without salt or gravy.* Unluckily the Orpheus sprung her foremast, which obliged her to give up pursuing those Republican ragamuffins, and returned here.

During her absence, one of the most atrocious infringements on the liberty of British subjects, and the most daring extension of arrogated power that has yet occurred among us, was practised, by our Colonial Tribunal, on the persons of three sailors belonging to the African Queen.

These thoughtless sons of Neptune came on shore to regale themselves with a walk while their master was away (I believe at Bance Island) and as they strolled through the town, wantonly killed a duck belonging to one of the Settlers; they were immediately apprehended, and taken before the Chief Magistrate, who committed them to prison, and the subsequent day they were tried, not by their Peers, but by *Judge* McAuley, and a *Jury of twelve blacks*, who, without any evidence or defence from the prisoners, found them guilty of stealing and killing the *duck*. The *self-created Judge* then sentenced one of them to receive thirty-nine lashes by the common whipper, fined the other two in a sum of money each, and ordered them to be confined in irons, on board the York, till their fines were paid.

These sentences were accordingly put in execution; poor Jack was dreadfully mortified at being whipped by a black man; but his punishment being soon over, I considered it the lightest, for his fellow sufferers were kept ironed in the close hold of a ship, already infested with disease, upwards of three weeks, till the Orpheus returned; when the master of the African Queen presented a petition from them to Captain Newcomb, who did not hesitate to interpose his authority. He came on shore, waited on the Governors, and without waiting for compliments or paying any himself, he demanded of them, by what authority they tried white men, the subjects of Great Britain, by a *Jury of blacks*; it was so novel a circumstance, that it struck him with astonishment. "By Act of Parliament," answered Mr. McAuley.—"Shew me that Act of Parliament," replied Captain Newcomb, The Act for incorporating the Company being produced, Captain Newcomb read it over carefully, and finding there was no sanction given for holding any Courts of the kind, exclaimed, "Your Act of Parliament mentions nothing of the sort—your Court is a mere usurpation, and a mockery on all law and justice, I desire the prisoners may be released instantly." This, you imagine, was very unpalatable language to our *mighty men*; but they were forced to stomach it, and comply with the orders of their superior.

It is much to be wished, a ship of war was always stationed here; the very sight of her would restrain the exercise of similar abuses, or any extravagant stretches of undelegated power.

The first Sunday in every month is the day appointed for holding this *sham* Court, which, withal, serves very well for regulating any internal quarrels or misunderstandings among the Settlers, by whom it is credited; but extending its functions beyond them, is most iniquitous presumption.

Letters arrived by the African Queen from Mr. Clarkson, saying he was coming out immediately. The joy this news produced was of short continuance, and suddenly damped by dispatches from the Directors, mentioning Mr. Clarkson being *dismissed,* and succeeded by Mr. Dawes. This cannot in any way be rationally accounted for, but it is universally supposed the Directors have been betrayed into an act so prejudicial to their interests, and the welfare of their Colony, by listening to some malicious, cowardly representations, sent home by certain persons here, who are fully capable of assassinating the most immaculate character, if thereby they can acquire latitude for their boundless ambition, or, for a moment, quench their unconscionable thirst for power.

No language can perfectly describe how much the generality of people are chagrined on this occasion; they have added to their petition the most earnest solicitation for Mr. Clarkson to be sent out again.

Numbers, hopeless of such an event, are about to quit the Colony, and ever since the news transpired, they have harrassed Mr. Dawes with insults, in hopes he may take it in his head to be disgusted and march off. They even went so far as to write a letter, reminding him of the recent melancholy fate of Louis XVI. and threatning something similar to him, if he did not instantly acquiesce with some demand they made relating to provisions, and which I learn he complied with, without hesitation. I should not be surprised, after obtaining one demand so easily, if they repeated their threats, until all the promises made them were fulfilled: but they say it was the want of provisions, that incited them to *frighten* the Governor, and they will now wait peaceably till their Deputies return from England, or till they know what the Directors mean to do for them.

It will be a monstrous pity if this Colony does not succeed after the immense sum of money expended on it; the original theory of its establishment (so generally known) was praise worthy and magnanimous, nor do I suppose such a scheme by any means impracticable; but injudicious management, want of method, anarchy, perpetual cabals, and cavils, will thwart the wisest and noblest intentions, which I predict will be the case here, unless some speedy salutary alterations are adopted; if the present system is continued, not only the settlers, but the natives will be provoked; all kind of confidence will cease, the Companys funds will be fruitlessly exausted, and more than probable, before ten years, we may hear that the Colony is dwindled into a *common* slave factory: some situations make it necessary for superiors to be feared, and all situations require they should be loved; but if the present managers continue here, their life-times, they will never experience the pleasure of the latter, or the honor of the former; and retire when they like, I very much question whether they will leave one friendly thought towards them behind: for this (tho' an idea, well meaning men would blush to foster) must ensue, where the seeds of dissention and rancarous[119] jealousy are sowed and encouraged by those whose provice should be to suppress their growth.

The Amy tis said will sail in a week, she carries a small cargo of about 1500l. value, a laughable return for upwards of 100,000l. Being the first remittance; I dare say it will be well puffed off in your news-papers; to see one of those puffs, would put me in mind of a persons face, distorted with a forced laugh, when the heart felt nought but emotions of agony: for here is a capital stock of more than 200,000l. Half expended, and this first harvest, I suppose, will barely defray the disbursements of shipping and carrying itself; what is more lamentable, such as it is cannot be often repeated, for the property is mostly sunk in such a way, that no probable or real advantages can ever revert from it, without the aid of an immense sum most judiciously applyed.

The periodical rains are just commencing, and seem to set in very severe, but I am in hopes of escaping its inclemency, being about to turn my back on them, and bid adieu to this distracted land, so you may probably hear of our arrival in England very shortly after the receipt of this letter, although we are to take a round about voyage by way of Jamaica. Mr.—— had taken our passage in the Amy, but the Discontents, about to leave the Colony, are so numerous, that she will be greatly crowded, and as the Nassau has excellent accommodations, sails well and immediately, he thinks we will be more comfortable in her, and less liable to fall in with French Pirates, than we should in the former, which is a dull sluggish vessel, though it is a prevailing opinion here, should she (the Amy) meet with a French man of war, she will be in no danger, as the National Convention have offered protection to all the Company's ships; how true this may be, I cannot say; but it is probable enough, as two of the Directors were some time since nominated Members of the Convention.[120]

We are to sail in a day or two, and I am very much hurried in packing up, and preparing for our voyage, therefore must bid you farewell, &c. &c.

LETTER XIII.

Swan with Two Necks, Lad-lane,
LONDON, 11th *October,* 1793.

My Dear Madam,

I hasten to acquaint you, that after a passage of nine weeks and four days, in the Alexander (Shaw) from Jamaica, we landed safe at Dover, the 9th instant. My heart jump'd with joy, when I found myself once more treading the sod of Old England, which at one time during our voyage, I did not expect would ever be the case, for an ill-natured contagious fever, (when we had been but a few days at sea), discovered itself in the ship, and, before it could be checked, scourged almost every person on board; however, by the skill and vigilance of the ship's surgeon, only one death happened. We had been out about three weeks, when it attacked me, and was it not for the good nursing and attention I had from every one, particularly the Captain, Surgeon, and my own good man, in all human likelihood I should have fallen a victim to its barbarity; indeed, Captain Shaw's impartial kindness to his sick, was beyond every thing I ever witnessed before, and, in my opinion, stamps him a man of genuine humanity.

Our ship was armed with two and twenty guns, and had between fifty and sixty men on board. We sailed from Kingston the 3d of August, and the following day fell in with thirteen sail of Spanish ships, under convoy of a frigate, who was so very negligent of her charge, as to permit us to intercept seven of them, which, had they been French, we must have taken in spite of all she could have done, being at that time so far to leeward, as to be scarcely discernable. A Liverpool ship, bound home, had joined them the preceding day, and now begged to be taken under our protection; this was granted, and she kept company with us until we got into the chops of the Channel.

The fever that infested us, broke out among her crew, and hurried a fourth of their number into the other world. Here Captain Shaw displayed his humanity again, in a high degree, by waiting several hours every day, and thus prolonging our voyage, to the prejudice of his own interest, merely for the purpose of rendering them what assistance he could; had he not, their situation would certainly have been extremely comfortless, as the calamity I have just mentioned was aggravated by the ship being so leaky, that the master and crew had it frequently in contemplation to abandon her.

We had little bad or boisterous weather during our voyage, and the time pleasantly vanished after health was restored in the ship; scarcely two days passed away without meeting one or more vessels; we always brought them too, and although none of them were of the sort wished for, they amused and furnished us with news of some kind. Clearing ship, when a strange sail was seen, as if we really expected a rencounter, and exercising our guns, once or twice a week, with all the manoeuvres practised in an engagement, were sources of amusement altogether new to me. At first, when a broad side was fired it operated like an electrical shock, but habit soon made it familiar, and at last I was less sensible of vibration from it, than the awful tremendous thunder we oftentimes had off the coast of America, which was more severe by far, than any I ever heard on the coast of Africa. This being the substance of every thing worth notice on our way home, I shall therefore turn back to my quiting Sierra Leone, and say something of what occurred from that time till my departure from Jamaica.

We embarked and sailed on the ninth of June; nothing could have reconciled me to the idea of taking my passage in a slave ship, but Mr. — being with me, for I always entertained most horrid notions of being exposed to indelicacies, too offensive for the eye of an English woman, on board these ships; however, I never was more agreeably disappointed in my life. In the centre of the ship a barricado was run across, to prevent any communication between the men and women; the men and boys occupied the forward part, and the women and girls, the after, so I was only liable to see the latter, who were full as well habited as they would have been in Africa, and I had very comfortable apartments in the round house, where I could retire, when I chose to be alone.

Having heard such a vast deal of the ill treatment to slaves, during the middle passage, I did not omit to make the nicest observations in my power, and was I to give upon oath what those observations were, I would declare, I had not the slightest reason to suspect any inhumanity or mal-practice was shewn towards them, through the whole voyage; on the contrary, I believe they experienced the utmost kindness and care, and after a few days, when they had recovered from sea sickness, I never saw more signs of content and satisfaction, among any set of people, in their or any other country. We had not our compliment of slaves by one-third, consequently there was abundance of room for them. Regularly every day their rooms were washed out, sprinkled with vinegar, and well dried with chafing dishes of coal; during this operation the slaves were kept on deck where they were allowed to stay the whole day (when the weather would permit) if they liked it, and in the morning before they came up, and in the evening, after they retired to rest, our deck was always scrubed and scowered so clean that you might eat off it.

Their provisions were excellent, consisting of boiled rice and English beans, sometimes separate, sometimes mixed, cleanly dressed, and relished with a piece of beef, salf fish, or palm oil, the latter seemed generally to have the preference; a superabundance of this was their constant breakfast and supper; between the two meals each slave had a large brown biscuit, and commonly a dram of rum. Great attention was paid the sick, of which however there were few, a mess of mutton, fowl, or some fresh meat, was daily prepared for them, and we arrived in Jamaica on the 13th of July, with the loss of only one boy who was ill before we left the coast, and the remainder of the cargo in much higher health than when they embarked.[121]

Whether slaves are equally well treated in common, I cannot pretend to say, but when one recollects how much the masters are interested in their well doing, it is natural to suppose such is the case, for self-interest so unalterably governs the human heart, that it alone must temper the barbarity of any man, and prevent him from committing violence on, or misusing his own property, and every cargo of slaves is more or less that of the ship master's.

A few days before our arrival at Kingston, Mr. W—lb—ce and Tom Paine were burnt in effigy. It would have hurt me had I seen the former coupled with such an incendiary, and thus exposed to public ignominy; for, in my conscience I believe he was impelled by too keen notions of humanity, and too zealous a desire of doing good, to take so active a part as he has done for the abolition.

For a length of time I viewed the Slave Trade with abhorrence—considering it a blemish on every civilized nation that countenanced or supported it, and that this, our happy, enlightened country, was more especially stigmatized for carrying it on, than any other; but I am not ashamed to confess, those sentiments were the effect of ignorance, and the prejudice of opinion, imbibed by associating with a circle of acquaintances, *bigoted for the abolition*, before I had acquired information enough to form any independent thoughts upon the subject, and so widely opposite are my ideas of the trade from what they were, that I now think it in no shape objectionable either to morality or religion, but on the contrary consistent with both, while neither are to be to found in unhappy Africa; and while three-fourths of that populous country come into the world, like hogs or sheep, subject, at any moment, to be rob'd of their lives by the other fourth, I say, while this is the case, I cannot think the Slave Trade inconsistent with any moral, or religious law,—in place of invading the happiness of Africa, tends to promote it, by pacifying the murdering, despotic chieftains of that country, who only spare the lives of their vassals from a desire of acquiring the manufactures of this and other nations, and by saving millions from perdition, whose future existence is rendered comfortable, by the cherishing hands of Christian masters, who are not only restrained from exercising any improper or unjust cruelties over their slaves, by the fear of reciprocal injury, but by the laws of the land, and their religious tenets.[122]

All the slaves I had an opportunity of seeing in Jamaica, seemed vastly well satisfied, their conditions appeared to be far preferable to what I expected, and they discovered more cheerfulness than I ever observed the Blacks shew in Africa, unless roused by liquor.

The Kingston markets are as abundantly supplied with vegetables, both in variety, and quantity, as any I ever saw; and I was informed, wholy from the industry of slaves at their by-hours, for their own emolument; and I further heard, that notwithstanding many of them have, in this way, amassed money enough to purchase several slaves, yet few instances occur where they shew even a desire of ransoming themselves. This is not a matter of much astonishment, when we reflect how little slaves in our Islands are embarrassed with worldly cares: that they are fed when hungry, cloathed when naked, and kindly nursed, with every medical care, when sick, solely at their master's expence, who only exact honesty, and a reasonable task of labour in return, after which, if attended to, they have nothing to fear, but, on the contrary, are certain of being rewarded and encouraged by extraordinay indulgencies; and when the thread of life is spun out, they leave this world with the pleasing thoughts that an interested, if not a naturally humane and indulgent master or mistress will supply their place, and prevent their children from experiencing any want of a father or mother's fostering hand.

How very few of our labouring poor can boast, when their mortal bodies become tenants of the grave, that their children have such certain provision secured them, and probably thousands and thousands of themselves may go supperless to bed this very night, and rise tomorrow, not knowing where to get a breakfast, or without the means of acquiring a morsel of bread to allay the gnawings of hunger—whether then are their situations, or those of slaves, having Christian masters, most preferable? The question, in my opinion, requires but little consideration.[123]

Pray do not misinterpret my arguments, and suppose me a friend to slavery, or wholly an enemy to abolishing the Slave Trade; least you should,

I must explain myself,—by declaring from my heart I wish freedom to every creature formed by God, who knows its value,—which cannot be the case with those who have not tasted its sweets;[124] therefore, most assuredly, I must think favourably of the Slave Trade, while those innate prejudices, ignorance, superstition, and savageness, overspread Africa; and while the Africans feel no conviction by continuing it, but remove those errors of nature, teach them the purposes for which they were created, the ignominy of trafficking in their own flesh, and learn them to hold the lives of their fellow mortals in higher estimation, or even let me see a foundation laid, whereupon hopes itself may be built of their becoming proselytes to the doctrine of Abolition; then, no person on earth will rejoice more earnestly to see that trade suppressed in every shape; nor do I apprehend it would be impracticable, or even difficult to effect it, for I still admit what I said upwards of two years ago, to be strictly just.— "That Nature has not endowed the Africans with capacities less susceptible of improvement and cultivation, than any other part of the human race,"—and I am sure they thirst for literature; therefore, if seminaries were established on different parts of the coast, and due attention paid to the morals and manners of the rising generation, I do not question but their geniusses would ripen into ideas congenial with our own; and that posterity would behold them, emerged from that vortex of disgrace, in which they have been overwhelmed since time immemorial, establishing social, political, and commercial connections throughout the globe, and even see them *blazing* among the *literati* of their age.

I am heartily glad to get rid of this subject, and am surprised how I came to entangle myself in it: but trust no expressions have slipped from me which will reproach my humanity or sensibility, for the wrongs of mankind; if there have, impute them to mistaken notions of happiness and misery, for I am not conscious of meaning ill.

You will observe, I was in Jamaica from the 13th of July to the 3d of August, and perhaps may expect some opinion of the country, people's manners, &c. from me, but any remarks of mine cannot be otherwise than trifling, and confined, as my stay was too short, and Kingston, with a little of its environs, were the only parts I had a chance of seeing.

Kingston stands on the brink of a bay which forms the harbour; its situation is varied, being partly low and partly high. I suppose it to be about a mile in length, and rather more than half in depth; a regular well built town, with streets intercepting each other at right angles; but I think many of them quite too narrow for that climate. I am told it is the largest, best built, most opulent, and populous town we have in the West-Indies. The merchants mostly have small country villa's, within a couple of miles round, which are called Pens, whither they retire, between three and four o'clock in the afternoon, when all business for the day is compleated.

I found the heat much more oppressive than I ever felt it in Africa, where I was, including both voyages, upwards of two years, without perceiving my skin in any way discoloured by the weather, but before I had been in Kingston a week, I was tan'd almost as brown as a mulatto. This I charge in a great measure to living on the sea side, open to the violent breeze, which sometimes blew a very storm, and which, I am persuaded, is intensely acid, for I never could leave a key, knife, or any piece of steel exposed to it for half an hour without getting rusted. The people dress mostly after the custom of this country, and their manners are much the same, except in hospitality, which surpasses all I ever met with.

I used commonly to ride out from five to seven o'clock in the morning and then return to breakfast; in those rides I often observed the country tore up into deep furrows, which I conjectured were passages of rivulets dried up, but was informed they were occasioned by heavy inundations, during the rains; notwithstanding this, I found the roads remarkably good, particularly the road to Spanish Town, which is, without exception, the best I ever travelled upon; but understand, it was made at a prodigious expence, being a great part of the way through a morass, which laying to windward of Spanish Town, must contribute to make that place very unwholesome; This is the Capital of Jamaica, about thirteen miles from Kingston, but in comparison with the latter, very insignificant; several public offices, the assembly of the island, and courts of justice are held there; it is also the residence of the Governor, whose house is both spacious and elegant;* a marble statue of our late gallant Rodney is erected there, in memory of that ever famous action on the 12th of April, 1782;[125] its ornamental effect is greatly lost by being placed in an obscure corner. I am much surprised it was not raised at Kingston, where certainly it would have appeared to more advantage and notoriety; but the house of assembly determined that it should grace the former, being the metropolis.

I have already told you what excellent vegetable markets there are at Kingston; its flesh markets likewise are very good, plenty of fat beef, but rather dark coloured and coarse grained, excellent mutton, pork, and poultry of all kinds; turtle in high perfection, and a variety of fine fish may be had every day.

Kingston swarmed with emigrants from St. Domingo,[126] whose miseries and misfortunes did not fail to draw compassion and charity from its humane inhabitants, who subscribed most liberally to meliorate their sufferings, and I was credibly informed, that even the French prisoners have so handsome an allowance as three and sixpence currency each per day, from the island of Jamaica, for their maintenance. Are not these proofs of generosity? can a doubt exist that those people who not only assist the oppressed and injured, but provide so bountifully for their very enemies, are not alive to the nicest definition of humanity? only in minds warped by ignorance or prejudice, I presume, and the opinions of such are very immaterial.

---

*   It is said to have cost 30,000l. Jamaica currency—21,4281. 11. 6d. sterling.

A very galling and extraordinary misfortune befel me while at Kingston, which I cannot refrain mentioning to you. After we had been there about eight or ten days, a genteel dressed man took lodgings in the same house with us, and the following day we went to dine and stay the night at a gentleman's in the country, when this fellow availed himself of our absence, broke into my bed chamber, and rifled a small casket, containing nearly all the trinkets and valuables I had, to some considerable amount; be assured I felt prodigiously mortified at my loss, which was not a little aggravated by finding the knave had eloped, leaving behind him, a trunk *half full of stones*, in lieu of his spoils.

Tricks of this sort occur so rarely there, that it had made not a little noise, and the town vestry offering a handsome reward, for apprehending the thief, I had the satisfaction of hearing, just before we sailed, that he was taken, but this was all, for he had disposed of what he stole from me, at least none of the articles were found in his possession; however, it was supposed he would be convicted of other burglaries charged to him, and I cannot say, I should be hurt to hear that the world was rid of such a nuisance.

I believe I have now noticed every circumstance meriting attention, from the time of leaving Sierra Leone, until our arrival here, and having spun this letter out to a greater length than was either expected or intended, I must therefore hurry it to a conclusion, and shall only observe that I understand the Amy is arrived, with the two black Deputies from Sierra Leone, but I am not informed what kind of reception they have met with from the Directors, none of whom I've yet had the pleasure of seeing.

Mr.—— has some business with them, which he is in hopes of accomplishing shortly, we then intend paying a visit to you and the rest of my friends in Bristol.

Adieu.
Believe me always
Your's sincerely.

LETTER XIV.

"Even the declarations made by themselves, seem wholly new and strange to them; they forget not only what they have seen, but what they have said." Wilberforce, on the Slave Trade. 18th April, 1791.[127]

LONDON, 23d *Dec.* 1793.

My dear Madam,

I concluded my last by telling you Mr.—— had some business to settle with the Directors, part of which was on account of what they were, and yet are, indebted to me as the widow of Mr. Falconbridge, for money left in their hands, and for salary due to him when he died.[128]

About a week after we came to town, I called at Mr. Henry Thornton's, but not finding him at home, left my address with a message, that I wished to see him on business. Several days elapsed without a syllable from Mr. Thornton, and conjecturing the servant might have omitted delivering either my card or message, I called again, when his house-keeper assured me he had received both, but was then at his country seat at Clapham; I now left a note mentioning the circumstance of having waited on him twice, and beging to be acquainted when I could have the pleasure of seeing him; four or five days more passed away without any answer, which puzzled me very much to account for. Unwilling, however, to nurse any suspicion that either insult or injury could possibly be intended me, by a man who had spontaneously made such declarations of friendship as Mr. Thornton did to me, before I went last to Africa, and whose character is currently reported, to possess as little alloy as frail man can be charged with, I therefore determined to venture another letter before I formed any opinion; the consequence of this was an answer that staggered me a vast deal more than his silence; he informed me I would find him at his banking house, in Bartholomew lane, from ten to twelve the following day, if I *chose to call there*. I was vexed at receiving so affronting a note from Mr. Thornton, because it gave me room to question his veracity, and the Directors good intentions towards me; nevertheless, a consciousness of having done nothing to merit such rudeness, and my interest requiring me to see him, I curbed my nettled pride, collected as much composure as it was possible, and met the gentleman on his own ground. I believe he neither expected or wished for this meeting; when I entered his counting room, he blushed confusion, and with some difficulty stammered out, "pray madam, what is your business with me?" "I have been induced to take so much pains to see you, Sir, to request you will get the Directors to settle Mr. Falconbridge's accounts, and pay what is owing me," answered I, "why," said he, "Mr. Falconbridge kept no books, and he appears to be considerably in debt to the Company." "Kept no books, Sir, how can that be, when I have a copy of them this moment in my hands, a duplicate of which, I know your Accountant at Sierra Leone (in whose possession the original books are) has sent the Directors." "I have never seen them; pray what is the amount of your demand?" replied Mr. Thornton. I then produced an abstract account stating the sum; "why" says he, its a large amount; I did not know Mr. Falconbridge left any money in our hands, I thought he had received it; and his accounts for the Lapwing's first voyage were never settled." This language startled me a good deal, but I refreshed his memory regarding the money left with the Directors; and told him he also laboured under a mistake respecting the Lapwing's accounts, for he must recollect they were settled, and that he, fortunately, paid the balance of 74l. 19s. 6d. to myself. Naked truths thus staring him in the face, made him at a loss what to say;

however after a little reflection, he told me, "whatever is due to you, madam, must be paid; if you will walk into another room, and wait a few moments, I will send for Mr. Williams, the Secretary, who will see every thing set right."

I was then shewn into a large cold room, covered with painted floor cloth, where, after waiting some time half frozed, Mr. Williams came. His behaviour was gentlemanlike: when I had recapitulated nearly what I said to Mr. Thornton, he enquired if Mr. Falconbridge left a will in my favour? which having answered in the affirmative, he wished me joy, as it would prevent others from sharing of the little property he left—desired me to get the will proved, and when that was done there would be no impediment whatever in my way, and I should be paid immediately.

In a few days after, Mr.—— saw Mr. Williams, who told him, he had better omit proving the will till the Court exactly ascertained what amount I had to receive, as it would save expence.

Perhaps Mr. Williams intended a kindness by this admonition, for he must have known then, what I am now sure of, that the Directors mean, if they possibly can, to withhold every sixpence from me; at least, there is great reason to suppose so from their quibbling conduct.

After detaining us here all this time, and shuffling Mr.—— off from one Court to another, without assigning any honest, business like reason, for doing so; they now wind up their prevarications, by saying, they must wait for further information from Sierra Leone, which I look upon tantamount to a positive refusal; indeed, it would have been much handsomer had they candidly declared at once, that it was not their intention to pay me—for their evasive answers have increased the injury, by prolonging our stay here to the overthrow of some plans Mr.—— had in contemplation.

What do you think of their charging me with the presents they particularly directed, I should purchase for, and make, Queen Naimbana; with the stores granted by the Court for me to take to Sierra Leone, my journey to Bristol and Falmouth, and every little donation they made, either to Mr. Falconbridge, or myself.

But besides these paltry, pitiful charges, they bring forward three others of much greater consequence, though founded on equally shameful and frivolous grounds, viz. the Lapwing's cargo, with all the expences of her first voyage, and for eight months before she left the river Thames;—the goods sent in the Duke of Buccleugh, together with the freight and passage money paid Messrs. Anderson's, and the Amy's cargo when we last went to Africa.

They might, with as much propriety, have included the whole of the Company's funds that have been thrown away;—yes, shamefully so,—no set of raw boys just let loose from school, could have disposed of them more injudiciously.—What had Mr. Falconbridge to do with the disbursement of the Lapwing? Her master was the ostensible person. The trifling goods sent out in her and the Duke of Buccleugh, were all appropriated conformable to the instructions Mr. Falconbridge received; they were not intended for trading with, but merely as gifts of charity, and bribes, to pacify the covetous natives; therefore, if Mr. Falconbridge had not accounted for them, it would be very easy to find out whether they had been disposed of that way: but I know every thing was settled previous to our second voyage, and it is only a poor, mean finesse in the Directors to say otherwise.

As to the Amy's cargo, true—it was consigned to Mr. Falconbridge; but that consignment was done away, when he received his fresh instructions, after we arrived at Sierra Leone; and before that vessel left Africa, the Master of her got a receipt for his whole cargo, from the Governor and Council, which receipt the Directors have at this moment.

I will not interrupt your time with this subject longer than to give you the sentiments of the late Governor of Sierra Leone, who says, in a letter of the 15th instant, to Mr.———, "I am sorry the Directors should give you so much trouble, and particularly about the cargo of the Lapwing for her first voyage. They certainly are unacquainted with the circumstances, and the situation of Falconbridge on his first voyage, or they would never be so minute, particularly with his widow, who experienced such unheard of hardships.

"I hope I speak truth, when I pronounce their late Commercial Agent an honest man, but a very unfortunate one, not in the least calculated for the station he filled, which men of discernment might have discovered at first view. I assure you, had I been on board the Lapwing, on her first voyage, by myself, in Sierra Leone river, without a person in the neighbourhood likely to befriend me (which was the case with Falconbridge), knowing the country as I do, I should have thought myself extremely happy to have returned safe to my native country, without any cargo at all."

I shall now leave you to make what comments you please on the vexatious treatment I have received from those Gentlemen, and to turn in your mind what my prospects would have been had I come home implicitly confiding in the profusion of friendly promises they bestowed on me (unsought for) when last in England.

I certainly had a right to build some expectations from them; but in place of any, you find those *paragons of virtue and human excellence*, unwilling to do me common justice, refusing to pay me what is religiously my right—a little pittance, which God knows, I gave the highest price for!

However, if there is any comfort in having company in one's misfortunes, or ill usage, I have that satisfaction.—Their treatment to Mr. Clarkson (the late Governor), and others, has been highly discreditable, but their behaviour to the two Deputies from Sierra Leone,[129] and consequently to all their constituents, is the most inconsistent part of their conduct, because any injury done them must annoy and jar the Company's interest.

These unfortunate oppressed people (the Deputies) have related to me most minutely every circumstance that has befallen them since their arrival in this country; and, as you seem interested in their behalf, and desire to know what success they have met with, I will repeat their narrative nearly in their own words.

"We landed *pennyless* at Portsmouth," I think they said "the 16th of August, but we had a small bill on the Directors for the amount of what our fellow sufferers subscribed before we left Free Town. The Company's Agent at Portsmouth gave us two guineas to pay our way here, which were deducted from our bill when it was paid. As soon as we came to Town, we went to Mr. Thornton's house, and delivered our Petition to him, he read it over, and seemed at first to be very kind, and to compassionate us very much, but, in two or three days time, he told us the Directors had received letters from Africa, stating that our complaints were frivolous and ill grounded.[130] After this we saw several of the Directors, who told us the same. We asked who the letters came from, but this they would not tell, however we are sure Dawes and McAuley are the authors, because they must write all the —————they can think of to excuse themselves.

"When we had been here about three weeks, finding our money almost exhausted, we applied to two of the Directors, namely, Mr. Thornton and Mr. Parker, and requested them to supply us with a little." The latter said, "Yes, I will let you have money, if you will mortgage, or sell the lands due you by the Company," but the former had *more humanity*, he recommended us to go and labour for our support. To this we replied, we were willing to work, if we knew where to get employment.—Mr. Thornton then said, "You shall be at no loss for that, I will give you a line to a person who will employ you."—"This we gladly accepted of, and accordingly got into service, where we wrought for near a month, without hearing the most distant hint of an answer to our Petition. We then began to grow very uneasy, and quite at a loss what to do, having no friend to advise us.

"The Directors never would give us Mr. Clarkson's address, though we asked for it frequently; however, in the midst of our distress, accidentally hearing he lived at Wisbeach,[131] we wrote him without hesitation, enclosed a copy of our Petition, requested he would interpose his influence with the Directors, and in vindication of his character, endeavour to get justice done us. We told him, all we required was the fulfilment of his promises, which the Gentlemen at Sierra Leone had assured us he made without authority. When Mr. Clarkson received this letter, he wrote to Mr. Thornton, begging the Directors would appoint some early day to meet him and us together, that he might explain his promises, and thereby acquit himself from having acted dishonorable, in any shape, to the people he carried from America to Sierra Leone.

"We suppose the Directors did not like to see Mr. Clarkson and us face to face, for Mr. Thornton never answered that letter, which obliged Mr. Clarkson to write another; this he sent unsealed, under cover to us, that we might be convinced of his good intentions and integrity towards us."

They shewed me a copy of the letter, which having read, I also transcribed, as I now do again word for word.

"WISBEACH, *Nov.* 11, 1793.

"*My dear Sir,*

"As you have given me no answer to my letter, wherein I requested a day to be appointed for the Directors, myself, with Messrs. Anderson and Perkins, the Deputies appointed by the inhabitants of Free Town to meet, to explain the promises you authorised me to make them, I am induced to take this method to convince the people at large of your Colony, that I have done all in my power, since I have been in England, to forward the performance of the promises I made them, with as much zeal as I used when I was on the spot; and as I cannot bear to be suspected by them, or the inhabitants of Nova Scotia, who were witnesses of my exertions in their behalf, I am induced to take this method of assuring them of the sincerity of my professions, as well that the promises I made them were from the Directors of the Sierra Leone Company, and that they have as great a right to the performances of them as they have to dispose of their own property.

"I send this letter to you (unsealed) under cover to Messrs. Anderson and Perkins, for their perusal, that they may assure those they represent, I have done all in my power to perform my engagements with them, consistent with honour and honesty.

I am, Dear Sir,
Your's sincerely,
(signed) JOHN CLARKSON.

To Henry Thornton, Esq.

Chairman of the Court of Directors
of the Sierra Leone Company, London."

"We attended," continued the spokesman, "the first Court after receiving this letter, and delivered it. The Directors did not seem well pleased, but they made no observations on it to us. Before we left the Court, we were informed one of the Company's ships was to sail for Sierra Leone immediately—that we were to return in her, and when *embarked*, we should have an answer to our petition.

"We thought it very strange, they should put off giving us an answer till we had embarked, and therefore objected, saying, we wished not only to have, but to consider, the answer before we left this country, and were proceeding to say much more, when the Court prevented us, by saying, "Whatever objections you have to make, or whatever you wish to tell us, you must do it in writing."—In consequence whereof, on the next Court day, we presented an Address as follows:

Anna Maria Falconbridge

"To the Honourable the Chairman and
Court of Directors of the Sierra Leone
Company.

"Honourable Sirs,

"You have desired us to commit to writing what we wish to tell you.

"We did not think, Gentlemen, any thing more was necessary than the petition we brought, and delivered to you from the people we represent; but as you do not seem to treat that petition with the attention we expected, you oblige us to say something more on the subject, for we would be very remiss were we to leave this country, without doing all in our power to get some satisfaction, not for the trouble we have been at, but such as will be pleasing and comfortable to our countrymen, and at the same time serviceable to your interest.

"The Settlers at Free Town (those brought from America we mean), whose thoughts we now speak, always believed the promises made them by Mr. Clarkson, in Nova Scotia, were your promises. We are now convinced of the truth of this, by the letter from Mr. Clarkson, which we delivered you on Friday last.

"We certainly hope your Honors intend making good those promises, and we beg to know whether you do or not?—We beg to have Grants for the land we at present occupy, and a promise in writing for the remainder, or the value, to be given at a future time named in that instrument of writing.

"When we are able, we shall consider ourselves bound to contribute what we can, towards defraying the expences of the Colony; but this never can be the case until your promises are fulfilled to us; at present you are obliged to give us daily wages, to do work, from which no advantage can ever be derived, either to the Company or the Settlers; and we have no choice, but to do this work, or starve; whereas if we had our lands, and that support from the Company, which was promised, there would be no necessity for employing us except at such work as was really wanting; and we might do as we please, either work on our own lands, or the Company's, whereby there would be a mutual advantage, and in a few years, with industry and good management on our parts, the produce of those lands would yield a profitable trade to the Company, and we should have the pleasure of knowing we were providing comfort for our children after us.

"We always supposed we were sent from Nova Scotia to Sierra Leone, by his Majesty, (God bless him) the King of this Country; who, no doubt, expected our situation would be made better, from the assurances he had received of what your Honors were to do for us. We wish the Governor of our Colony should be appointed by his Majesty, whose subjects we consider ourselves, and to whom we shall be happy at all times of shewing our loyalty and attachment.

"If we are not of importance enough to this Country, to deserve a Governor authorised by the King, we, with due respect to your Honors, think we have a right to a voice, in naming the man who shall govern us, but by this we do not mean to say, that we have a right to interfere with the person whom you may chuse to direct or manage your property.

"We *will not* be governed by your present Agents in Africa, nor can we think of submitting our grievances to them, which we understand is the intention of your Honors, for it is inconsistent to suppose justice will be shewn us, by the men who have injured us, and we cannot help expressing our surprise that you should even hint such a thing.

"Our Countrymen have told you, in the petition we delivered to his Honor the Chairman, that they will wait patiently till we returned, that their religion made them bear the impositions of your Council, and prevented them from doing any thing that might be considered improper, till they heard from your Honors, being convinced they would then have justice shewn them; but we are sorry to say, we do not think you seem disposed to listen to our complaints, and if we are obliged to return to Sierra Leone, impressed with those sentiments, and without obtaining any satisfactory answer to the complaints and representations we have made, it is impossible for us to say what the consequences may be, but we will make bold and tell your Honors, on the answer we get, *depends the success of your Colony.*

"We wish to return to our families by the Amy, and therefore beg to have your answer time enough for us to consider on it, before we leave this Country.

"We hope your Honors will not think we have said any thing here but what is respectful and proper; we thought it our duty to tell you the truth; we want nothing but justice, which cannot surely be refused us. We have been so often deceived by white people, that we are jealous when they make any promises, and uneasily wait till we see what they will come to.

"We shall conclude gentlemen, by observing, since we arrived here, we have avoided giving you trouble as much as possible; we did not come upon a childish errand, but to represent the grievances and sufferings of a thousand souls.

"We expected to have had some more attention paid to our complaints, but the manner you have treated us, has been just the same as if we were *Slaves*, come to tell our masters, of the cruelties and severe behaviour of an *Overseer*.

"You will pardon us gentlemen, for speaking so plain; we do not think it has proceeded[132] from any inclination to wrong us, but from the influence and misrepresentations of evil minded men, whose baseness will some day or other be discovered to you, for the Great Disposer of events will not suffer them to be hidden long.

We are Gentlemen,
With all possible respect,
Your faithful Servants,

(Signed)

ISAAC ANDERSON,   ⎰ Representatives
                 ⎱ for the Inhabitants of
CATO PERKINS.   Free Town."

"When they had read this over, they seemed very much out of humour, and we were desired to leave the Court room, but in a few minutes Mr. Thornton sent us this letter."

"Messrs. Anderson and Perkins.

"In consequence of an address sent by you to the Court of Directors this day, I desire to be informed in writing, what are those promises of Mr. Clarkson, which you say, were made to you, in Nova Scotia, and are still unfilled."

I am,
Your obedient humble servant,

(Signed)   H. THORNTON.

SIERRA LEONE HOUSE,
19*th Nov.* 1793.

"Here is our answer to Mr. Thornton."

To HENRY THORNTON, ESQ. Chairman,
of the Court of Directors of the Sierra
Leone Company.

"Sir,

"As you desire to be informed in writing, what were the promises made by Mr. Clarkson to us (the inhabitants of Free Town) in Nova Scotia, we have to acquaint you, they were to the following purpose:

"That his Majesty having heard of the abuses we met with in America, and having considered our loyalty and services, in the late war, wished to make some amends, and proposed, if we were inclined to go to Africa, we should be carried thither free of expence.

"That the part of Africa we were to be carried to, was called Sierra Leone, where a Company of the most respectable gentlemen, in England, intended to form a settlement for the purpose of abolishing the Slave Trade.

"That he (Mr. Clarkson) was authorised by the Directors of that Company, to say, each head of a family should have a grant of not less than twenty acres of land, for him or herself; ten acres for a wife, and five acres for each child.

"That those grants should be given directly on our arrival in Africa, free of any expence or charge whatever.[133]

"That we should be provided with all tools wanted for cultivation, and likewise the comforts and necessaries of life, from the Company's stores, at a reasonable rate, such as about ten per cent. advance, upon the prime cost and charges, and should not be distressed for the payment of such goods, until enabled by the produce of our lands; but when we became comfortably settled, we should be subject to such charges and obligations as would tend to the general good of the Colony.

"That we should be protected by the laws of Great Britain, and justice should be indiscriminately shewn Whites and Blacks.

"As far as we can recollect those are the heads of Mr. Clarkson's promises to us; almost the whole of which remain unfulfilled. There has been one fifth part of the lands distributed to most of the settlers, but they are in general, so mountainous, barren, and rocky, as to be of little or no use to them; nor was the surveying of that fifth part compleated when we left Sierra Leone, at which time the rains had set in, therefore it was impossible to clear or make much progress this year, and you must be sensible, Sir, of the injury we sustain by loosing two years in the improvement of those lands.

"We are charged extravagantly for all the goods we purchase from the stores, which we consider, not only a breach of promise, but an unjust and cruel way of imposing a tax on us.

"We certainly are not protected by the laws of Great Britain, having neither Courts of Justice, or officers appointed by authority of this government. But even the Police which we have formed among ourselves, has not distributed justice impartially to Blacks and Whites, due, as we suppose, to the influence of your Agents; and we think it an unsufferable cruelty, that at the caprice or whim of any Gentlemen in office, at Free Town, we, or any of us, should be subject, not only to be turned away from the service, but prevented from purchasing the common necessaries from the Company's stores, for the support of our families, while it is not in our power to procure them by any other mode.

We are Sir,
Respectfully,
Your obedient, humble servant,

(Signed)

ISAAC ANDERSON, { Representatives
  for the People of
CATO PERKINS. Free Town."

LONDON, 20*th Nov.* 1793.

"What was the consequence of this letter? said I—"Why the Directors were no better pleased with it than the first, they seemed quite in a quandary; were very anxious to know whether any person had assisted us in collecting and reducing our thoughts to writing, interrogated us separately on the subject, and appeared greatly disappointed with our answers."

"Have you had any answer from them? No, Madam, and imagine they do not intend giving any; indeed we have heard that they mean to keep us from going to Sierra Leone again; if so, it no doubt is a stratagem, to dupe and lull our Countrymen, who have said they will wait peaceable, until we return; but such a poor little artifice is so very unbecoming the characters of gentlemen, that we can hardly believe it; however, if it is the case it cannot avail much, and will in the end, do them more injury than us; we have already wrote to our brethren, warning them of our suspicions, and guarding them against signing any paper or instrument of writing, as we have reason to think some thing of the sort will be asked of them, to contradict what we have done; it will be a great hardship on us to be kept here from our families, yet, if it ultimately tends to obtain justice for our constituents, or to secure freedom and happiness to them and their children, we shall think it no sacrifice."

This is fully the substance of the information I have from time to time had, from the two Deputies.*

Is it not almost incomprehensible that Thirteen Men, whose reputations in private life (one or two excepted) have hitherto been esteemed so spotless, that the tarnishing blasts of fame, or the venom'd shafts of malevolence, have seldom ventured to attack them, should, as a corporation, act incompatible with common sense and common —————— ?

The Directors conduct must really be a subject of consternation wherever it is known; and should they not, of their own accord, fulfill Mr. Clarkson's promises to their settlers, which they certainly seem inclinable to, I really think, in my humble opinion, this government ought to feel it a National concern, and enforce a performance.

His Majesty, no doubt, expected he was doing those poor people an actual

---

* Those two men returned to Sierra Leone, in February or March last, but two others have arrived on the same errand, and are just now (August 1794) in London: I am told they have many new complaints, among which is one of a serious nature, viz. That an enormous tax of two bushels of neat rice, equal to 130lb. has been demanded per acre for their lands, notwithstanding those lands were promised them, *free of every expence, or charge whatever.* Now rice is sold from the Company's store-house, at Sierra Leone, at the rate of sixteen and eight-pence per hundred pounds, consequently this tax would amount to 21s. 8d. per acre.

service, by removing them to a country, which gave birth, not only to their fore-fathers, but many of themselves, and more especially so as they were to be taken under the wing and protection of such patrons of humanity, as the gentlemen conducting the affairs of the Sierra Leone Company *professed* themselves to be, otherwise, he never would have hazarded their happiness, by taking them from America, where they were mostly comfortably settled;—where they might have been useful and valuable subjects, and where they had been, long before their removal, really an acquisition, besides subjecting this Country to the expence of upwards of 20,000l. for their transportation.**

Do you not think that immacculate Member of the House of Commons, who is obstinately persisting to abolish the Slave Trade, would be better employed, and would discover more real humanity, if he exerted himself in getting justice done these poor blacks, whose happiness and comfort he has, in some measure, though innocently, been the means of destroying?[134]

Until all the promises made them are performed, or, at least, a sincere inclination shewn to perform them, no kind of confidence can exist between the Company and the Colonists; and, unless that is quickly secured, the Colony must fall to nought. It may not be amiss here to give you the sentiments of a Gentleman, zealous for its success, and intimately acquainted with the Directors, and with the progress of the Colony, from its birth.[135]

He says, in a letter to a friend of his at Sierra Leone, "I am fearful your present Governors will forget the situation the Nova Scotians were in formerly; the number of times they have been deceived, and will not make allowances for the great change they have made; and I am more fearful of their not having patience or moderation enough to put up with their ignorance. It is an easy thing for the Governor and Council to leave them to themselves, if they are wickedly inclined; but I I should consider such behaviour as the greatest species of wickedness on their parts, (the Governor and Council) and should think their education ill bestowed upon them, and their religion but skin deep. What! are they not sent out to instruct them, and to set a good example to the unenlightened Africans? Ought they not to make the same allowances for them as our schoolmasters did for us in our infancy? and ought they not to know, that ignorant people, situated as they are, with the bad example set before their eyes by those who were sent out to instruct them at the commencement of the Colony—are liable to be riotous and unruly—particularly when so many have resided together, and but little employment to keep their minds amused? with the promises made them by the Company entirely neglected, and not the least appearance of a speedy completion, or even a *desire* to perform them. I say, had the Nova Scotians acted different from what they have done, under all these circumstances, it

---

** Those are a part of the very people, whom America (it is said) is asking compensation for.

would have astonished me, and I should have requested those, who consider themselves more enlightened, and stood forward as their friends and protectors, to have taken a lesson from so singular an example.

"Should you quarrel with the Nova Scotians, who do you think I shall blame? Your Government and the Company;—your *Government*, for want of patience, and for not shewing an inclination to perform promises, which will always set ignorant people at variance with their leaders, and particularly those who have been so often deceived before; and the *Company*, for not enforcing their orders relative to promises, and for their dilatory manner of sending out the means to perform them with dispatch.

"If you should have a war with the Natives, it will certainly be the fault of your Government; because, you have it in your power, by a particular conduct, to make your Colony unanimous,—and then you have nothing to fear.—You can always keep the natives quiet, if you have peace at home, which you may do, and at the same time gain their esteem and confidence; and if your Government should not, in every instance, do their utmost to preserve peace and harmony, and make every degree of allowance for the ignorance and bad example hitherto set to the poor natives, and, I may add, the Nova Scotians, they will, in my opinion, have a greater crime to answer for, than they may be aware of—for should your Colony, from bad management not succeed, after *all the advantages it has had*, the friends to the civilization of Africa, will have reason to repent of their having made an attempt to instruct that unenlightened part of society; it will depress the spirits of those whose hearts were warmly engaged in the cause, and deter them from making future attempts.

"These considerations have been so forcibly impressed on my mind, that I do not remember, since my arrival in England, of having ever written to, or conversed with the Directors, either as a body, or in private; but I have taken care to enforce, in as strong language as I could, the necessity of performing, as soon as possible, their promises to the Nova Scotians.

****

"I have been almost ready to expose people who are deserving of blame, but the situation of the Colony is such, that I am obliged to be silent, for it has many enemies in this Country, who would be rejoiced at having an opportunity to prejudice the minds of the Subscribers, against the measures adopted by the Directors."

I have given you those extracts, corroborant to many assertions I have made, that you may not impute any of them to a wrong cause; and I must give you another from the same letter, very interesting to the company's servants and officers employed in the Colony.

"I find there is a religious influence in the Colony, that will carry every thing their own way with a majority of the present Directors, and whatever they say, will be a law with them; and I really believe, that religion, which ought to have been the support and sheet anchor of the Colony, will be its ruin, from its being practised with too great enthusiasm and inconsistency; and I am fearful, that those possessed of honest hearts and independent spirits, who will speak their sentiments as truth dictates, will always be neglected by the Government there, and the Directors at home; and will never be done that justice which their readiness and exertions on every occasion to promote the prosperity of the Colony, entitles them to."

Can the Company ever expect to prosper, or have officers of probity or worth, while such is the case? No,—Sycophantic Hypocrites are the only servants who will continue in their service, and those will always drain the purses of their employers, by any means, however scandalous or dishonorable, to fill their own.

ADIEU.

To HENRY THORNTON, *Esq.* M. P.
and Chairman of the Court of Directors of
the Sierra Leone Company, *&c. &c.*

BRISTOL, *April* 4, 1794.

SIR,

Being earnestly solicited, by several friends, to publish the History of my *Two Voyages to Africa*, and having, with some reluctance, consented, I feel it incumbent on me to address this letter to you (which is hereafter intended for publication), by way of acquiting a tribute truth and candor demands, in support of what I have, necessarily, mentioned regarding the Directors behaviour to me.

It is needless, Sir, to take a more distant retrospect of the subject matter, than to the time of our arrival from Sierra Leone, in 1791.

If you will turn over to that period, and search into your personal behaviour, as well as the Court of Directors, to Mr. Falconbridge, I am persuaded you will find it marked with repeated testimonies of approbation and applause, for the services you were pleased to say he had rendered the common interest and original views of the Company.

For what purpose did the Directors vote us a compensation for our losses? Or for what purpose did they remove Mr. Falconbridge, out of his particular province as a medical man, and make him their Commercial Agent?

Were these not tokens of satisfaction, and rewards for his extraordinary exertions to serve the Company; or were they mere tricks of chicane and deception, to inveigle him to return to Africa, and answer the desirable end of securing a footing for the Emigrants, then expected from America? Let your own heart, Sir, decide upon these questions.

I understand the Directors persist to say, Mr. Falconbridge had not settled the accounts of his first voyage before he left England the second time; and that they impeach his memory, by saying he has not accounted for the cargo of the Amy, consigned to him as Commercial Agent. Is it so, Sir? Are these the paltry subterfuges made use of for withholding the poor pittance I am entitled to?—If they are? I shall charitably suppose, for a moment, they proceed from error, and endeavour once more to set you right,—though, believe me, not with the smallest expectation of profiting thereby.

To the first I shall observe,—You must labor under the misfortune of a very careless memory, if you cannot recollect that all Mr. Falconbridge's accounts, anteceding the 25th of December, 1791, were adjusted to that time, and that I received from *yourself* a balance of 74l. 19s. 6d. which appeared on the face of the account in his favor.

Can you deny the truth of this assertion, and say there was no such settlement? If you can, I will not attribute it to any harsher cause than bad memory, for I yet think it is impossible, Mr. Thornton would be so pitiful, *willingly*, to utter an untruth.

But if this pointed circumstance had not happened, and I was wholly ignorant of the affair, I should suppose men of business (as some of the Directors must be) would never have suffered him, or any person else, to commence the transactions of a new concern 'till those of the old were clearly concluded, but more especially so in this instance, as the charities Mr. Falconbridge had the distribution of on his first voyage, were the property of the St. George's Bay Company, whose original funds and effects were taken in account by the Sierra Leone Company, upon their incorporation, and therefore it was certainly necessary that the Directors should be made acquainted with the true state of their affairs.

To the second, I have to remind you, that Mr. Falconbridge never received the Cargo of the Amy, and consequently cannot account for what he was not in possession of; upon his arrival in Africa he got instructions from the Directors, placing him entirely under the control of the Superintendant and Council, and the property of the Company solely under their direction, consequently the first consignment and unlimited instructions given him became nugatory; furthermore, the master of the Amy got a receipt for his whole Cargo from the Governor and Council, previous to his leaving Sierra Leone, which is just now in possession of the Directors.

Mr. Falconbridge had no independent authority or management over the company's goods after he received those instructions, nor did he give any orders of himself, as other hair-brained members of council did, but got written instructions from the Superintendant and Council for every sixpence worth he had, either from ship-board or else where, all of which is accounted for in his books, delivered Mr. Grey by the particular desire of Mr. Dawes.

I am inclined to believe the Directors are already acquainted with these circumstances, indeed it is almost impossible they can be ignorant of them.

But admitting they are, what excuse can they have for swelling up an account against me with fictitious niggardly charges, such as charging me with disbursements for the Lapwing's first voyage, not only during her voyage, but for six or seven months before she left the river Thames. The freight and passage money of the Duke of Buccleugh paid Messrs. Anderson. The presents I was desired to purchase and make Queen Naimbana, for which I have your letter as authority. The stores I was allowed to take with me for our use at Sierra Leone. Our Journey to Bristol, Falmouth, &c. &c.?

How can your *Honorable* Court, formed, as it is, of Members of Parliament, Bankers, and some of the first Merchants in the City of London, all professing the quintessence of philanthropy, thus depreciate its worth by being guilty of such gross meanness? I verily believe it would be impossible to cull from the Migratory Chapmen of *Rag Fair*, any number of men who would not blush to be detected in a similar transaction.[136]

That the Directors had cause to be displeased with Mr. Falconbridge for not extending their commercial views, may be in some measure true; but tied up as he was, to obey the dictates of the Superintendant and Council, who would not listen to any arrangements of the kind, until comfort and regularity were established in the Colony—What was he to do? however if he was altogether in fault, was he not punished by annulling his appointment as Commercial Agent? could the Directors do more? If they had blindly (as they certainly did in many instances) made improper appointments: What more could they do than annul them when they discovered their mistake?

But I should suppose it did not require any great discernment, to know that a Surgeon, unacquainted with mercantile affairs, would make but as poor a figure in that line, as a Merchant, who had not studied physic or anatomy, would make in the practice of surgery.

Mr. Falconbridge's dismission did not charge or accuse him with any *crime*, but wanting knowledge of his business; and what information the Directors could get on that score must have been from a quarter as ignorant, if not more so than himself;—but surely, it was their province to have convinced themselves, when they made the appointment, whether he was equal to it or not.

Did not Mr Falconbridge's dismission stipulate, that his salary was to continue till the Governor and Council procured him a passage to England? Could there have been the smallest idea, at that time, of detaining either the money left in the hands of the Directors, or his wages? Surely not.—Then why do the Directors now (he is no more) withhold payment from me?

For shame, Mr. THORNTON, for shame! ! !—How can you wink at my being so shabbily treated, after the unexampled sufferings I have undergone, and after the prodigality of fair promises I had from you, to induce me to return a second time to Africa. Did you not tell me, if any accident befell Falconbridge, I should be handsomely provided for by the Company? Surely, you cannot forget making such a promise;—which you not only forego fulfilling, but shamefully keep back (all I require of you) the trifling sum so justly due to me.

If the Directors were not fearful of subjecting their conduct (towards me) to the investigation of impartial men, they never would have refused submitting the affair to arbitration, as was offered; nor would they have threatened, or boasted, that they would ruin me, with an expensive law-suit, in Chancery, when I signified my intention of trying the cause at Common Law, if they meant to do the fair thing.

I cannot help forming those conjectures, for how are we to calculate the principles of men but by their actions? Though, believe me, Mr. Thornton, notwithstanding all I have said of the Court of Directors, I yet firmly believe, if the decision was left wholly to yourself, I should have ample justice, and I cannot avoid thinking, from the opinion I have heretofore formed of your benevolence of heart, that you are secretly ashamed of the Directors nefarious treatment to me.

I will not trespass on your time any longer, but shall quit the subject, with referring my cause to the loftiest of Tribunals, where reigns a Judge of mercy, vengeance, and justice, who, I am persuaded, will not let such turpitude go unpunished, and who has, probably, already began to shew his displeasure.

Pray, Sir, receive this letter with temper, and consider it comes from a Woman, aggravated by insults and injury.

I am, &c. &c.

ANNA MARIA ——— .

Henry Thornton, Esq. M. P.
King's Arms Yard, Coleman-street,
London.

FINIS.

APPENDIX.[137]

In the Preface, the Public is referred to the Directors of the Sierra Leone Company, for the authenticity of the Author's assertions, who now thinks proper, as a further vindication, to annex the following letter, which speaks for itself.

Moreover, she avails herself of this supplement to express her vexation at the number of typographical errors throughout the foregoing pages; besides those enumerated, she has discovered several others, such as,—Preface, *allmost* for almost; page 35, *spinnage*, for spinage; page 80, *maddern* for madder; page 176, *least* for last—and one or two more, which she hopes the reader has mercifully looked over, and not charged to her pen.

Bristol, *August* 11, 1794.

SIR,

Your not answering my last letter, and the disdain you have shewn me on other occasions, since I came last to England, has not deterred me from doing what I considered honorable and upright.

Conscience, never wandering Monitor, advised me I should fall short of that sincerity I boast to possess, and proudly nourish, if I omitted sending you a copy of my Voyages to Africa, before they were presented to the World.

This admonition (which no doubt grew from a desire "to hide the fault I see," and a persuasion of having adhered most scrupulously to truth) prompted me to present a Copy, to that valuable and ever to be esteemed Divine Mr. GILBERT, who will give the same to you, for your perusal, immediately on his arrival in London, for which place he sets off this morning.

Would to God! you may read with calmness! but I fear a prepossession of the Author's obscurity and insignificance will betray you; nay, I already anticipate your reproachful smiles at my mean diction and trite remarks, but remember, Sir, Truth, though unadorned, never fails to attract notice—it carries its own value—always shelters the innocent, and brands conviction on the malefactor's threshold.

Search the secret recesses of your bosom, and enquire if the Directors conduct to me, has not been a violation of those fundamental principles, which *should* govern the actions of every man, or body of men?—Yes, Sir, ask there, if I am not an injured Woman?

Remember, for a moment, my little patrimony has been expended in your service:—remember my matchless sufferings;—and remember likewise your own honour and credit, I say, remember these things, and they may point out what you ought to do.

The second document of Christianity is to make contrition for our offences. *All*, from the Palace to the Cottage, are liable to err, and none of us should blush to confess our penitence; however, let the impulse of your own heart guide you.—What I have done exonerates mine.

I am, Sir,
Your obedient Servant,

ANNA MARIA ———— .

To Henry Thornton, Esq.
  M.P. and Chairman of
  the Court of Directors of
  the Sierra Leone Company.

EDITOR'S NOTES

1. In her letter to Thornton, dated August 11, 1794, Falconbridge sends him a pre-publication copy of the book. The second edition of 1802 omits the letter to Thornton, but the date of the Dedication is altered from June to August.

2. John Matthews was an unemployed naval officer turned slave trade agent. In 1788 he published his successful *A Voyage to the River Sierra-Leone, on the Coast of Africa* (London: B. White, 1788). A second edition appeared in 1791, with plates, and a French translation in 1797-98 (i.e. L'an v). In 1791, just before his brother set sail for Sierra Leone, Thomas Clarkson told him to 'read over Matthews's Book, and examine each Chapter most minutely if it be true' (British Library, Clarkson Papers, MS Add. 41263, vol. 1).

3. St. George's Bay Company was the name of the trading company Sharp set up in 1790 for the first settlers. Its charter modestly confined it to helping the early settlement. Sharp's City friends who contributed to its establishment later petitioned for incorporation by Act of Parliament as the Sierra Leone Company.

4. Factory: trading station, from licensees' setting up stations under a representative or factor. The Anderson brothers had owned Bance (Bence, Bense, Bunce) Island since 1785. The Island was first settled and fortified by the Royal African Company in the 1670s. By the early eighteenth century, Company employees were dwindling, and the Island given over to private traders.

5. A revealing crack in the epistolary facade (see *Plate* 2). The date should read 1791; see also Letter III, which ought (incidentally) to have been numbered Letter IV. These 'errors' of date were corrected in the 1802 edition.

6. It was later to be said against Falconbridge that his 'conduct & professions gave the slave traders great reason to believe that nothing less was intended than to ruin them if possible by the most unfair means, as by enticing away their seamen, inveigling their slaves, encouraging the natives to cut off slave ships &c' (Abolition and Emancipation, Part 1, Reel 6, Zachary Macaulay's Journal, 1793). Given the precariousness of the settlement, the Directors felt that a more temperate and conciliatory approach was needed; see footnote 63 below.

7. 'ingenuously' in the 1802 edition.

8. Jemmy succeeded to King Tom, who had put his mark to the first treaty drawn up by Captain Thompson. Clarkson worked hard to dispel Jemmy's distrust of the settlers; see E. G. Ingham ed., *Sierra Leone after a Hundred Years* (London: Frank Cass, 1968), pp. 18–19, 21.

9. 'was not the least inclined' in the 1802 edition.

10. Ballingall is not named in the 1802 edition.

11. The *Lapwing*, seized by the British Government for smuggling, was purchased by the Sierra Leone Company out of the condemned hold; see Prince Hoare, *Memoirs of Granville Sharp* (London: Henry Colburn, 1820), p. 349.

12. Zachary Macaulay, later Governor, did not find the young John Tilley 'genteel', but praised him for avoiding his usual swearing and obscenities whenever they were together. Tilley even attended church when he stayed at Freetown (see Ellen Gibson Wilson, *The Loyal Blacks* (New York: Putnam, 1976), p. 310). Like all

the white slave traders on Bance Island, Tilley was no friend to the colony. See A. P. Kup ed., *Adam Afzelius: Sierra Leone Journal, 1795–1796* (Uppsala: Studia Ethnographica Upsaliensia, 1967), p. 62 (hereafter Afzelius, *Journal*).

13. Naimbana, or Nemgbana, was ruler of the Koya Temne from 1775 until his death in 1793. Granville Sharp described him as 'a very reverend old man' who had allowed the settlement to continue, acting as its landlord and protector. Elliotte Griffiths was one of the original settlers, a valet by trade educated by Sharp. Naimbana offered to build him a large school so that he could teach English to those who were willing. He married Clara, Naimbana's daughter; see Hoare, *Memoirs*, pp. 343, 321.

14. cry: like a wake, often accompanied by puncheons of rum and great quantities of tobacco.

15. palaver: African court.

16. Another son of this local chief appears to have gone to England for his education. In 1797 Anthony Domingo wrote to Sharp expressing gratitude to the Directors of the Sierra Leone Company for his education (see P. Edwards and J. Walvin, 'Africans in Britain, 1500–1800', in *The African Diaspora: Interpretive Essays*, eds. M. Kilson and R. Rotberg (Cambridge, MA: Harvard University Press, 1976), p. 191).

17. 'Present possession is the only tenure they [the natives] allow of in the occupying of lands. If a man quits his situation, another may immediately take possession, provided he is a native; for they are extremely tenacious of their rights, and will not suffer any strangers to settle among them without their consent and approbation'; see Matthews, *Voyage*, pp. 78–79. An authoritative paper on the issue of land tenure is V. R. Dorjahn and C. Fyfe, 'Landlord and Stranger', *Journal of African History*, 3 (1962), pp. 391–97.

18. Robanna, on an island near the shore opposite Robaga.

19. Thomas Winterbottom described the Queen as a 'Canny old woman' (see Afzelius, *Journal*, p. 85). Of polygamy Winterbottom writes: 'The women, by habit and education, are so much accustomed to the practice, that a younger rival scarce excites in them any emotion of jealousy', in *An Account of the Native Africans in the Neighbourhood of Sierra Leone, to which is added An Account of the Present State of Medicine among them*, 2 vols. (London: C. Whittingham, 1803), vol. 1, p. 146. Winterbottom was an amiable and skilful young doctor who stayed four years in the colony.

20. Of the native men on the coast, Winterbottom wrote: 'Those who can afford it are fond of indulging their vanity in imitating the European mode of dress, and of displaying all the finery they can procure. They love to deck themselves in tawdry embroidered silk clothes, with a profusion of gold and silver tinsel, which often give to the wearers a very ludicrous appearance' (Winterbottom, *An Account*, vol. 1, p. 98; cf. also Matthews, *Voyage*, pp. 4–5).

21. Captain Thomas Boulden Thompson, who was in charge of transporting the first settlers, knew the west coast well because he had been employed by Government throughout the 1780s to find a suitable site on coastal Africa for Britain's surplus convicts; see Mollie Gillen, 'The Botany Bay Decision, 1786:

Convicts, not Empire', *English Historical Review*, vol. 47, no. 385 (October, 1982), pp. 751–58.

22. European traders were generally considered depraved dogs by the natives (see e.g. Winterbottom, *An Account*, vol. 1, pp. 209–210 and Matthews, *Voyage*, p. 96).

23. Also spelt grisgris, grigris, or gregory, a European term of African origin meaning fetish (from *feiticaria*, witchcraft). These were amulets to ward off the effects of witchcraft or the malice of evil spirits (Winterbottom, *An Account*, vol. 1, p. 99). Matthews wrote: 'To remove one of them, even unknowingly, is a great offence, and subjects the aggressor to a *palaver*, or action in their courts of law' (Matthews, *Voyage*, p. 67).

24. Palm produce was to become an important export commodity during the nineteenth century.

25. raree-show: originally, a show contained or carried about in a box; a peep-show, or spectacle.

26. 'When we sat down to dinner, the queen with her daughters and other attendants sat down on the ground outside the tent' (Clarkson's Journal, quoted by Ingham in *Sierra Leone*, p. 27).

27. 'After a certain age the title of pa, or father, is prefixed to the names of the men, as a token of respect' (Winterbottom, *An Account*, vol. 1, p. 211).

28. Larger than Bance Island, Tasso possessed a rich and well-drained soil. The Company tried to 'purchase' it, but the slave traders on Gambia Island out-bid them; see Ellen Gibson Wilson, *John Clarkson and the African Adventure* (London: Macmillan, 1980), p. 88.

29. An island, Marabump (or Marrabump); called Mabenka Island on nineteenth-century Admiralty Charts. According to Thomas Winterbottom, it had some native towns upon it (Thomas Winterbottom, *An Account*, vol. 1, p. 19). Zachary Macaulay mentions it in his Journal as a place associated in some way with Tilley's slave-trading operations (Abolition and Emancipation, Part 1, Reel 7).

30. This should be Letter IV, an error which was not corrected, even in the 1802 edition.

31. Matthews and Winterbottom expand on its symbolic significance. Cola, writes Matthews, 'is presented to guests at their arrival and departure – sent in complimentary presents to chiefs – is a considerable article of inland trade ... and frequently made the token of peace or war' (Matthews, *Voyage*, p. 60). 'Kola is always presented to the guests, in visits of ceremony or of friendship, and is looked upon as a mark of great politeness ... at public meetings, or palavers between different nations, it is a substitute for the olive branch. Two *white* kola ... betoken peace and a continuance of friendship, while two *red* ones are considered as an indication of war' (Winterbottom, *An Account*, vol. 1, p. 77). Kola also formed an important part of the red water ordeal (Afzelius, *Journal*, p. 25).

32. Among native African women, hysteria, 'and the whole train of nervous diseases are totally unknown' (Winterbottom, *An Account*, vol. 2, p. 205).

33. made our congees: to take ceremonious leave, or make a retiring bow.

34. Falconbridge's high opinion of Bance Island sociability was not, on the whole,

shared by other colonists. Her friend, the botanist Afzelius, knew when he was amongst slave traders 'for besides their cursing and swearing, they had all on check shirts, a black handerkerchief round the neck and another round the waist, all insignia of the bloody trafic in human flesh'. Macaulay also thought Bance Island 'a most unpleasant place ... a scene of continual dissipation and confusion ... few of them are long lived' (Afzelius, *Journal*, pp. 135, 83).

35. The French had been on this island since 1785, when Naimbana granted it to them. Renaud ('Rennieu'), the Agent in Falconbridge's time, was on good terms with the colony. In 1796, despite being at war with all British shipping in the area, the Frenchman was reluctant to attack the settlement (Afzelius, *Journal*, pp. 151, 167).

36. Also known as John Henry Naimbanna, or the 'Black Prince' (1767–1793). Zachary Macaulay published an account of his life in 1796, entitled *The African Prince*, reproduced in full in P. Edwards and J. Walvin ed., *Black Personalities in the Era of the Slave Trade* (London: Macmillan, 1983), pp. 204–10. For an account of his extempore speech after visiting the House of Commons to hear a debate on the slave trade, see P. Edwards and D. Dabydeen (eds), *Black Writers in Britain, 1760–1890* (Edinburgh: Edinburgh University Press, 1991), pp. 99–100.

37. Salt 'is an article so highly valued, and so eagerly sought after, by the natives, that they will part with their wives and children, and everything dear to them, to obtain it, when they have not slaves to dispose of; and it always makes a part of the merchandize for the purchase of slaves in the interior country' (Matthews, *Voyage*, p. 146). 'Refuse slaves' was a slave-trader's term for the physically worthless. One of Thomas Clarkson's queries for his brother John was, 'whether having old slaves to sell they [the Africans] put them to Death when they cannot find a Purchaser, or put them into their Plantations to work' (British Library, Clarkson Papers, MS Add. 41262A, vol. 1).

38. Falconbridge's account has been treated with great scepticism in some quarters. For some reasoned objections, see C. Fyfe, *A History of Sierra Leone* (London: Oxford University Press, 1962), p. 17. In weighing up the arguments on each side, it is worth remembering Lord Sydney's design in 1786 of enslaving Polynesian women for the new colony at Botany Bay to keep the transported men from 'gross irregularities and disorders' (Robert Hughes, *The Fatal Shore: A History of the Transportation of Convicts to Australia, 1787–1868* (London: Collins, 1987), p. 245).

39. Under Sharp's eccentric constitution of 'Frankpledge', all householders were obliged to participate in 'watch and ward', i.e. serve as militiamen for the protection of the community.

40. 'Lions are said to be on the heights of Sierra-Leone; but I never yet saw any myself, nor have any persons upon whose veracity I could depend; but they have leopards in abundance, equally fierce and rapacious as the lion' (Matthews, *Voyage*, pp. 39–40).

41. Lascar: an East Indian sailor, 'a tent-pitcher', an inferior class of artilleryman, or in the Portuguese *laschar*, native police or soldier (OED).

42. Sierra Leone is spelt a number of different ways, sometimes, as in this text, Sierra Leone and Sierra Leona; in earlier publications the name was Sierraleon, Serre-Lions, or Siera Liona. In John Ogilby's *Africa* (London: T. Johnson, 1670), this last spelling is translated '*The Mountain of the Lioness*', a name thought to derive from the 'terrible noise, like the furious roarings of a robbed Lioness' made by the combined uproar of the sea and winds beating on the hollows of the concave rocks.

43. Winterbottom does not dispute this theory (Winterbottom, *An Account*, vol. 2, p. 221).

44. The hospitality of the natives is mentioned by most writers familiar with the coast.

45. Palaver sauce was the name given by whites to the boiled leaf of a plant somewhat resembling spinach (Winterbottom, *An Account*, vol. 1, p. 64).

46. Winterbottom thought the women used palm oil 'to preserve the velvet smoothness and softness of their skins' (Winterbottom, *An Account*, vol. 1, p. 102).

47. red pepper: *capsicum frutescens*, or bird pepper, which Winterbottom considered very 'wholesome' in preventing gout and 'intermittents' (i.e. ague). It is so highly esteemed by the natives, he wrote, that 'it is used not only as seasoning to their food, but enters largely into the composition of their medicines' (Winterbottom, *An Account*, vol. 2, pp. 44–45).

48. Red water was made from an infusion of the bark of *Erythrophleum guineense*. Winterbottom gives more information on this custom in *An Account*, vol. 1, pp. 129–33.

49. Matthews claimed that, 'among the great who keep a number of wives', every married woman had her 'cicisbeo'. He also asserted, contra Falconbridge, that African women 'never attempt to impose on their husbands by introducing a spurious offspring into his family, but always declare before they are delivered who is the father' (Matthews, *Voyage*, pp. 120–121).

50. Although the land on Gambia Island is high, 'the shore is covered with mangroves and ooze; and as its situation, in a kind of bay, half surrounded by very high hills, renders it extremely hot, it has always proved very unhealthy' (Winterbottom, *An Account*, vol. 1, pp. 18–19).

51. The Cape Verde Islands lie in the Atlantic Ocean, 620 kilometres off the African coast, directly west of Senegal. The archipelago consists of 10 islands and 5 islets. Praia (Porta Praya), the principal town, is on Sao Tiago (Saint Jago), one of the four leeward islands. The Portuguese brought Africans to the islands to work as slaves in their plantations.

52. Possibly an allusion to his excessive drinking.

53. A kind of coarse linen originally made in Osnabrück, a town and district in North Germany (in English known as Osnaburg).

54. This island is one of the six islands in the windward group of the Cape Verde archipelago.

55. One of the four leeward islands of the Cape Verde archipelago.

56. *Teixo*, a yew tree (Portuguese).

57. John Nicholson Inglefield (1747–1828) published *Captain Inglefield's Narrative of the Loss of the Centaur, in 1782 ... a literal extract of his letter to the Admiralty, written from Fayal in 1782. Also, a copy of the ... court martial ... officers of the Centaur* (London: J. Murray and A. Donaldson, 1783). This was a much reprinted shipwreck narrative.

58. A nice reversal of the stereotypically dramatic encounter between the secluded, unfree foreign woman, and the publicly visible, 'free' English woman.

59. Granville Sharp, Chairman of the Committee for the Relief of the Black Poor in 1786, was instrumental in setting up the original 'Province of Freedom' in Sierra Leone; see my Introduction.

60. Henry Thornton (1760–1815), wealthy banker, MP, philanthropist, and driving force behind the Sierra Leone Company. His home at Clapham was the meeting place for an influential group of Evangelicals, including William Wilberforce, Hannah More and Zachary Macaulay.

61. John Frederick fell sick on the return voyage from England in 1793 and died shortly after landing. His family believed at first that the Company had killed him, a factor which exacerbated the already tense situation following the recent death of his father.

62. Joseph Hardcastle, one of the Company's Directors, wrote: 'he promises to be a valuable man & has an uncommon thirst for knowledge ... a suitable instrument to civilize his Countrymen' (British Library, Clarkson Papers, MS Add. 41262A, vol. 1).

63. Three months later, in December 1791, Thornton wrote to Thomas Clarkson: 'We were at first considerably pleased with him – & after a few weeks enquiry & deliberation were so far satisfied as to appoint him chief Commercial Agent at a Salary of £250 per ann: adding £100 of present also – We discovered in him however by degrees a great constitutional warmth of temper which has rather alarmed & made us fear, lest with power in his hands he should be carried to any sudden act of violence – A want of punctuality & of regular commercial habits has also made us think him unfit for the Leader in a commercial Factory, tho notwithstanding both these points we are disposed to think favorably of him in the general & we are grateful to him as I am sure we ought to be, for the services he has rendered to the Company' (British Library, Clarkson Papers, MS Add. 41262A, vol. 1).

64. See the next letter for his decision that their behaviour was indeed 'juggle and chichane'.

65. To Thornton, John Clarkson wrote: 'Eight gentlemen, all invested with great power, each of them acting from himself, and none of them accountable to the other, form to be sure, a system of government, as pregnant with contradictions and inconsistencies as can be imagined' (Ingham, *Sierra Leone*, pp. 53–54).

66. Clarkson believed that the portrait had done 'more in our favour than the most sanguine of us could have expected' (Ingham, *Sierra Leone*, p. 150).

67. 'irresistibility' in the 1802 edition.

68. The Company's surveyor was James Cocks, a post later taken by Richard Pepys, chief engineer.

69. Clarkson shared Falconbridge's contempt for the majority of the Council: 'their brains have been turned, from being allowed to wear a flaming sword and cockade, with a fine coat and epaulette, when a jacket and trousers would have been more consistent for those employed in founding a new settlement' (Ingham, *Sierra Leone*, pp. 65–66).

70. Dr John Bell, despite some obvious drawbacks, was appointed by the Directors because of his experience in tropical medicine. Thornton's introduction of him was not promising; to John Clarkson he wrote: 'I am sorry to have to hint to you that I have heard some things of an unpleasant nature said concerning him, particularly that he has been observed to be in liquor once or twice' (31st Dec. 1791; British Library, Clarkson Papers, MS Add. 41262A, vol. 1).

71. 'inebriety' in the 1802 edition.

72. Reverend Nathaniel Gilbert, son of a wealthy Antigua planter.

73. According to Winterbottom, the funeral, or cry, was not solemnized 'until near three years after the body had been buried' (Winterbottom, *An Account*, vol. 1, p. 243).

74. The Bananas are not described by Matthews in any detail at all, but he does reproduce 'A View of the Island of Bananas' in the 1788 edition of his *Voyage*.

75. Like Alexander Falconbridge, Clarkson was very reluctant to go on board slaving ships, or in any way be 'under a compliment' to their captains.

76. The surveyor, James Cocks, nicknamed by his fellow councillors 'Captain of the soldiers'.

77. 'in consequence of too much wine' in the 1802 edition.

78. Perhaps the most quoted line from Falconbridge's narrative.

79. 'momentarily' in the 1802 edition.

80. Certainly Clarkson had little sympathy with the Company's emphasis on trade. He believed it was much more important to settle the Nova Scotians on their lands, agriculture being a much more improving activity than trade, which would ensure only 'gain and laziness' to the settlers (Ingham, *Sierra Leone*, pp. 136–37).

81. Thomas Winterbottom, who arrived in mid-July 1792 (see note 19).

82. 'my ghastly figure' in the 1802 edition.

83. In November 1791, six men—Henry Hew Dalrymple, Lieutenant Philip Beaver, Sir William Halton, John King, John Young and Robert Dobbin—formed a committee at Old Slaughter's Coffee-house for the colonization of Bulama. A Constitution for the settlement was drawn up in February 1792. The plan was to grow sugar and other tropical plantations (see my Introduction). Dalrymple, an unemployed army officer who had served on the west coast of Africa at Gorée, was the prime mover behind the plan.

84. Lieutenant Philip Beaver (1766–1813) was the younger son of a Somerset clergyman. His career resembled John Clarkson's, to whom he was well known. They had both entered the navy as fatherless young boys, served on the same ships and been retired on half pay in the 1780s. In 1805 Beaver published an account of the failed colony in his *African Memoranda: relative to an attempt to establish a British settlement on the island of Bulama, on the western coast of*

Africa, in the year 1792 (London: C. & R. Baldwin, 1805).

85. A third of those on the *Calypso* died of fever during the six weeks before she sailed to England.

86. In his first address to the colony after receiving his new instructions, Clarkson argued that 'though I have it in my power to do as I please ... I detest an arbitrary government' (Ingham, *Sierra Leone*, p. 97).

87. Isaac DuBois was responsible for building Harmony Hall. It was later burnt by the French.

88. Clarkson wrote of this period: 'We are now tormented with ants ... crickets, cockroaches, spiders, etc., are driven out of their crevices and jump about the floor in a distressing situation amongst their enemies' (Ingham, *Sierra Leone*, p. 137).

89. 'The *tenneé*, when full grown, is from fifteen to twenty feet long, and about three feet round .... The natives even assert that they are so large in the savannahs, in the interior country, that they will swallow a buffalo' (Matthews, *Voyage*, pp. 43–44).

90. The botanist was Adam Afzelius, student of Linnaeus, who later taught at the University of Uppsala. Recommended to the Company by Banks, he planned to write an ambitious natural history of Sierra Leone. The mineralist was Augustus Nordenskiold, a Swedenborgian alchemist and visionary who, together with C. B. Wadstrom, dreamed in the 1780s of a free Church in West Africa. Together (with others) they wrote the utopian document, *Plan for a Free Community upon the Coast of Africa, under the Protection of Great Britain; but intirely independent of all European Laws and Governments* (London, 1789); see my Introduction.

91. 'where he anticipates success' in the 1802 edition.

92. Wilberforce wrote to John Clarkson, 'I regret very sincerely that in my public capacity I have been compelled to consent to the Measure of his Removal. But in these Cases we must be ready to sacrifice our private feelings no less than our personal Interests' (British Library, Clarkson Papers, MS Add. 41262A, vol. 1). His successor Wallace ('Wallis') was an unseemly choice of employee, having spent the last 25 years in the slave trade; he also drank too much. His sole qualification for the post of Commercial Agent seems to have been his extensive knowledge of the coast.

93. 'He has been killing himself by slow degrees for the last three months, and for some days past his Bones have been through his skin in several parts of his Body. He died this eveng. at six o'clock a very happy release both to him and those about him' (John Clarkson's Journal, 19 Dec. 1792, quoted in Wilson, *John Clarkson*, p. 117).

94. Thornton wrote of Horne that he was 'in some degree of connection with Mr Wesley tho' he is of the Church of England'. A man of 'extraordinary zeal', Thornton believed he would 'be the delight of the Methodistical part of the Blacks' (British Library, Clarkson Papers, MS Add. 41263, vol. 1). William Dawes (1762–1836), officer of marines, scientist and administrator, who had recently served in Port Jackson. He was to take over as Governor of Sierra Leone after Clarkson's departure in December 1792.

95. corrected to 'off' in the 1802 edition.
96. In the 1802 edition Falconbridge appended the following explanatory footnote: 'Mr. Clarkson had wrote a day or two before this to Mrs. Wilson, offering *her* a passage in the Harpy, and at the same time informing Captain Wilson, she was to sail in a few days, if he wished to write'.
97. Clarkson also commented on the absurdity of this, in a country where it rained for almost half the year (Ingham, *Sierra Leone*, p. 145).
98. Nordenskiold died 10 December 1792, having returned gravely ill from a journey of several months, during which he was robbed by natives and persecuted by slave traders. Officially he was looking for gold, but the urgency with which he set out on his travels suggests he may also have been hoping to verify Swedenborg's vision about the New Church of Jerusalem in Africa's interior.
99. James Watt, plantation manager; at one point he was also in charge of the hospital at Savoy Point. By 1803 he had joined the slave trade.
100. Richard Pepys had taken over the surveying of land. Rather than the Nova Scotians receiving their lots straightaway as promised, the rumour started up that the land would not be cleared for another year. DuBois, busy with a number of public works, complained bitterly about the uselessness of the fort. Stripped of workmen from his own projects, he jokingly described Dawes and Pepys as 'Fort Mad' (British Library, Clarkson Papers, MS Add. 41263, vol. 3).
101. Clarkson's plantation was a square mile rented by Governor Clarkson towards the end of November 1792.
102. DuBois spent the evening on board this slave ship, writing letters to friends in England and in the West Indies; he 'drank bad wine got a violent head ache & came home sick' (British Library, Clarkson Papers, MS Add. 41263, vol. 3).
103. An abbreviated version of the Act of Parliament incorporating the Sierra Leone Company can be found in Carl Wadstrom, *An Essay on Colonization, particularly applied to the Western Coast of Africa, with some free thoughts on Cultivation and Commerce; also Brief Descriptions of the colonies already formed, or attempted, in Africa, including those of Sierra Leona and Bulama* (London: Darton and Harvey, 1794–1795).
104. The chief suspect was Naimbana's interpreter, Elliotte Griffith, an 'assured Rogue' according to DuBois and Clarkson; apparently Dawes could not see the dangerous extent of Griffith's sway over the settlers (British Library, Clarkson Papers, MS Add. 41263, vol. 3).
105. Zachary Macaulay (1768–1838) had returned to England in 1792 after a stint as book-keeper, then manager, of a slave estate in Jamaica. His experience gave him a detestation of slavery, but John Clarkson came to believe that 'arbitrary Power is what Mr McAuley approves of' (letter to DuBois, July 1793; British Library, Clarkson Papers, MS Add. 41263, vol. 3).
106. Winterbottom wrote of Naimbana's death that it was 'much and deservedly lamented' (Winterbottom, *An Account*, vol. 1, p. 260).
107. The botanist Adam Afzelius succeeded in witnessing one of these trials; see his detailed eye-witness account in Afzelius, *Journal*, pp. 21–30.

108. In a letter to Clarkson, John Gray, the colony's accountant, relayed King Jemmy's joke about Horne's fruitless missionary efforts: 'this Country People no like dry Palavers'. Gray thought the focus should be on the native children, and that they should be trained up 'into plantation workers' (Feb. 15, 1793; British Library, Clarkson Papers, MS Add. 41263, vol. 3). Clarkson believed Horne's time would be more profitably spent instructing the settlers to read and write (see Ingham, *Sierra Leone*, p. 146).

109. Morley was Falconbridge's brother (see my Introduction). Despite his involvement in the slave trade, Morley was later to warn Governor Macaulay of a possible French attack on the colony in May 1796 (Afzelius, *Journal*, p. 149).

110. In his journal DuBois boasted of this wedding feast that 'such a dinner in all probability never was seen on the Grain Coast of Africa'. This was a second marriage for DuBois as well (British Library, Clarkson Papers, MS Add. 41263, vol. 3).

111. In addition to Anglicans, there were a number of evangelical groups, such as Methodist, Baptist and Huntingdonian. The importance of these sects in helping to define a separate and cohesive black identity in Nova Scotia is discussed in James W. St. G. Walker, 'The Establishment of a Free Black Community in Nova Scotia', in *The African Diaspora: Interpretive Essays*, ed. M. Kilson and R. Rotberg (Cambridge, MA: Harvard University Press, 1976), pp. 216–19.

112. 'is it not a pity that religion should be a cloak to vice and idleness' (DuBois, Journal, Jan 23, 1793; British Library, Clarkson Papers, MS Add. 41263, vol. 3).

113. After this incident DuBois noted in his journal: 'Memorandum—He Richard Pepys is as black a Hearted insinuating a Villain as this day exists' (British Library, Clarkson Papers, MS Add. 41263, vol. 3). Perkins and Anderson, the settlers' delegates who travelled to London in 1793 to petition the Directors, spared Clarkson the exact details of Pepys's speech. They wrote in a letter to him: 'we are sorry to tell you that the Gentlemen you left behind you speaks mightily against you and we was present when Mr Pepys told all the people that you had no authority for the Promises you made us in Nova Scotia ...' (in *'Our Children Free and Happy': Letters from Black Settlers in Africa in the 1790s*, ed. C. Fyfe (Edinburgh University Press, 1991), p. 35).

114. 'one of his daughters was accused of bewitching him & drank red water in consequence—she escaped its effect—several people have been taken up supposed to have used Witchcraft or Poison on the Person of the King, & no doubt some will loose their lives' (John Gray to John Clarkson, 15 Feb, 1793; British Library, Clarkson Papers, MS Add. 41263, vol. 3).

115. One reviewer made the gross error of thinking that she had changed her name 'from Falconbridge to Dawes' (see *British Critic*, vol. 4 (July–Aug, 1794), p. 555). Clarkson had wanted the couple to wait a decent interval before marrying, but after an argument between the lovers on 6 January, in which Falconbridge got 'quite in a *pet*' and accused DuBois of 'indifference towards her', they agreed to be married the following morning (DuBois's Journal, British Library, Clarkson Papers, MS Add. 41263, vol. 3).

116. For the full text of their petition, see '*Our Children Free and Happy*', pp. 35–40. Isaac DuBois helped the settlers compose their petition, but he does not appear to have satisfied everyone. According to Macaulay, some of the settlers complained of 'an artifice practiced upon them by Mr DuBois'. It was alleged that, when they complained about some passages, he agreed to strike them out, but then sent off the original unaltered. By the time Perkins and Anderson arrived in London, Macaulay had ensured that the Directors were already in possession of a more 'authentic' petition (Abolition and Emancipation, Part 1, Reel 6, Macaulay's Journal, 25 June, 1793).

117. Hummum is a variant of hammam, a Turkish bath. 'The Hummums', which housed several of the Company's officers, was obviously named, jokingly, after 'The Hummums' in Covent Garden, a place to sweat and bathe in the early eighteenth century. It subsequently became a hotel. Macaulay, who moved into the Hummums after DuBois and Falconbridge left, was distinctly unimpressed by the building, complaining to the Directors in London not to be taken in by DuBois's 'pompous description' of it; of all houses it was the 'least fitted in the colony to exclude the rains' (Abolition and Emancipation, Part 1, Reel 6, Macaulay's Journal, 1793).

118. It is very likely that this incident refers to another of Falconbridge's brothers, by the name of Horwood (Horwood and Captain Morley may have been half-brothers). On 1 May 1793, DuBois wrote to Clarkson of Dawes's oppressive and arbitrary conduct, citing as the most recent incident 'the dismissal of Mr Horwood Mrs DuBois's brother without assigning any reason whatever for so doing – and after dismissing him telling him he might *be reappointed* in the Service if he chose' (British Library, Clarkson Papers, MS Add. 41263, vol. 3).

119. 'rancorous' in the 1802 edition.

120. In October 1792, the Convention conferred French citizenship on Clarkson and Wilberforce, together with Tom Paine, Joseph Priestley and George Washington; see Ellen Gibson Wilson, *Thomas Clarkson: A Biography* (London: Macmillan, 1989; 2nd edn, 1996), p. 79. It is true that there were informal negotiations between the Company and France regarding immunity for the colony, but this did not prevent Freetown from being totally destroyed by the French in late September 1794 (Wilson, *Loyal Blacks*, pp. 316–17).

121. 'Cargo' was a common enough term for slaves. It was also used of convicts. When the *Lady Juliana* arrived in Port Jackson in June 1790, the colony's chief legal officer complained: 'a cargo so unnecessary and unprofitable as two hundred and twenty-two females, instead of a cargo of provisions' (David Collins, *An Account of the English Colony in New South Wales* (London, 1798), pp. 118–19).

122. Matthews argued that religious wars conducted in the interior resulted in numerous prisoners-of-war, all of whom would be put to death were it not for the option of slavery offered by trade with the Europeans (Matthews, *Voyage*, pp. 167–69).

123. This was a common argument of the pro-slavery faction, one which could of course be stood on its head for the purposes of revolution at home. See my Introduction for discussion of Coleridge's anti-slavery lecture in Bristol, 1795.

124. The freeman 'who has felt and enjoyed the sweets of liberty, to him the deprivation of it ... must no doubt be painful: but the man who is born a slave ... who never even in idea felt the sentiments which liberty alone can inspire ... is not so great an object of our commiseration' (Matthews, *Voyage*, pp. 173–74).

125. George Brydges Rodney (1719–1792), promoted to Admiral in 1778. When Gibraltar was blockaded by the Spaniards in 1780 he routed them and became a national hero. This fame was cemented in 1782 when he prevented a large French fleet from capturing Jamaica. In gratitude for this decisive victory, known as 'The Battle of the Saintes', the Jamaican legislature voted £3,000 for the erection of a statue. He was elevated to the peerage in June 1782.

126. There had been a massive slave uprising on French-controlled St Domingo in August 1791. At this time, Britain was attempting to capture the French slave islands, including St Domingo.

127. From 'Debate on Mr. Wilberforce's Motion for the Abolition of the Slave Trade, 1791', in Hansard, *The Parliamentary History of England from the Earliest Period to the Year 1803* (London: T. C. Hansard, 1817), vol. 29, p. 256. Here Falconbridge takes Wilberforce's forceful criticisms of the pro-slavery faction and levels them against his closest allies (and her powerful enemies), England's leading abolitionists.

128. In a letter to DuBois, dated 1 July 1793, John Clarkson wrote that Alexander Falconbridge had made a will before his last trip out, and that the Company 'had money of his in their Hands' owed to Anna Maria. Astutely, and with some prescience, he warned the couple that 'the Company are now so very, very frugal that I should not wonder if they hesitated paying the money as they all exclaim against Falconbridge and say he has deceived them so much, and run them to such immense expenses' (British Library, Clarkson Papers, MS Add. 41263, vol. 3).

129. Cato Perkins and Isaac Anderson. Perkins, born into slavery in Charleston, North Carolina, was a pastor in the colony. Anderson, a free man, also from Charleston, was to be executed in 1800 after leading a rebellion against the Company's government.

130. Armed by Macaulay with a supposedly more 'authentic' petition, Thornton wrote dismissively of Perkins and Anderson in a letter to John Clarkson: 'They pleaded a number of vague promises of yours such as your having promised that bread should be as cheap at Sierra Leone as in America & the price of labor as good &c &c What they say in other points is as vague as in this' (British Library, Clarkson Papers, MS Add. 41263, vol. 3).

131. 'we did not know where to write to you till Mr Duboz [DuBois] let us ...' (*'Our Children Free and Happy'*, p. 35).

132. 'however, we do not think your conduct has proceeded' in the 1802 edition.

133. The quit-rent imposed upon their lands by the Company stood at the heart of their grievances. Thornton reasoned thus to Clarkson in his letter of 31st Dec, 1791: 'On the whole we have proposed rather to indemnify ourselves for all our huge expenses at the first by a rent on the lands, which will be more easy to

collect than by high profits on trade. I trust the blacks will not consider this as a grievance especially as it will be very light at first & that they will consider themselves as thereby paying the necessary expence of government & return to the English subscribers who have stood forth so liberally to save them' (British Library, Clarkson Papers, MS Add. 41263, vol. 1).

134. The allusion is, of course, to William Wilberforce, one of the Company's Directors.

135. John Clarkson is the anonymous 'gentleman' cited here; see p. 36, n. 18.

136. Rag Fair was a second-hand clothes market in Houndsditch, a poor part of London.

137. This Appendix is dropped from the 1802 edition.

A

VOYAGE

ROUND THE

WORLD,

IN

THE GORGON MAN OF WAR:
CAPTAIN JOHN PARKER.

PERFORMED AND WRITTEN BY HIS WIDOW;

FOR THE ADVANTAGE OF A NUMEROUS FAMILY.

———

DEDICATED, BY PERMISSION,

TO

HER ROYAL HIGHNESS
THE PRINCESS OF WALES.

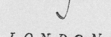

LONDON:

PRINTED BY JOHN NICHOLS, RED-LION-PASSAGE, FLEET-STREET.

AND SOLD BY

Mr. DEBRETT, Piccadilly; Mr. PRIDDEN, No. 100, Fleet-Street;
Meffrs. WILKIE, Paternofter-Row; and Mr. RICHARDSON,
at the Royal Exchange. 1795.

Plate 21 Title-page of Mary Ann Parker's *A Voyage Round the World* (1795).
Source: Australian National Library.

TO

HER ROYAL HIGHNESS

THE PRINCESS OF WALES,

WITH GRATEFUL THANKS

FOR HER CONDESCENDING PERMISSION,

THE FOLLOWING WORK

IS MOST HUMBLY DEDICATED

BY HER ROYAL HIGHNESS'S

MOST DEVOTED,

AND MOST OBEDIENT SERVANT,

MARY ANN PARKER.

No. 6, *Little Chelsea, June* 25, 1795.

PREFACE

It having been most unjustly and injuriously reported, that the Authoress is worth a considerable sum of money; she thinks it her duty thus publicly to avow, that nothing but the greatest distress could ever have induced her to solicit beneficence in the manner she has done, for the advantage of her family.

If this traducing report originates (and it can no otherwise) from Captain Parker's being entitled to a share of prize-money, accruing from successes in the West-Indies; she has to lament, that his debts are unfortunately too considerable to give his children one hope of any thing coming to them after they are discharged.—It is her duty to bring them up not to expect any thing, as it is her first wish that the creditors should be justly reimbursed their demands.

The unhoped-for success she has met with in Subscriptions to this publication demands her acknowledgements; and she trusts her situation as a nurse, and being obliged to attend so much to her domestic concerns, will be accepted as an apology for the brevity and other greater demerits of the book.

List of Subscribers

A

Sir Joseph Andrews, Bart. of *Shawe.*
Lieut. Colonel Affleck, 23d Dragoons.
Captain John Arbuthnot, Royal Artillery.
Lieut. Anstruther, Royal Navy.
William Arbuthnot, Esq. *Cariacou, West Indies.*
George Arbuthnot, Esq. *Navy Pay-Office.*
Robert Arbuthnot, Jun. Esq.
Captain Askew, Romney Fencibles.
Alexander Adair, Esq. *Pall-Mall.*
S. Aldersey, Esq. *Navy Pay-Office.*
Mr. Edmund Antrobus, *Strand.*
Mr. Joseph Ainsworth, *Blackburn.*
Mr. William Aspinall, *Ditto.*
Mr. Frederick Accum.
Mr. Richard Atkinson.
Mr. Thomas Aloes.
Mr. Adams.

B

Right Hon. Earl of Banbury.
Sir Joseph Banks, Bart.
Lady Banks.
Colonel Bishopp, *Knightsbridge.*
Lieut. Col. Braddyll, M.P.R. Lancashire Militia.
Hon. Major Bridgeman, M.P. Ditto.
Hon. Mrs. Boscawen, *South Audley-Street.*
Major Byron, late of the 12th Regiment.
Captain Burnett, Bengal Artillery.
Captain Bootle, Royal Lancashire Militia.

Captain Bristow, Wiltshire Militia.
Miss Bristow.
Mr. Bristow.
Captain Robert Burrows, *Francis East-Indiaman.*
Francis Barker, Esq. *Knightsbridge.*
Rev. T. Brown, *Dornsby, Lincolnshire.*
Nicholas Bond, Esq. *Sloane-Street.*
Richard Barker, Esq. 2d Life Guards.
Robert Barnwell, Esq.
Jeremiah Berry, Esq. *Norfolk.*
John Beddingfield, Esq. *Navy Pay-Office.*
T. D. Boswell, Esq. *Ditto.*
William Barclay, Esq. *Ditto.*
William Bankes, Esq. *Winstanley.*
David Bull, Esq.
Edward Blair, Esq. *Horksley.*
Mr. Joseph Budworth, F. S. A. *Sloane-Street.*
Mrs. Budworth.
Rev. W. Beloe, F.S.A. *James-Street, Westminister.*
Mr. George Barke, *Brompton.*
Mr. Edward Bill, *New Bridge-Street.*
Mr. John Berwick, *Pall-Mall.*
Mr. Browell, *Scotland-Yard.*
Mr. Barke, *Knightbridge.*
Mr. Arthur Brocas, *Francis East-Indiaman.*
Mrs. Brocas.
Mr. J. Bainbridge, jun. *Sloane-Street.*
Mr. Battey, *Ditto.*
Mr. Bisset, *Ditto.*
Mrs. Barley.
Mrs. Bell.
Miss Blashfield, *Sloane-Street.*
Mr. John Blackwell.
Mr. Biddulph.
Mr. Browne.
Mr. Barlow.
Mr. Blackett.
Mr. Alexander Butler, *Blackburn.*
Mr. Richard Birley, *Ditto.*
Mr. Samuel Bower, *Ditto.*
Mr. Robert Broadbelt, *Ditto.*
Mr. David Blessett, *Ditto.*
Mrs. Brook, *Ditto.*
Miss Babington, *Sloane-Street.*
Mrs. Bosquet.

Mr. Thomas Burch.

C

Right Hon. Lord Compton.
Admiral Sir Roger Curtis.
Colonel J. F. Cradock.
Major Clayton, *Wigan*.
Captain Chesshyre, Royal Navy.
Captain Crooke, Royal Lancashire Militia.
Captain Christian, Royal Navy.
Lieutenant Clotwyk, South Hants Militia.
Richard Cardwell, Esq. *Blackburn*.
Richard Cardwell, Jun. Esq. *Ditto*.
Henry Cranstoun, Esq. *Navy Pay-Office*.
Christopher Cook, Esq. *Ditto*.
John Church, Esq. *Ditto*.
S. Child, Esq. *Ditto*.
William Cresswell, Esq. *Ditto*.
John Clarke, Esq. *Knightsbridge*.
Thomas Carter, Esq. *Sloane-Street*.
Richard Henry Croft, Esq. *Pall-Mall*.
George Cloake, Esq. *Turnham-Green*.
William Cowan, Esq.
Mr. William Close, *Pall-Mall*.
Miss Cocks, *Sloane-Street*.
Mr. P. Cooper, *Arundel-Street*.
Mr. Carrol, *Sloane-Street*.
Mr. Codd, *Hans-Place*.
Mr. Charles Cullen.
Mr. Capel.
Mr. Chalmers.

D

Colonel Delhoste, R.M.V.
Captain Drummond, *Knightsbridge*.
Captain Darby.
John Davies, Esq. *Navy Pay-Office*.
Richard Draper, Esq, *Ditto*.
Mr. R. Dolton, at Mr. Glover's, *Knightsbridge*.
Mr. James Dewar, *Clement's Inn*.
Mr. Thomas Docker, Surgeon in the Army.
Mr. Joseph Docker, *Pall-Mall*.
Mr. H H. Deacon, *Sloane-Street*.

Mr. William Dawes, *Fenchurch-Street*.
Mr. Thomas Dowding.
Mr. Douglas.
Mr. Dunell.

E

Major John Edwards.

F

Sir James Foulis, Bart.
Captain Frith, North Hants Militia.
George Fennell, Esq. *Navy Pay-Office*.
T. Fitzgerald, Esq. *Ditto*.
Edward Boscawen Frederick, Esq. *Berkeley-Square*.
C. W. Flint, Esq.
Samuel Felton, Esq. F.R.S.
E. Foulker, Esq.
James Fallowfield, Esq.
John Foster, Esq.
Rev. Mr. Ferrers, *Bath*.
Miss Fernside.
Mrs. Fowden, *Wigan*.
Mr. Henry Fielden, *Blackburn*.
Mr. John Fielden, *Ditto*.
Mr. William Fielden, *Ditto*.

G

Capt. Lord Viscount Garlies, Royal Navy.
Sir Nigel Bowyer Gresley, Bart.
Colonel Gledstanes.
Mrs. Gledstanes.
Lieutenant Colonel Henry Grey.
Major Thomas Grey.
Captain William Grey.
Captain George Grey, Royal Navy.
Major Grymes, *Sloane-Street*.
Captain Grueber, *Ditto*.
Captain Gage.
Captain Gillam, Madras Infantry.
William Gillam, Esq.
G. J. Gascoigne, Esq. *Navy Pay-Office*.
J. Glover, Esq. *Jobbing's Buildings, Knightsbridge*.

Rev J. Gamble, *Knightsbridge*
Lieutenant John Gardiner, Royal Navy.
William Gardiner, Esq.
Jasper Leigh Goodwin, Esq.
William Gresley, Esq. *Twickenham.*
Thomas Gardnor, Esq. *Upper Grosvenor-Street.*
Rev. Mr. Gamman, *Cheapside.*
Mrs. Gines.
Mrs. Gresley.
Mr. Thomas Gill.
Mr. Goldney.
Mr. John Grant, *Cockspur-Street.*
Mr. Isaac Glover, *Blackburn.*
Mr. Green, *Dartford.*
Mr. Robert Gray.
Mr. Gray.
Mrs. Gray.

H

Right Hon. Lady Caroline Herbert.
Charles Herbert, Esq.
Honorable Lady Honeywood.
Colonel Stephens Howe, *Aid de Camp to His Majesty.*
Colonel Henderson.
Colonel Otho Hamilton, *James Street, Westminster.*
Captain Hamilton, 3d Life Guards, *Ditto.*
Captain Howarth.
Dr. Harrington, M.D. *Bath.*
Captain Hopwood, Royal Lancashire Militia.
Lieut. Thomas Hitchbone, late of 12th Reg.
D. Harmood, Esq. *Navy Pay-Office.*
William Hutton, Esq. *Ditto.*
Alexander Hislop, Esq. *Ditto.*
William Hamerton, Esq.
William Higden, Esq.
John Hale, Esq.
John Fowden Hindle, Esq. *Blackburn.*
Hugh Robert Hughes, Esq. *Pall-Mall.*
Rev. E. Harris, *Sloane-Street.*
Mrs. Harris.
Miss Harris.
Miss Sophia Harris.
Rev. Mr. Harrison, *Brompton.*
Rev. James Holme, Vicar of *Shap, Westmorland.*

Miss Catherine Hunter, *Adelphi*.
Mr. Thomas Hollis, *Park-Place, Knightsbridge*.
Mr. Peyton Hadley.
Mr. Howison, *Hammersmith*.
Mrs. Holland, *Hans Town*.
Miss Holland.
Mr. Holme, *Thames-Street*.
Mrs. Hockley, *Blacklands*.
Mr. Harding.
Mr. Ham.
John Hull, M.D. *Blackburn*.
Mr. William Hornby, *Blackburn*.
Mr. John Hornby, *Ditto*.
Mr. Hicks.

J

Captain Jekyll, 43d Regiment.
George Jeffries, Esq. *Sloane-Street*.
George Jeffries, Esq. Jun.
Mr. Jackson, *Knightsbridge*.
Mrs. Jackson.
Mrs. Jarvis.
Mr. Johnston.

K

Mr. Kelly, *Sloane-Street*.
Mrs. Kearsley, *Wigan*.

L

Captain Sir Wilfred Lawson, Bart. R.L.M.
Lady Lawson.
Captain Lyons, 11th Dragoons.
Mrs. Lyons.
Captain Lane, *Sloane-Street*.
Captain John Larkins, *Greenwich*.
Lieut. Lutwidge, R. Lancashire Militia.
Library *at Bampton Vicarage, Westmorland*.
William Lockhart, Esq. *Navy Pay-Office*.
—— Lewis, Esq.
Miss Eliz. Locker, *Greenwich*.
Mr. Ralph Lattic, *Blackburn*.
Mr. John Livesay, *Ditto*.

Mr. Lonquet.
Mr. Long, *Upper Brook Street.*
Mr. Henry Longbottam, *Borough.*

M

Sir John Miller, Bart.
General Melvill.
Honourable Captain Murray, Royal Navy.
Captain Richard Morrice, Ditto.
Captain Simon Miller, Ditto.
Captain Maude, Ditto.
Mrs. Maude.
Captain Machell, R. Lancashire Militia.
Dr. Moore.
Miss Hannah More, *Bath.*
Thomas Maberley, Esq.
Thomas Maude, Esq. *Downing-Street.*
Henry Grey Mainall, Esq. M.D.
Samuel Maskall, Esq.
John Minyer, Esq.
D. Minors, Jun. Esq.
Miss Merry.
Mr. Mash, *St. James's Palace.*
Miss Murray, *Clarges-Street.*
Rev. James MacQuhoe, *Blackburn.*
Mr. William Miller, *Bond Street.*
Mr. John Marshall, *Aldermary Church-Yard.*
Mrs. Marshall.
Mr. Michie, *Sloane-Street.*
Mr. William Maude, Royal Navy.
Miss Milles.
Mr. Mills.
Mr. Maundrill, *Knightsbridge.*
Mr. Maundrill, Jun.
Mrs. Middleditch.
Mr. Donald Maclean, *Blackburn.*
Mr. Bertie Markland, *Ditto.*
Mr. Charles Morgan, *Ditto.*

N

Ensign Neville, 3d Guards.
—— Norris, Esq.
J. Nesbitt, Esq. M. P.

William Newton, Esq. *Sloane-Street.*
Mr. John Neville, *Blackburn.*
Rev. R. Nares, F.S.A. *James-Street, Westminister.*
Mr. John Noble. *Fleet-Street.*
Mr. William Noble, *Pall-Mall.*
Mr. Deputy Nichols.
Miss Nichols.
Mr. John-Bowyer Nichols.
Mr. Naylor, *Mile End.*

O

Rev. George Ogle.
Mrs. Orrell.
Mr. Thomas Oldfield, *Union-Street.*

P

Viscountess Palmerston.
N. Pierce, Esq. *Navy Pay-Office.*
C. Purvis, Esq. *Ditto.*
G. Player, Esq. *Ditto.*
Roger Palmer, Esq. *Oxford-Street.*
Francis Palmer, Esq. *Sloane-Street.*
William Pollock, Esq.
Joseph Potter, Esq. *Chelsea.*
Charles Phillips, Esq.
Thomas Poole, Esq.
Captain Parker, 11th Light Dragoons.
Rev. John Pridden, M.A.F.S.A.
Miss Phillips, *Sloane-Street.*
Mr. William Parrys, *Knightsbridge.*
Mr. Plaskett.
Mr. James de la Pryme, *Blackburn.*
Mr. John Parkhouse.
Mr. Peyton, *Navy-Office.*
Mr. Edward Powell.
Mr. Palmer, *St. James's Street.*
Mrs. Pocock.
Mr. Pettiwood.
Mr. Parsons.
Mr. J. Plumridge, *Sloane-Street.*
Mr. Charles Pincent, *Edward-Street.*
Mr. Edward Powell.
Mr. G. Pusser, *Knightsbridge.*

R

General Rainsford.
Mrs. Rainsford.
Captain Edward Ridgway, R. Lancashire Militia.
Lieutenant Radford, Ditto.
Kemys Radcliffe, Esq. *Navy Pay-Office.*
Walter Reed, Esq. *Ditto.*
George Ross, Esq. *Duke-Street, Adelphi.*
Major Andrew Ross, *Ditto.*
William Roberts, Esq.
John Reid, Esq.
Rev. Dr. Reynett, *Prescott-Street.*
Mrs. Reynett.
Mr. J. A. Rucker, *Sloane-Street.*
Mrs. Russell.
Mr. Rieman.
Chevalier Ruspini, *Pall-Mall.*
Mr. Ramsay Robinson, *Kensington.*
Mr. Thomas Richardson.
Mrs. Ricketts, *Lower Seymour-Street.*
Mr. William Rothwell, *Sloane-Street.*
Mr. Randoll.

S

Right Honourable the Earl of Scarborough.
Colonel Hans Sloane, M. P. *Upper Harley-Street.*
Lieut. Colonel William Skerrett.
Major Smith, Royal Artillery.
Captain Squires, Royal Navy.
Captain John Schank, Ditto.
Captain Skinner.
Dr. Shusan, *New Bridge-Street.*
Mrs. Stephens, *Adelphi.*
Miss Stevens.
George Swaffield, Esq. *Navy Pay-Office.*
John Swaffield, Esq. *Ditto.*
James Slade, Esq. *Ditto.*
Henry Slade, Esq. *Ditto.*
Walter Stirling, Esq. *Ditto.*
Thomas Sermon, Esq.
Walter Stott, Esq. *Liverpool.*
Henry Sudell, Esq. *Blackburn.*
Samuel Swinton, Esq. *Sloane Street.*

Alexander Scott, Esq.
William Smith, Jun. Esq. *Lombard-Street.*
James Symes, Esq.
Robert Saunders, Esq. *Southend, Kent.*
Rev. Mr. Symes.
Edward Gray Saunders, Esq. *Oxford-Street.*
Rev. Thomas Staikie, M. A. Vicar of *Blackburn.*
Edward Stuart, Esq.
Mr. Sealey.
Mr. Seaman, *Strand.*
Mr. Thomas Somers.
Mrs. Saunders, *Sloane-Street.*
O. B. Smyth, M.D.
Mr. Henry Stacie, late Soldier 58th Regiment.
Mrs. Smith, *Woodstock.*
Mrs. Sones.
Mrs. Stuart.
Mrs. Shepherd, *Kelvedon.*
Mrs. Seaten, *Suffolk-Street.*
Mrs. Shricol, *Westham.*

T

Admiral Charles Thompson.
Captain Thornton, Royal Artillery.
Captain Thomas, 11th Light Dragoons.
Captain Trotty, Royal Navy.
Captain Taylor *Carteret Packet.*
Alexander Trotter, Esq. *Navy Pay-Office.*
William Taylor, Esq. *Ditto.*
William Taylor, Jun. Esq. *Ditto.*
Adam Thomson, Esq. *Ditto.*
Mr. Charles Tweidie, *Ditto.*
Charles Tweedie, Jun. Esq. *Ditto.*
Rev. Dr. John Trotter, *Hans Square.*
John Turing, Esq. *Sloane Street.*
Mrs. Turing.
Miss Turing.
William Thompson, LL. D.
John Thoyts, Esq. *Merton.*
Rev. Mr. Thomas, *Strand.*
Mr. Thomas Turner, *Blackburn.*
Miss Travers, *Ditto.*
Mr. Thomas Thompson, *Castle-Street.*
Mr. F. Trecourt, *Sloane-Street.*

Mr. John Townsend.
Mr. Richard Twiss.
Mr. Toulmin.

U

Capt. Vesey, 39th Regiment.
Lieut Upton, R. Lancashire Militia.
G. Urquhart, *Navy Pay-Office*.
Mr. Virtue, *Hammersmith*.

W

Major Wathen.
Captain Charles White, Royal Navy.
Captain Williamson, Royal Lancashire.
Captain Wright, 99th Regiment.
Thomas Wilson, Esq. *Navy Pay-Office*.
Thomas Walker, Esq. *Ditto*.
Mr. William Ward, *Ditto*.
Willliam Webb, Esq. *Conduit-Street*.
William Walter, Esq. *New Bridge-Street*.
Thomas Watsan, Esq.
—— Walker, Esq.
J. Warner, Esq. *Knightsbridge*.
Jekyll Wyatt, Esq.
Thomas Watson, Esq.
Mrs. Wallace, *Sloane-Street*.
Mr. Wilmot, *Thornhaugh-Street*
Mr. Watkins.
Mrs. Welcher, *Sloane-Street*.
Miss Welcher.
Mr. Richard White, *Piccadilly*.
Mr. John Wright, *Old Bond-Street*.
Miss White, *Bath*.
Mr. William Ware, *Sloane-Street*.
Mr. White.
Mr. Richard Wimburn.
Mr. Wagner, *Pall-Mall*.

CONTENTS

CHAP. I.

Reasons for undertaking the voyage—set out for Portsmouth—passengers on-board—sail from Spithead—arrive at the island of Teneriffe—pay a visit to the Governor—description of the town of Santa Cruz—an excursion to Puerto Oratava—a laughable occurrence—Lieutenant Rye—another excursion—return to the ship—and set sail.

CHAP. II.

Ceremony of crossing the Equator—arrive at St. Jago—description of the Portugueze inhabitants—a violent gale—see the island of Saint Trinidad—a description of that island—arrive at Simon's Bay—set out for the Cape.

CHAP. III.

Set off for Cape Town—stop at False-bay—meet a party of Soldiers—reflections—arrive at the Cape—Mrs. De Witt—shipwreck of the Guardian—Lieutenant Riou—a Cape breakfast—observations on the town and its inhabitants.

CHAP. IV.

Visit Colonel Gordon—arrival of the Neptune—receive intelligence from New South Wales—arrival of Captain Patterson and his Lady—a Cape dance—a Hottentot Song—visit Mr. Vandrian's brewery—prepare for our departure.—Set sail.

CHAP. V.

The voyage continued—a melancholy accident; singular instance of fraternal affection—death of Lieutenant Ross—a dreadful storm—the falling of a ball of fire—observations and reflections.

Mary Ann Parker

CHAP. VI.

Arrive at Port Jackson—Governor King and Captain Parker wait upon Governor Phillip with the dispatches—account of ships arrived in the harbour; and of a dreadful mortality which had taken place on-board the transports—interesting particulars respecting the propriety of establishing a whale fishery on the coast of New Holland.

CHAP. VII.

Governor Phillip breakfasts on-board—visit Sidney Cove—go on shore—short description of shrubs—birds, beasts, &c. of Botany Bay—excursion to, and description of, Paramatta—visit the Governor.

CHAP. VIII.

Description of the inhabitants of New South Wales—their huts—their extraordinary honesty—account of Banalong—an instance of his sensibility—observations on the Slave Trade.

CHAP. IX.

Preparations for our departure—repair on-board—set sail—see Lord Howe's Island—Mount Lidgbird—Mount Gower—Three King's Head Island—New Zealand—Cape Maria.

CHAP. X

The voyage continued—discover a number of Ice-islands—description of them—singular story of a Shark—with an anecdote relative thereto.

CHAP. XI.

Arrive at Table-Bay—take up our abode at Mr. Peter de Witt's—mild treatment of the Slaves at the Cape—a Gentoo—a visit to Constantia—return to Cape Town.

CHAP. XII.

Some account of Cape Town—departure from the Cape—Ascension Road—the voyage continued—reach Saint Helens—land at Portsmouth—arrive in London—Conclusion.

Narrative of a Voyage Round the World

Chap. I.

*Reasons for undertaking the voyage—set out for Portsmouth—
passengers on board—sail from Spithead—arrive at the island of
Teneriffe—pay a visit to the Governor—description of the town of Santa
Cruz—an excursion to Puerto Oratava—a laughable occurrence—
Lieutenant Rye—another excursion—return to the ship—and set sail.*

On the *first* day of January 1791, my late husband, Captain John Parker,[1]
was appointed by the Right Honourable the Lords Commissioners of the
Admiralty to the command of His Majesty's ship the Gorgon—On the
second he received his commission. The ship was then lying at her
moorings off Common-hand in Portsmouth harbour, refitting for her
intended voyage to New South Wales, and exchanging the provisions she
then had, for the newest and best in store.

There were embarked for their passage to the aforenamed colony, a part
of the new corps that had been raised for that place, commanded by Major
Grose.[2] By the last day of January the ship was ready for sea; and on the
first day of February the pilot came on board, in order to conduct her out
of the harbour to Spithead.

When things were in this state of forwardness, it was proposed to me to
accompany Captain Parker in the intended expedition to New Holland. A
fortnight was allowed me for my decision. An indulgent husband waited my
answer at Portsmouth: I did not therefore take a minute's consideration; but,
by return of post, forwarded one perfectly consonant to his request, and my
most sanguine wishes—that of going with *him* to the remotest parts of the
globe; although my considerate readers will naturally suppose that my
feelings were somewhat wounded at the thoughts of being so long absent
from two dear children, and a mother, with whom I had travelled into
France, Italy, and Spain; and from whom I had never been separated a
fortnight at one time during the whole course of my life.

Attended by an intimate friend, I repaired to the West end of the town, and set off for Portsmouth the next morning. We remained at Spithead until the 12th of March. In the interim orders had arrived to receive on board Captain Gidley King, of the Royal Navy, the intended Lieutenant Governor of Norfolk Island in the Pacific Ocean, together with Mrs. King and their family;[3] also to disembark Major Grose, and such part of the corps as were on board, except Mr. Burton a botanist, Mr. Baines the chaplain, and Mr. Grimes, who, with their attendants, were directed to be continued on board, and to take their passage for the new settlement.[4]

On Tuesday, the 15th of March, we sailed from Spithead, by way of St. Helens; and, after a fortnight's seasoning and buffeting in the channel, I began to enjoy the voyage I had undertaken; and with the polite attention of the officers on board, and my amiable companion Mrs. King, we glided over many a watery grave with peace of mind, and uninterrupted happiness; although many calms tended to render our passage to the island of *Teneriffe* somewhat tedious.[5]

We arrived, however, safe in the bay of *Santa Cruz* on the *fifteenth* of April; and captain Parker sent the second lieutenant on shore, to acquaint the Governor of our having put into that port for refreshment, and offered to exchange salutes, provided his Excellency would assure him the return of an equal number of guns from the garrison; at the same time informing him that he should have the honour, together with the officers, of waiting on him the ensuing day; and that lieutenant governor King of Norfolk Island was a passenger, and also intended to do himself the honour of paying his respects to his Excellency.

The officer returned with the Governor's answer, that whatever the ship stood in need of, she might have; and that an officer should be sent on-board, to signify the time when it would be most convenient for His Excellency to receive the compliments we had been so polite as to offer, of waiting on him; but that he had orders from his Court not to return any salute to a foreign Ship of War.

About half an hour after the return of the officer, one of the Governor's Aid-de-Camps came on board: he congratulated us, in his Excellency's name, on our safe arrival, and informed us that the Governor would be happy to see us, and requested that we would favour him with our company to dine with him on the ensuing day.

The invitation was accepted. Our party consisted of Lieutenant Governor King, his lady, our officers, together with Mr. Grimes, and Mr. Baines. The company at Don Antonio di Gutierez (that was the name of the Governor) were; the former Governor the Marquis di Branciforti, the Lieutenant Governor and his lady, with several other officers and their ladies.

The reception we met with, and particularly the compliments *di los manos,** would have struck me by their singularity, had I not resided when

* A compliment paid in Spain by the ladies to each other on entering a room. The last comer just touches the hand of every lady, at the same time curtseying and repeating continually '*di los manos*'.

very young upwards of three years in Spain; during which time I had every reason to believe them particularly attentive to the *English ladies:* and I hope it will be allowed me to remark the great satisfaction which they expressed at my being capable of conversing in their own language—a pleasure which I could not help participating with them, from having it in my power to be of some service, as *Interpreter General* to the party with whom I had the satisfaction of sailing.

It being Passion-week, the dinner, although sumptuous, consisted of many dishes dressed with oil.—After having, from hunger and politeness, ate more than we wished of the least rancid dishes, not expecting any plain ones to make their appearance; we were quite surprized when a large roasted Turkey, dressed quite in the English fashion, was brought on the table:—had it made an earlier entrance, it would have been well finished, but, unfortunately, it came so unexpectedly, that our appetites had been satisfied, with a previous course of rancid plenty.

After dinner our formidable party paraded the town, which I suppose to be very near a mile in length, and about half a mile in breadth. There are several neat churches in it, but only one good street which is remarkably broad:—the rest are generally very narrow, and abound in beggars, who are extremely troublesome to travellers.

At sun-set we returned on board, well satisfied with the reception we had met with; and on the following day, the same party dined at Mr. Rooney's, a Gentleman in partnership with the English house of Mess. Little and Co. and to whom Captain Parker had been introduced by means of a letter from Sir Andrew Hammond. From a desire of making me acquainted with some Spanish ladies, Mr. Rooney engaged us in an afternoon's walk to visit Captain Adams, the Captain of the Port, and there I had the pleasure of meeting with several females. They seemed highly delighted with my hat and dress, and took singular satisfaction in repeatedly taking off the former, and in examining my coat, which was half uniform. My having formerly travelled in Spain, and consequently having acquired a tolerable knowledge of their language procured me unusual attention, such as I shall ever remember with pleasure, though mingled with a degree of regret, arising from the improbability of my ever revisiting a country, in which I had the happiness to meet with unlimited kindness.

The next morning we were presented with sallads, fruits, lemons, &c. from different inhabitants of the town, who seemed to vie with each other in presenting us with those salutary refreshments.

The following day was fixed for an excursion to *Puerto Oratava.*[6] Accompanied by Governor King, his lady, our first Lieutenant, and a young gentleman belonging to Mess. Little and Co. we went on shore at day-break, and after breakfasting mounted our buricos or donkeys. The roads (hardly deserving that appellation) were rugged indeed; in some places the stones were sufficiently out of the ground to afford us seats, but the good humour which reigned amongst our party made ample amends for any trifling difficulty of that nature—and indeed little difficulties make social excursions more interesting.

Our first halting-place was a small hut, where Mr. Malcolme, a gentleman belonging to the same house, had taken care to provide us with biscuits, wine, &c. Having refreshed ourselves we continued our ride until *meridian*, when it was judged prudent for us to tarry during the heat of the day. Here Mr. Malcolme had also procured a cold collation, or a first dinner.—Two sultry hours having passed away very cheerfully, we again mounted our buricos, and, upon my making use of the Spanish method of quickening their pace, my animal set off on full speed, left the muleteer staring with astonishment and poor me rolling down a steep hill; but perceiving the party, who had not got up with us, coming rapidly to my assistance, fearful lest they should gallop over me, I arose as quickly as possible, and scrambling to a stone sat myself down upon it, and laughed as heartily as I ever recollected to have done in my life. This little accident let my muleteer into the secret of my having understood the chief of his conversation with the other, who had the honour of attending my companion Mrs. King, which was "his inclination to stop at all the *posadoes*, or public houses, we had passed by."

At a short distance from this laughable scene, we were met by Mr. Little, who very politely conducted us to his town residence, where he had prepared a most splendid entertainment replete with every delicacy of the season. The fruits and vegetables were luxuries indeed to us, who had been accustomed to little choice during our passage.

From this town, on the same evening, one of our officers, Lieutenant Rye, accompanied by Mr. Burton the botanist, took his departure for the Peak of Teneriffe, in which enterprize, notwithstanding the great danger pointed out to him at that season of the year, he was fortunate enough to succeed, and arrived at its summit.

On his return to England, his excursion was published; and I recommend it to the perusal of my readers; yet must at the same time take the liberty of observing, that although he has been minute as to particulars that tend to the information and benefit of such as may hereafter wish to visit the Peak, he has been too diffident in mentioning the extreme fatigues and difficulties which he underwent in the accomplishment of his wishes.[7] The inhabitants spoke of his courage in terms of astonishment—too much cannot be said in praise of his perseverance, it is sufficient of itself to convince us that no difficulties are insuperable to the prudent and brave, and at the same time brings to my remembrance the following lines of Mr. Rowe:

> "The wise and prudent conquer difficulties
> By daring to attempt them: Sloth and folly
> Shiver and shrink at sight of toil and hazard,
> And make th' impossibility they fear."[8]

We were the next morning regaled with a breakfast equally profuse and delicate as the preceding meals. The greater part of that day being too sultry to walk, we were much indebted to the polite and respectful attention of the aforementioned gentlemen, who, studying our amusement, proposed an evening excursion to their country residence, situated at a short distance from the town. It is a small neat house, standing upon a hill, commanding an extensive view of the Bay of Santa-Cruz; the garden is enclosed with myrtle hedges, the walks were shaded with vines, and lofty lemon trees, and the parterre before the door arranged with pots of most beautiful carnations.

Having comfortably regaled ourselves, we returned back to tea and supper; retired early, and arose at four the next morning. After breakfasting we set out upon our return; at *eleven* we stopped to partake of some refreshments, and then proceeded *two* leagues farther, when we again alighted to avoid the intense heat; during which time Mrs. King and myself strolled to several little huts. The inhabitants were surprized at seeing strangers of our sex alone; but their astonishment soon subsided when I spoke a few words to them in Spanish;—from this moment pleasure was visible in every countenance; in proof of which, although their spot of ground was small, their kindness induced them to present us with some sage, and an egg apiece—the *little* all they had to proffer us; and I make no doubt but we were remembered by them the remainder of the day; nay I will even think they have not yet forgotten us.

Returning to our party, and finding all ready, we remounted, and after riding a few miles our English friends took leave of us. Their uniform attention has induced me to name them so often in this narrative—the only return I shall ever have it in my power to make them.

It may afford a smile to my readers to add, that, after it was found out that I could speak Spanish, I entered into conversation with my muleteer, which made him so proud of his charge, that, previous to our entering any town or village, he, with great form, requested me to sit upright, and then spread my hair very curiously over my shoulders.—Poor fellow! could I be displeased with his request; since it arose, without doubt, from a desire of making me appear to the greatest advantage?

Thus, by the favour of a serene evening, we returned to Mr. Rooney's, who wished us to sleep on shore, as the wind began to blow fresh, and the surf rendered it very unpleasant for us to go on-board; but having resolved prior to my leaving England, to bear every difficulty, if possible, and determined to start none, I, with my good friends, took leave; and, after a few lifts over a heavy sea, we reached the wished-for vessel.

The next morning we paid a visit to the Spanish Lieutenant Governor's Lady, who introduced us to several ladies. The following day Mr. Rooney and Mr. Malcolme favoured us with their company on-board. After dinner they took leave of us, and shortly after we received from them a present of some lemons, and such other fruit as they deemed most acceptable for our intended voyage.

On the 24th of April we attempted to sail; but unfortunately the anchor of our vessel hooked the cable of a Spanish brig, owing to a strong tide; which broke the window, and carried away part of our quarter gallery. This accident detained us until the following day, when we sailed with a fresh and favourable breeze, and saw the Peak many leagues distant.

CHAP. II.

Ceremony of crossing the Equator—arrive at St. Jago—description of the Portugueze inhabitants—a violent gale—see the island of Saint Trinidad—a description of that island—arrive at Simon's Bay—set out for the Cape.

On the 27th of April we got into the Trade-Winds. On the 29th we crossed the line, and paid the usual forfeit to Amphitrite and Neptune. Those sailors who had crossed the line before burlesqued the new-comers as much as possible, calling themselves Neptune and Amphytrite with their aquatic attendants. They have the privilege to make themselves merry; and those who have never been in South latitudes purchase their freedom by a small quantity of liquor. But the sailor or soldier who has none to give is the object of their mirth; and, the more restive he is, the more keen they are to proceed to business. A large tub of salt water, with a seat over it, is placed in the fore-part of the ship, on which the new comer is reluctantly put—the seat is drawn from under him; and, when rising from the tub, several pails of water are thrown over him—he is then pushed forward amongst his laughing shipmates, and is as busy as the rest to get others in the same predicament.[9]

The *first* of May we expected to make the island of *Sal*—saw many porpoises, and, having had moderate breezes, arrived at *St. Jago* on the *third*. Being advised not to go on shore, we waited till we had procured abundance of all kinds of refreshments; in particular, fruit, poultry, and goats; all of which articles were very scarce at Teneriffe, owing to its being so early in the Spring. The turkeys upon this island are remarkably fine, and would do credit to the plumpest that Norfolk could produce.

The ships then in Port Praya Bay were The Phoenix and Lord Camden East Indiamen; and, during our short stay, The Dutton, Albemarle, Barrington, and Active transports, arrived. Here we had the pleasure of becoming acquainted with Captain Patterson, of the New South Wales corps, and his Lady.[10] We treated ourselves with cocoa-nuts and pineapples, of which there are great abundance in this island. The Portugueze inhabitants have chiefly been defaulters in their native country; and the sallowness of their complexions proves what a sickly climate they have to buffet with. The black inhabitants are robust, and much inclined, like their masters, to take advantage of strangers; nay, I have been credibly informed, that they make no ceremony of cheating one another, whenever a suitable opportunity occurs. They are fond of old cloaths in their exchange for fruit, &c. and a shabby suit of old black is esteemed twice as valuable as any other colour.

We left this island on the 6th of May—had fresh breezes and violent heat until the 10th. Many sharks were caught, and the tails of the youngest of them eaten by the men: porpoises were seen rolling about with great force all around us.

We experienced much heat between the trade-winds, until the 19th, when, for a change, we were overtaken by a most violent squall of wind, attended with thunder, lightning, and rain, and the ship pitched very much.

The greatest inconvenience I suffered from these squalls was the necessity we were under of having in the dead lights, which are strong shutters wedged in to prevent a following sea from breaking into the ship. The noise made by the working of the vessel, and the swinging of the glass shades that held our lights, rendered the cabin very dismal.

This squally weather continued, with little variation, until the 23d, when we spoke with a French ship, bound to Port L'Orient. They had nothing to dispose of; but sent us a fine turtle, which was a great treat to those who were fond of the variety of good food it contains.

On the 29th we saw the island of Saint Trinidad, which appears a very beautiful little spot: Captain D'Auvergne, in a cutter belonging to Commodore Johnstone's fleet, was cast away here.[11] I am told they made themselves quite comfortable, as they saved great part of their stores; and, having some garden seeds, they grew up quickly, and cabbages thrived particularly well. This island is about nine miles in circumference, well wooded, and watered with fertile valleys; and the English colony, who were the only inhabitants, left it with regret. We saw a great quantity of birds hovering all around; and, as they are not often disturbed by man, they range in native freedom. The sea-birds have plenty of food, from the variety of fish, particularly the Flying-fish, which is constantly tormented both by Bonetas and Dolphins, and the birds darting upon them, in their flying efforts to escape.

On the 30th the weather was very squally, and the sea rough. We saw pintado-birds, and others usual in these latitudes; also Mother Cary's Chickens—small birds, that fly very fast, and are not unlike the swallow: they are seldom seen but in rough weather; and sailors say they are the attendants upon storms—of course they are not partial to them.

This weather continued several days; once we were obliged, on account of the roughness of the sea, to dine on the deck in the cabin; but these little difficulties were scarcely felt, the party being in good humour, and our spirits well supported by good broth, roast pig, and plumb-puddings—thanks to my caterer, who had so well provided for so long a voyage.

With little variation, we sailed till the 19th of June, when land was once more in sight. At ten the next morning the *Bellows Rock* opened to view; and on the 21st, at *four* in the afternoon, we arrived, at *Simon's Bay;* this being the Bay where ships generally lay during the winter-season, as the sudden hurricanes, which sweep round the mountains at this period, make the Bay at Cape town too dangerous to risk a vessel at.

An officer was sent on shore, to inform the Commandant of our having put in for refreshment: he shortly returned, and brought us word, that every thing wanted should be readily supplied; and the next morning the Commandant paid us a visit on board.

Governor King also wrote to Mr. Peter de Witt, a merchant at the Cape of Good Hope; in consequence of which he waited upon us, and brought with him two carriages to conduct us to the Cape; the one a chaise, drawn by four, the other a kind of waggon, drawn by eight horses.

On the 23d, eager for a little shore amusement, we rose early, and, after breakfasting upon rolls, and such fruit as we had procured from the Bay, Lieutenant Governor King, Mrs. King, our first Lieutenant, Captain Parker, and myself, went on shore—the fort saluting with fifteen guns, and our ship returning the compliment with an equal number.

CHAP. III.

Set off for Cape Town—stop at False bay—meet a party of Soldiers— reflections—arrive at the Cape—Mrs. De Witt—shipwreck of the Guardian—Lieutenant Riou—a Cape breakfast—observations on the town and its inhabitants.

I could not help being well-pleased at finding myself once more safe landed. We loitered some time at Mr. Brank's, where we met Colonel Burrington, of the Bengal army, who was then at the Cape, for the re-establishment of his health. In a short time we set off for Cape Town, Captain King and Mr. De Witt in the chaise and four, and the rest of us in the carriage drawn with eight horses, somewhat resembling a covered waggon, except having seats within, and little gaudy decorations.

The road was excessively bad, and the carriage not being hung with springs rendered travelling most joltingly disagreeable. After having rode about eight or nine miles, we arrived at a house situated in the bottom of *False Bay*, called *Mussleburg*: this house, when first built, was intended by the Governor and Council, as a temporary residence, being situated in a good fishing neighbourhood, and as a place of refreshment to travellers passing to and from Cape Town and Simon's Bay.—After the jolting of our vehicle, we had reason to think it a place of relief; and when we arrived there, we found several officers, with their wives and children, at dinner. We had also met several different parties of soldiers on the road; upon enquiry, we found it was a regiment marching to Simon's Bay, in order to be embarked on-board a Dutch Indiaman bound to Batavia; there having been recently at that place a great mortality amongst all classes of Europeans, said to be caused by the Malays, the natives of Java, having poisoned the waters.[12]

In relating this circumstance, I cannot but feel myself deeply affected, as it brings to my mind the recollection of similar embarkations that have lately taken place for those cruel islands, where so many brave men have fallen victims to that worst of all distempers, the Yellow Fever—a distemper, the fatal effects of which I have so heavily experienced, as it has deprived me of a beloved husband, the tender partner of my life, and my only support in the time of trouble and affliction. When I reflect on his many virtues, and on the irreparable loss which I have unexpectedly sustained, I cannot help saying, with General Draper, on a similar occasion:

> "Why to such worth was no duration given?
> Because perfection is the choice of Heaven."[13]

But to proceed—During our ride, we noticed some remarkable small birds with beautiful plumage; but which are not known to sing: their chief support is supposed to be from a flower that grows plentifully in the neighbourhood, somewhat resembling a tulip; from this flower issues a juice equal in sweetness and thickness to syrup; and, when boiled, it is good for complaints in the breast, and also for young children.

The remainder of the road from Mussleburg to Cape Town is, in general, very pleasant; numerous villas being interspersed on both sides of the road. In particular, as you round Table Hill, towards Cape Town, the rising appearance of Constantia, where the famous wine is made,[14] has a wonderful effect upon the traveller; the situation of it being under the Table-Mountain, about three miles from Musselburg, and ten from Cape Town.

At six o'clock in the evening we reached the end of our journey; most completely jostled and tired. We were all lodged at Mrs. de Witt's, mother to the abovementioned gentleman, well known by the English frequenting the Cape: her bulk, comparatively speaking, was nearly equal to that of a Dutch man of war, and, being remarkably low in stature, her size was rendered still more conspicuous. She received us with much complacency, and immediately procured a little cargo of bread and butter, which I believe we all relished very much, having had no overplus in that article during our passage. The countenance of the good lady was pleasing, her manner engaging, and her motherly attention, during our short *séjour* at her habitation, such as I shall ever remember with the greatest degree of satisfaction. Miss J. de Witt did not make her appearance that evening; the eldest daughter was not very conversible; and a young lady, a relation, was remarkably bashful. Thus situated, we were obliged to amuse ourselves with our own private remarks, until supper was ready; a meal which, in this town, is distinguished for substantial dishes; and, what is always most welcome to voyagers, plenty of vegetables, which are as sweet as they can possibly be; for the situation of this climate is so happy, that all European and most tropical fruits and vegetables grow as well as in their native soils.

On the 24th of June, after a good night's repose, I arose particularly thankful to Providence for His protection; and offered up my daily supplication for the health of the affectionate ties I had left in England. Curiosity then directed my steps to a window, whence I beheld the small remains of his Majesty's ship the Guardian, commanded by Lieutenant Riou, an officer conspicuous for presence of mind in the most imminent danger, and for feelingly recommending his mother and sisters to the notice of his honourable employers. By dint of the greatest exertion he brought his ship to the Cape, and saved the lives of those of the crew who remained with him: as a reward for his services, he has since been made a post-captain.[15] To avoid as much as possible any disagreeable reflections which might arise from the idea of a probability of our sharing the fate of the above vessel (as the Gorgon was the first ship commissioned for the relief of the colony, after the fatal loss of the Guardian), I hastened to my companions, and was, for the first time, surprized with a Cape breakfast, which certainly merits many encomiums: it is customary to arrange out the table as for dinner, except its being covered with all sorts of fruit; against each person is placed a knife, a plate, and a napkin; thus seated, the lady of the house makes tea and coffee at a side-table, which the slaves hand round to the company.

The day being very rainy, and our baggage advancing slower than we had done, it was mutually agreed to remain at home. We were visited by Mynheer Van Graaffe, the Governor, who was at that time about to resign; also by Colonel Burrington and other Gentlemen.

A description of Cape Town having repeatedly been given by authors of knowledge and taste; I only intend, with submission to my readers, to commit to paper my own slender remarks on the various objects which engaged my attention.

The town I thought both clean and pleasant; its environs afford several delightful rides: the road to the Company's house, by the sea-side, brought to my recollection one from Puerta Colonela, at Leghorn, round the Lazarettos, to Monti Negro. I was struck with the uncommon dexterity of the Cape-drivers, who manage eight horses in hand, and turn the corners with the greatest swiftness. The carriages used for these excursions are entirely open, and consist, some of two, and others of four seats.

In this town there are no public amusements, nor any particular promenades, excepting the Governor's garden, at the end of which there is a very large aviary. There are not any public shops, as in other towns: the merchants dispose of their goods, both by wholesale and retail, in the following method: if you wish to make any purchase you send for a large book, upon the leaves of which are pasted patterns of edgings, dimities, silks, muslins, &c. with the prices annexed; and if you make any large purchase, you go and view the different articles in the parlours. Butcher, baker, &c. are all equally private; in fact, the most pleasing sight is in the market-place at daybreak, when the slaves, mostly two by two, bring their baskets by the means of poles on their shoulders. Ostrich feathers are very plentiful. There is also every sort of fruit in great abundance; that which was most remarkable to me was the rose-apple, not having met with it in any of my former travels in France, Spain, and Italy: there is a faintness in the taste of this apple which few palates would approve of; but the odoriferous smell it disperses around renders it very acceptable when placed amongst other fruit.

The women of the Cape are remarkable for their bulk; which I am apt to attribute to their going without stays, and sitting much in the house with their feet continually lifted on a chair. They have good teeth, and in general their features are pleasing; after marriage they are totally neglectful of their persons.

Neither hat nor bonnet is fashionable amongst them; high caps, with cloaks or shawls, are worn in their stead; the latter they have frequent opportunities of receiving, in return for the hospitality shewn to our British East India ships.

The churches at Cape Town are open at eight in the morning, when the genteel classes go in sedan chairs, which are usually kept in the entrance of their houses.

CHAP. IV.

Visit Colonel Gordon.—Arrival of the Neptune.—Receive intelligence from New South Wales.—Arrival of Captain Patterson and his Lady.— A Cape Dance.—A Hottentot Song.—Visit Mr. Vandrian's Brewery.— Prepare for our Departure.—Set sail.

Our baggage arrived the next day, and we were busily employed, having engaged ourselves to dine with Colonel Gordon.[16] The hour of dinner was two o'clock; the Colonel obligingly sent his carriage for us, which was very acceptable, the weather being intensely hot, and the pavement intolerably bad. The Villa where the Colonel resides is situated a few miles from the town, on the summit of a hill commanding a most pleasant and extensive view by sea and land. The good Colonel is already well known for his Museum, and Manuscripts relative to Natural History, and his many enterprising journeys to the interior parts of that country; for which he was eminently qualified on account of his extensive knowledge of the language, manners, and customs of the Hottentots, by whom he is almost adored.—The respect and regard which I bear to this family forbids my passing over in silence the polite and friendly attention I received from Mrs. Gordon, who is a Swiss lady, and who most agreeably acquiesces in whatever may tend to render those comfortable who have the happiness of being ranked amongst her acquaintance. After what I have said, it will easily be supposed that their children are taught the same engaging attention to strangers.[17]

On the next day, the Neptune and the Lady Juliana anchored in False Bay;

both of them had been ships sent out by Government with Convicts and Stores to the colony of New South Wales, and, after having fulfilled their contract with Government, were permitted to go to China, to take in a freight of Teas on account of the East-India Company. We did not receive any favourable account of the place we were shortly going to visit; on the contrary, we learnt from the commander of the Neptune, Mr. D. Trail, that, on his leaving it, there were only six months provisions in the Settlement, at full allowance; we also learnt the disappointment of the Governor and Officers of that Colony at the non-arrival of the Guardian:—in short, every circumstance served to assure us how anxiously they waited the appearance of our happy bark; and made Captain Parker as anxious to relieve them.

About this time the arrival of the Britannia and Albemarle transports was announced: this circumstance afforded us considerable satisfaction, as we were in expectation of again meeting with Mrs. Patterson, the Lady of Captain Patterson of the new corps. This gentleman once accompanied Colonel Gordon in his excursion up the country.[18] An unexpected meeting with those of our kingdom is always agreeable to travellers: it proved so to us; and the more especially as it chiefly consisted of those who were engaged upon services, similar in their nature with our intended voyage.

But, though surrounded with novelties and amusements, I could not forget the perilous situation of my husband, who was gone to bring the ship round to Table Bay, the winter season rendering it very unsafe on account of the Monsoons which are prevalent at that time of the year; but, thanks to the Supreme Being! the ship appeared in sight on Sunday the 17th of July, and Captain Parker came on shore to dinner. We received another invitation from Mrs. Gordon, and accordingly went in the afternoon to Green Point to tea; after which, we returned home to supper, and the evening concluded with dancing, which they are remarkably fond of at this town; particularly a dance somewhat like the *Allemande*, excepting the figure, which is not variable, and the long continuance of turning round: it is surprizing that the ladies are not giddy with the swiftness of the motion; for it would certainly turn any person's head unaccustomed to it.

The next morning we again visited the hospitable villa, where we were regaled in a manner that bespoke the attention of the providers: during a desert that would have gained applause from the nicest Epicure, singing was introduced, in the course of which we were favoured with a *Hottentot* song from the Colonel: to describe any part of it would be impossible; but, without a wish to offend, I must say that it appeared to me the very reverse of all that is musical or harmonious; and the Colonel, who gave us strict charge not to be frightened with what we were to hear, seemed to enjoy the laughter it occasioned. Different songs having gone round, the Colonel's son amused us with several pieces upon the organ; and shortly after we were agreeably surprized with the bands belonging to the regiments without: nor did this conclude the amusement; for, after drinking coffee, we danced until our return into town, when the same music accompanied us, to prevent, I suppose, our spirits from drooping at the thought of leaving such good company.

The next day Captain Patterson and his Lady arrived from False Bay; who, fortunately for our little parties, remained at the house in which we resided. Through the friendly introduction of this gentleman I became one of the party at Mr. Vandrian's; and I cannot but acknowledge the polite attention I received from this family during my short acquaintance.

On the 24th, a select party of us dined at Colonel Gordon's, where we met Colonel Burrington,* Major De Lisle, with some other Dutchmen, and Mr. Pitt, a relation of Lord Chatham, who was fortunately saved out of the wreck of the Guardian. We were occupied in feasting and singing till the evening, when we returned home, and found the company waiting for us. Upon our arrival, the dances immediately began; and, after eating an excellent supper, we retired to our apartments; but, from the coolness of the night, the moon shining delightfully, and the music parading the streets, we were unwilling to consign ourselves to "dull oblivion."

The next day we visited Mr. Vandrian, at the Brewery; where we met with a welcome reception: the house and gardens are very pleasant; the brewery is an extensive building, situated between Cape Town and False Bay, very near the latter; and, strange to say, not far distant from Paradise! a spot of ground so called, from the situation; and about which the Silver Tree grows in great perfection: neither is it far from Constantia.

The Governor, having rode out that morning, stopped and joined the party, who were then at dinner; and, the evening proving rainy, we returned with him in his *voiture d'Hollande.*

The following day we were busily employed in getting our cloaths ready for sea, and in sending them on-board, as we expected to embark that afternoon; however, the business of the ship not being actually accomplished, we slept on shore that night; and on the ensuing morning, the 31st of July, we all repaired on-board, escorted to the key by the greater part of Mr. de Witt's family: Mr. Peter de Witt accompanied us on-board, and saw us under weigh.

Chap. V.

The voyage continued—a melancholy accident; singular instance of fraternal affection—death of Lieutenant Ross—a dreadful storm—the falling of a ball of fire—observations and reflections.

During our residence at the Cape, great care had been taken amply to

---

* Whilst writing the above, intelligence has been received of the death of this gentleman, in an engagement with the Rohilla Chiefs, on the 26th of October, 1794.

provide for the remainder of our voyage; the crew were well supplied with fresh provisions, and we returned to our little sea-amusements in peace and tranquillity of mind.

With my companion Mrs. King, and the society of the ship, I seldom, if ever, found any thing unpleasant, except the pitching of the ship, which motion proved very disagreeable to me to the end of our voyage.

We proceeded favourably on our passage, having, in general, good weather, and brisk winds, until the 7th of September, when we met with the following melancholy occurrences. At 6 o'clock, P.M. a carpenter fell overboard; the cutter was immediately sent to rescue him, if possible, from the merciless waves; but to no effect, the sea running high, and the wind blowing fresh: one dismal hour had scarcely elapsed when the cutter returned, and, while hoisting it in, another poor man fell overboard: the cutter was again sent out; but, alas! the earnest attempts of the sailors to save the life of their comrade unfortunately proved abortive; his brother, who was in the boat, had been rescued by the deceased from a similar accident only a few months before; his gratitude to, and affection for, this brother, lost before him, drove him into a delirium; in which dreadful state he continued for some time. A dismal sky and a deluge of rain concluded this disastrous and eventful night. The ensuing morning was equally stormy as the preceding evening, and the weather continued much the same until the 11th, when we saw the Coast of New Holland.

In the evening of this day we had the misfortune of losing Mr. George Ross, midshipman, after a severe illness since leaving the Cape. This young gentleman was the son of Lieutenant Ross of the Navy, and brought up at Portsmouth Academy; he was a very promising youth, and his death was sincerely regretted by all his shipmates, and the superior officers of the ship, for his attention to his duty. The same melancholy evening died suddenly James Key, a seaman. The ensuing day the bodies of the deceased were committed to the deep, after having performed the usual funeral service.

On the 12th we had fresh gales, with favourable weather, which continued until the 17th, when we came in sight of Mount Dromedary,[19] so called from the similarity of its shape. This day we were engaged to dine with the officers in the wardroom: under the expectation of arriving shortly at Port Jackson, the time passed away very sociably; but a sudden squall and perverse winds coming on, deprived us of the satisfaction of reaching the wished-for haven for three long days—at least they appeared so to every one of us; when we reflected that the colony stood in such great need of the supplies with which we were so plenteously stored: however, with patience, the sovereign remedy of all evils, and the travellers best support, I passed the time in adjusting the cabin, and in other preparations prior to our going on shore.

The ensuing day, being Sunday, was pleasant and serene, as if to afford us an opportunity of imploring a continuance of the Divine Protection, which we had hitherto experienced in a singular degree.

On Monday the 19th, at noon, we were in latitude 35°. 15″. S. and longitude 149°. 26″. E. from the meridian of Greenwich, when a point of land appeared in sight, called by Captain Cook *Long Nose*, on account of its pointed shape. At sun-set the hovering clouds seemed to forebode the event of the evening; at eight came on a tremendous thunder-squall, attended with most dreadful lightning and constant heavy rains, which continued upwards of an hour and a half. About *half* past *eight* the lightning struck the pole of the main-top-gallant-mast, shivered it and the head of the mast entirely to pieces; thence it communicated to the main top-mast, under the hounds, and split it exactly in the middle, above *one third* down the mast; it next took the main-mast by the main-yard, on the larboard side, and in a spherical direction struck it in six different places; the shock electrified every person on the quarter-deck; those who were unfortunately near the main-mast were knocked down, but recovered in a few minutes: this continued until about *half* past *ten*, when a most awful spectacle presented itself to the view of those on deck; whilst we who were below felt a sudden shock, which gave us every reason to fear that the ship had struck against a rock; from which dreadful apprehension we were however relieved upon being informed that it was occasioned by a ball of fire which fell at that moment. The lightning also broke over the ship in every direction: it was allowed to be a dismal resemblance of a besieged garrison; and, if I might hazard an opinion, I should think it was the effect of an earthquake. The sea ran high, and seemed to foam with anger at the feeble resistance which our lone bark occasioned. At midnight the wind shifted to the westward, which brought on fine clear weather,[20] and I found myself once more at leisure to anticipate the satisfaction which our arrival would diffuse throughout the colony; for, owing to the loss of his majesty's ship The Guardian, the governor and officers were reduced to such scanty allowance, that, in addition to the fatigues and hardships which they had experienced when the colony was in its infant state, they were obliged, from a scarcity of provisions, to toil through the wearisome day with the anxious and melancholy expectations of increasing difficulties. What then could afford us more heart-felt pleasure than the near event of relieving them? for it is surely happiness to succour the distressed; a satisfaction we fully experienced. Our desire of reaching the colony was also increased by the reflection, that the greater part of the marine officers were to return with us once more to visit Old England, and to render happy such of their friends and relations as had lingered out their absence with many an aching heart. With what anxiety did they await the ship's arrival! with what eagerness did they hasten on-board! The circumstances are too deeply engraven on my memory ever to be eradicated; but, alas! my pen is utterly incompetent to the task of describing our feelings on this occasion.

CHAP. VI.

Arrive at Port Jackson—Governor King and Captain Parker wait upon Governor Phillip with the dispatches—Account of ships arrived in the harbour; and of a dreadful mortality which had taken place on-board the transports—Interesting particulars respecting the propriety of establishing a whale-fishery on the coast of New Holland.

At sun-rise we saw the coast of New Holland, extending from South West to North West, distant from the nearest part about nine or ten miles. During the night we were driven to the Northward, and passed Port Jackson, the port to which we were bound; however, on the ensuing day, the 21st, we arrived safe in the above harbour. As soon as the ship anchored several officers came on-board; and, shortly after, Governor King, accompanied by Captain Parker, went on shore, and waited on his Excellency Governor Phillip, with the government-dispatches: they were welcome visitors; and I may safely say, that the arrival of our ship diffused universal joy throughout the whole settlement.

We found lying here his Majesty's armed tender The Supply, with her lower masts both out of repair; they were so bad, that she was obliged to have others made of the wood of the country, which was procured with great difficulty, several hundred trees being cut down without finding any sufficiently sound at the core.[21] Lieutenant Bowen, with four sail of transports under his direction, was arrived here; also The Mary-Anne, a transport-ship, that had been sent out alone, with only women-convicts and provisions on-board.

A dreadful mortality had taken place on-board of most of the transports which had been sent to this country; the poor miserable objects that were landed died in great numbers, so that they were soon reduced to at least *one third* of the number that quitted England.

"Their appearance," to use the words of Captain Parker, "will be ever fresh in my memory. I visited the hospital, and was surrounded by mere skeletons of men—in every bed, and on every side, lay the dying and the dead. Horrid spectacle! it makes me shudder when I reflect, that it will not be the last exhibition of this kind of human misery that will take place in this country, whilst the present method of transporting these miserable wretches is pursued; for, the more of them that die, the more it redounds to the interest of the ship-owners and masters, who are paid so much a-head by government, for each individual, whether they arrive in the colony or not."[22]

But to return to my narrative.—On the 25th, in consequence of the anniversary of his majesty's accession to the throne, his Excellency Governor Phillip gave a public dinner to all the army and navy officers in the colony. The Gorgon dressed ship as well as her scanty allowance of colours would permit; and, at the usual hour, fired twenty-one guns.

About this time, Mr. Melvin, master of The Britannia transport, arrived here; with this, and with several other gentlemen, Captain Parker held various conferences on the propriety of establishing a Whale-Fishery on the Coast of New Holland. Minutes of these conferences were preserved by my husband; and, as they appear to me rather interesting, I shall take the liberty of inserting them in this place.

"Mr. Melvin gave it as his opinion that a very good Whale-Fishery might be established upon this coast; and that fish were infinitely more numerous than on the American. In his passage from Van Deiman's Land to Port Jackson, he asserted that he saw more shoals of spermaceti whales in the course of that voyage, than in any one of a great number which he had made in the South Whale-Fishery. This afternoon he sailed, upon experiment, accompanied by the William and Anne, Edward Bunker, master. The day after their leaving Port Jackson, they fell-in with a shoal of whales; the boats belonging to the two ships struck seven of them; but the wind blew so hard that each ship saved but one; and, in consequence of the weather were obliged to return from the cruize.

As soon as the agreement between Government and the ships had ended, which was when they had landed their convicts and discharged their lading, the masters of them were at full liberty to proceed upon their owners' employ. Five of the number had permission from the East India Company to load with cotton at Bombay; the others, being fishery-ships, went out and returned frequently. During the time of our stay at Port Jackson, they saw abundance of fish; but, always meeting with tempestuous weather and a strong current setting to windward, their success was not adequate to their expectations. One of them, named the Matilda, took three fish, which yielded about thirty barrels of oil, and the master told me that it was in its quality more valuable, by *ten* pounds in the ton, than the oil which they procured on the coast of America. One of them gave me a small keg of it, which I brought home with me as a specimen. They also told me, that nothing but the fear of losing the time of their employers prevented them from continuing on this coast, for they had many good harbours to run into if need required; an advantage of considerable importance, as it enabled them always to have a good supply of water, which was not the case when fishing on the American coast: they had also great relief from wild herbs gathered here, particularly that called Sweet Tea, which makes a very pleasant and wholesome beverage.[23] These, with other considerations, were sufficient to influence those employed in the Whale-Fishery to prefer this coast to the other, where they have no port to go into, as, by treaty, they are not to approach nearer than one hundred leagues of the shore: in consequence of which, their crew must be greatly infected with the scurvy, for want of that assistance which they can so plenteously meet with on the coast of New South Wales. They have also an opportunity of keeping their ships in much better repair, having harbours to go into when necessity required, whereas on the coast of America it is quite the reverse.

New Holland abounds in good harbours; we have thoroughly investigated the greater part of them, and there are many others at present but imperfectly known; yet, if a Whale Fishery were once established, they would soon become familiar to us; and, if peculiar emoluments were granted to Ships that took fish on this coast in preference to that of America, great advantages might accrue to Government therefrom: the number of vessels which would be in that employ must greatly lessen the freight of transports, and give us continual opportunities of supplying the settlement at a moderate expence to government: it would also be an encouragement to settlers to go over; and until that takes place the maintaining the Colony of New South Wales will be a continually accumulating burthen to the mother-country. Were we to send settlers from England, with some little property of their own, [*Plate 22*] and to give the men sufficient encouragement by allotting them ground, building them convenient houses, allowing them a certain number of convicts, [*Plate 12*] giving them tools of husbandry, seeds of various kinds adequate to the number of acres in their possession, and victualling them and their men, for at least eighteen months, out of the public stores, at the expiration of which time they and their men were to provide for themselves—Were we to do these things, it might probably be able to support itself in a few years.

But to return to the Whale Fishery: it might be carried on by small vessels at the different harbours with which we are at present acquainted; if they contained casks enough to hold the blubber which two or three Whales might produce, and were able to carry three or four Whale-Boats, they would be sufficiently large. When they took any fish, if it were not convenient to run for Port Jackson, let them make any of the other harbours, immediately boil down the oil, and then watch for the opportunity to proceed to sea again. It is to be observed, that, at the full and change of the Moon, the weather is very tempestuous and unsettled on this coast, and also that there is a strong current always setting to windward; the harder it blows, the stronger it sets, and causes a turbulent, irregular, and very high sea. In the course of a season these small vessels would in all probability procure a sufficient quantity of oil to load such ships as should be sent from England to receive it; but, if any objection be made to small craft from the apprehension of convicts running away with them, let all the ships that Government take up belong to the Whale-fishery; let them sail from England in the Months of October, November, and December; and after having landed their stores, or whatever they may have brought out for Government, let them refit their ships and then proceed on the fishery, returning to Port Jackson when they want refreshments, or into any of the harbours with which we are acquainted. Lieutenant Bowen, of the Atlantic transport, discovered a bay, which, in honour to Sir John Jervis, he named after him. This bay has been since explored by Mr. Weatherhead, master of The Mary and Anne transport; who, in one of his cruizes after whales, was twice there, and has given me a draught of it.

Plate 22 Juan Ravenet (*c.* 1766–?), 'Ingleses enla Nueva Olanda' (1793).
Source: Dixson Galleries, State Library of New South Wales.

There are two other ports known to the Northward of Port Jackson; the first is *Broken Bay*, which has been well surveyed by Captain Hunter, of his majesty's ship The Sirius;[24] and is a very fine harbour, forming into different branches: one branch enters the river Hawkesbury; another runs to the Westward, and forms a fine piece of water, which has been named, by Governor Phillip, *Pittwater*. The next harbour to the Northward of this is Port Stephens, which has not been explored; but some of the fish-ships have been close in with it, and make no doubt but that it is a very good port."

Chap. VII.

Governor Phillip breakfasts on-board—visit Sidney Cove—go on-shore—short description of shrubs, birds, beasts, &c. of Botany Bay—excursion to, and description of, Paramatta—visit the Governor.

But to return to my narrative.—On the 30th Governor Phillip did us the honour to breakfast on-board; so did also Mr. Collins, Judge Advocate;[25] and Mr. Palmer, the Commissary.[26] The conversation was very interesting; the one party anxiously making enquiries after their relatives in England; and the other attentively listening to the troubles and anxieties which had attended the improvements made in that distant colony. When the company returned on-shore, we amused ourselves with the pleasing novelties of *Sidney Cove*, [*Plate 23*] so named by the Governor in honour of Lord Sidney: from this Cove, although it is very rocky, a most pleasant verdure proceeds on each side: the little habitations on shore, together with the canoes around us, and the uncommon manners of the natives in them were more than sufficient amusements for that day; the next was occupied in receiving visits from several officers belonging to this settlement.

When we went on shore, we were all admiration at the natural beauties raised by the hand of Providence without expence or toil: I mean the various flowery shrubs, natives of this country, that grow apparently from rock itself. The gentle ascents, the winding valleys, and the abundance of flowering shrubs, render the face of the country very delightful. The shrub which most attracted my attention was one which bears a white flower, very much resembling our English Hawthorn; the smell of it is both sweet and fragrant, and perfumes the air around to a considerable distance. There is also plenty of grass, which grows with the greatest vigour and luxuriance, but which, however, as Captain Tench justly observes, is not of the finest quality, and is found to agree better with horses and cows than with sheep.[27]

In Botany Bay there are not many land fowls: of the larger sort, only eagles were seen; of the smaller kind, though not numerous, there is a variety, from the size of a wren to that of a lark; all of which are remarkable

Plate 23 'A direct North General View of Sydney-Cove' (1794), oil painting based on a drawing by Thomas Watling.
Source: Dixson Galleries, State Library of New South Wales.

for fine loud notes, and beautiful plumage, particularly those of the paroquet kind. Crows are also found here, exactly the same as those in England. But descriptions, infinitely beyond the abilities of her who now, solely for the benefit of her little flock, is advised to set forth this narrative, having been already published, it would be presumptive to attempt any thing farther.

Our amusements here, although neither numerous nor expensive, were to me perfectly novel and agreeable: the fatherly attention of the good Governor upon all occasions, with the friendly politeness of the officers rendered our *séjour* perfectly happy and comfortable.

After our arrival here, Governor King and his Lady, resided on shore at Governor Phillip's, to whose house I generally repaired after breakfasting on-board: indeed it always proved a home for me; under this hospitable roof, I have often ate part of a Kingaroo, with as much glee as if I had been a partaker of some of the greatest delicacies of this metropolis, although latterly I was cloyed with them, and found them very disagreeable. The presents of eggs, milk, and vegetables, which I was often favoured with from the officers on shore, were always very acceptable; and the precaution which Captain Parker had taken, previous to our departure from the Cape of Good Hope, made me fully contented with my situation.

Our parties generally consisted of Mrs. King, Mr. Johnson,[28] and the Ladies who resided at the colony. We made several pleasant excursions up the Cove to the settlement called *Paramatta*.[29] The numerous branches, creeks, and inlets, that are formed in the harbour of Port Jackson, and the wood that covers all their shores down to the very edge of the water, make the scenery beautiful: the North branch is particularly so, from the sloping of its shores, the interspersion of tufted woods, verdant lawns, and the small Islands, which are covered with trees, scattered up and down.[30] [*Plate 24*]

Upon our first arrival at *Paramatta*, I was surprised to find that so great a progress had been made in this new settlement, which contains above one thousand convicts, besides the military. There is a very good level road, of great breadth, that runs nearly a mile in a straight direction from the landing place to the Governor's house, which is a small convenient building, placed upon a gentle ascent, and surrounded by about a couple of acres of garden ground: this spot is called Rose-Hill.[31] On both sides of the road are small thatched huts, at an equal distance from each other. [*Plate 6*] After spending the day very agreeably at the Governor's, we repaired to the lodging which had been provided for us, where we had the comfort of a large wood fire, and found every thing perfectly quiet, although surrounded by more than one thousand convicts. We enjoyed our night's repose; and in the morning, without the previous aid of toilet or mirror, we set out for the Governor's to breakfast, and returned with the same party on the ensuing day.

This little excursion afforded us an opportunity of noticing the beautiful plumage of the birds in general, and of the *Emu* in particular, two of which

Plate 24 'By water to Parramatta; with a distant view of the western mountains, taken from the Windmill-hill at Sydney', from *The Voyage of Governor Phillip* (1789), opp. p. 165.
Source: Rare Book and Special Collections Library, University of Sydney.

A non-descript BIRD found at BOTANY BAY,

in NEW SOUTH WALES.

From a Drawing made on the spot.

The Bird measured Seven Feet Two Inches in height, & Three Feet Nine Inches in length.

It approaches nearest to the Emu of South America, or the Cassowary of Java

London. Published Feb.y 1791 by J. Johnson N.o 72 S.t Pauls Church Yard & C.S talker Stationers Court.

Plate 25 'A non-descript Bird found at Botany Bay, in New South Wales. From a Drawing made on the spot' (1791).
Source: Mitchell Library, State Library of New South Wales.

we discovered in the woods: their plumage is remarkably fine, and rendered particularly curious, as each hen has two feathers generally of a light brown; the wings are so small as hardly to deserve the name; and, though incapable of flying, they can run with such swiftness that a greyhound can with difficulty keep pace with them. The flesh tastes somewhat like beef. [*Plate 25*]

In this cove there are some cool recesses, where with Captain Parker and the officers I have been many times revived after the intense heat of the day, taking with us what was necessary to quench our thirst.

Here we have feasted upon Oisters just taken out of the sea;—the attention of our sailors, and their care in opening and placing them round their hats, in lieu of plates, by no means diminishing the satisfaction we had in eating them. Indeed, the Oisters here are both good and plentiful: I have purchased a large *three-quart* bowl of them, for a pound and a half of tobacco, besides having them opened for me into the bargain.

CHAP. VIII.

Description of the inhabitants of New South Wales—their huts—their extraordinary honesty—account of Banalong—an instance of his sensibility.—observations on the Slave Trade.

The Inhabitants of New South Wales, both male and female, go without apparel. Their colour is of a dingy copper; their nose is broad and flat, their lips wide and thick, and their eyes circular. From a disagreeable practice they have of rubbing themselves with fish-oil, they smell so loathsome, that it is almost impossible to approach them without disgust.

The men in general appeared to be from five feet six to five feet nine inches high, are rather slender, but straight and well made: they have bushy beards, and the hair on their heads is stuck full with the teeth of fish, and bits of shells: they also ornament themselves with a fish-bone fastened in the gristle of the nose, which makes them appear really frightful; and are generally armed with a stick about a yard long, and a lance which they throw with considerable velocity.[32]

The stature of the women is somewhat less than that of the men—their noses are broad, their mouths wide, and their lips thick. They are extremely negligent of their persons, and are filthy to a degree scarcely credible: their faces and bodies are besmeared with the fat of animals, and the salutary custom of washing seems entirely unknown to them.

Their huts or habitations are constructed in the most rude and barbarous manner: they consist of pieces of bark laid together somewhat in the form of an oven, with a small entrance at one end. Their sole residence, however, is not in these huts; on the contrary, they depend less on them for shelter than on the numerous excavations which are formed in the rocks by the washing of the sea; and it is no uncommon thing to see fifty or sixty of them comfortably lodged in one of these caves.[33]

Notwithstanding the general appearance of the natives, I never felt the least fear when in their company being always with a party more than sufficient for my protection. I have been seated in the woods with twelve or fourteen of them, men, women, and children. Had I objected, or shewn any disgust at their appearance, it would have given them some reason to suppose that I was not what they term their *damely*, or friend; and would have rendered my being in their company not only unpleasant, but unsafe.

Before I conclude my description of the natives, it is but justice to remark, that, in comparison with the inhabitants of most of the South-Sea Islands, they appear very little given to thieving; and their confidence in the honesty of one another is so great, that they will leave their spears and other implements on the sea-shore, in full and perfect security of their remaining untouched.[34]

From the treatment which I invariably experienced, I am inclined to think favourably of them; and fully believe that they would never injure our people, were they not first offended by them.

I cannot help observing that one of the men had a most engaging deportment; his countenance was pleasing, and his manners far beyond what I could possibly have expected. He was pleased to seat himself by me, changed names with Captain Parker, and took particular notice of the travelling knife and fork with which I was eating, and which I did myself the satisfaction to give him: he paid us a visit on-board the ensuing day, and shewed me that he had not lost my present, but made use of it, though somewhat aukwardly, whilst he demolished *two* or *three* pounds of the ship's pork.

The natives very frequently surrounded our vessel with their canoes. The women often held up their little ones, as if anxious to have them noticed by us. Sometimes, for the sake of amusement, I have thrown them ribbands and other trifles, which they would as frequently tye round their toes as any other part of their person.

Since my return to England, Banalong, one of the natives brought hither by Governor Phillip, came to see me. [*Plate 13*] To describe the pleasure that overspread this poor fellow's countenance when my little girl presented to him the picture of her dear father, is impossible; it was then that the tear of sensibility trickled down his cheeks; he immediately recognized those features which will never be obliterated from my memory, and spoke, with all the energy of Nature, of the pleasing excursion which they had made together up the country. The above is one amongst many instances which I could relate of the natural goodness of their hearts; and I flatter myself that the time is hastening when they will no longer be considered as mere savages;—and wherefore should they?

> "Fleecy locks, and black complexion,
>   Cannot forfeit Nature's claim:
> Skins may differ, but affection
>   Dwells in white and black the same."[35]

CHAP. IX.

Preparations for our departure—repair on-board—set sail—discover Lord Howe's Island—Mount Lidgbird—Mount Gower—Three Kings Head Island—New Zealand—Cape Maria.

In the course of this month (October), the Britannia transport anchored at this place, as did also the Admiral Barrington. The arrival of the latter afforded us the pleasure of seeing Mrs. Patterson again, whose company added much to the happiness of our little parties. The 25th was quite a busy day with us, it being the commemoration of His Majesty's accession to the throne: after amusing ourselves in the morning with looking at some ships which were busily employed in going out of the cove on a fishing expedition, and the *full dress* of our bark in compliment to the day, we repaired to the Governor's, whose unremitting attention to his guests rendered the day very agreeable, could we but have forgotten that it was the eve of our separation from Captain King and his Lady, whose affability had so much contributed to the pleasantry of our voyage thus far; and who, with Captain and Mrs. Patterson and several other military officers destined for Norfolk Island, set sail the next day, accompanied to the end of the cove by the Governor, Judge Advocate, Captain Parker, and many others, who were anxious to be in their company as long as possible.

From the first of our arrival at Port Jackson, no time had been lost in preparing for our return to England. The embarkation of the marines,[36] with their wives twenty five in number, and their children forty-seven, the caulking of the vessel, the clergyman of the New Corps coming on-board to read divine service for the last time, in short every thing began to remind me of our departure.

The ship, when ready for sea, was very differently stored to what it was when we left the Cape of Good Hope in July. In lieu of live stock and all kind of necessary provisions, our bark was now crowded with Kangaroos, Opposums, and every curiosity which that country produced. The quarter-deck was occupied with shrubs and plants, whilst the cabin was hung around with skins of animals. We had also procured a variety of birds. I was so fortunate as to bring to England a bronzed wing, and two pair of Norfolk Island pigeons; they are now alive and well, and are, I believe the only birds of the kind ever brought to this country.[37]

The uniform attention which the Governor paid us during our short stay at the colony will always be remembered with singular satisfaction:—he may be justly called, like the Monarch of Great Britain, *"The Father of his People;"* and the Convict, who has forsaken the crimes that sent him to this country, looks up to him with reverence, and enjoys the reward of his industry in peace and thankfulness:—indeed, the kindness which we experienced from all around was such, that to have left the colony without a considerable degree of regret at parting from them would have shewn much ingratitude.

On the 17th of December, after supping at the Governor's, we repaired on-board, where every one was busily engaged in lashing and securing such things as were intended to be conveyed to England: it was my occupation to look after the birds, and to place them in the safest and most convenient manner I possibly could.

18th. Anchor being weighed, we set sail at 7 o'clock P.M.

19th. Fresh breezes, and rather squally.

20th. We found ourselves at the North Head of Port Jackson, with fresh breezes. At midnight hard squalls from all parts of the compass.

21st. At 4 A.M. heavy rain with lightning; at 6, violent squalls of wind, with a deluge of rain, severe thunder and lightning, the wind flying around the compass, and the ship labouring very much. At 10, we brought-to, the unsettled weather not permitting us to sail, except on the Southerly tack. At 8 P.M. the sea struck the vessel on the starboard quarter, which occasioned the plants on the deck to give way, the noise of which sounded so dismal in the cabbin, that I, who was at that time much oppressed with the sea-sickness, imagined that the fate of our bark was fast approaching.

22d. Still squally and much rain.

23d. The dead-lights in; every thing very wet from the quantity of rain which had fallen, and myself very sick.

24th. The weather moderate throughout the 24 hours.—On this day the ship's company were put to the allowance of *five* pints of water per day, as a necessary precaution against future accidents.

25th. Moderate and cloudy, with lightning to the Southward. On looking out for land, we saw Lord Howe's Island, a small spot discovered by Captain Wallis, and called, by the inhabitants of the Society Island, *Mophea*; it lies in South latitude 16° 46″, and West longitude 154° 8″. At 5 P.M. we saw Mount *Lidgbird* S.E. by E. The Cutters were sent on shore to seek for turtle; Lieutenant Ball having met with plenty when he first discovered this Island.

26th. We tacked the ship to the Northward of Lord Howe's Island. The Cutters returned without meeting with any success. There are goats, and a great number of brown birds about the size of our crows: the noise made by this bird is loud and unpleasant, and when dressed the flavour is strong and disagreeable.[38]

27th. At 4 A. M. we saw Mount *Gower*, distance about 8 or 9 leagues N.N.E. from *Ball's Pyramid*. At 6 A. M. we discovered Ring's Point. At noon we met with fresh breezes and squally weather, which continued with little variation to the end of the month.

On the 1st day of January, 1792, about midnight, a large Meteor was seen in the South-West quarter, which took its course towards the North-West. Until the 5th instant, we had moderate weather, which afforded me the satisfaction of partaking in the chearful parties of those who were within our wooden walls. Upon looking out for land, we discovered the *Three Kings Head* Island off the North end of New Zealand. At 4 we saw the Coast of New Zealand. At half past 4, saw Cape Maria, at which time Van Dieman's land bore S. by W. and the North Cape S. E. by E. distant 7 or 8 leagues. It is remarkable that the land from Cape Maria to the North Cape appears to be desolate, barren, and rocky, without the least verdure or tree, excepting on the summit of a hill over *Sandy Bay*, where there appear *five* or *six*.

CHAP. X.

The voyage continued—discover a number of Ice-islands—description of them—singular story of a Shark—with an anecdote relative thereto.

I shall not here trouble my readers with the regular dates and little variations customary in these distant latitudes; but simply notice the weather, which was mostly fresh breezes, hazy, and squally—splitting of sails, passing rock-weed, sea-weed, and such like occurrences, met with by voyagers in general.

On the 14th we saw several whales, much rock-weed, and birds of different sorts.

16th. Cloudy, with a heavy swell from N.E. Saw a number of silver birds.

17th. Observed a curious porpoise, with a white bill and under-jaw, also a number of brown-winged birds around the ship.

18th. Fresh gales and squally; passed a number of porpoises.

19th. At 4 P.M. the wind shifted suddenly with a heavy squall from N.N.E. to W.S.W. and continued so the remainder of the night.

20th. The same uncomfortable weather, with a long Westerly swell. Saw several whales. This weather continued with little variation during the remainder of the month.

The beginning of February, we had frequent squalls and heavy seas, with rain, hail, and sleet.

On the 7th, we discovered *Tierra del Fuego*, and *York Minster*, bearing N.E. by N. distant about 7 or 8 leagues.

8th. Fresh breezes and hazy; York Minster bore N. N. W. $\frac{1}{4}$ W. 8 or 9 leagues.—In the afternoon of the same day, the central Isle of *Il de Fonzo* bore N. N. W. $\frac{3}{4}$ W. 8 or 9 leagues. At 4, land was seen at the mast-head, supposed to be the Island *Diego*. The extreme land to the N. W. $\frac{1}{2}$ W. was supposed to be *Cape Horn*, and that to the Eastward *Barnwell Islands*. At $\frac{1}{2}$ past 5, the land supposed *Cape Horn* bore W. N. W. 6 or 7 leagues.

The 12th was thick and foggy, with rain and fresh breezes. We saw albertrosses, penguins, and apparently some land-birds, supposed to come from Saint George's or Falkland Islands.

14th. We had almost a calm, saw some land-birds, and caught one which was rather larger than a full-sized pigeon. Passed Willis's Island, South Georgia, East 125 leagues.

16th. Discovered penguins and various other birds. The sea ran very high, and a hard gale struck the ship violently.

17th. The same blustering weather, with increasing gales. Saw several seals, penguins, and porpoises, whales and sea-weed.

The ensuing morning, at 4 o'clock, several Ice-islands appeared in sight. By the advice of Captain Parker I arose to partake of this uncommon *spectacle*. The course of one hour brought *seven* to our view, bearing E. by N. to N. N.W. distance from the nearest *three* leagues. From this time until 10 o'clock several ice-islands were seen. In order to support my drooping spirits, I retired for a short time to strengthen my resolution, a precaution by no means unnecessary, as I could not help reflecting on the number of navigators who had been arrested and frozen to death in the midst of these tremendous masses; it was in this manner that the brave Sir Hugh Willoughby was lost, with all his crew, in 1553,[39] and in like manner Lord Mulgrave in the year 1773 was caught in the ice, and nearly experienced the same unhappy fate.[40]

If it were possible for voyagers to divest themselves of the horror which the eventful expectation of change must ever occasion; the view is at once both beautiful and picturesque, even to the most incurious eye: the forms assumed by the ice are extremely pleasing and grotesque; the water which dashes against the ice freezes into a variety of forms, and almost into every shape which the imagination can frame.[41]

The novelty of the sight engaged the attention of every one on-board. About 7 o'clock we beheld no less than *fifteen* of these tremendous islands at one time, which obliged us to haul our wind, and bear up frequently in order to sail clear of them. Between the hours of 8 and 10 we passed *nine* more, and at that time a large body or field of ice appeared from North to W.N.W. our distance from it was about 9 miles. We hauled our wind to W. S. W. which course we ran for *seven* or *eight* miles; the northernmost part of the field then bore N.N.E. $\frac{1}{2}$ E. and the westernmost N. W. $\frac{1}{4}$ W. One of the Islands was $17\frac{3}{4}$ miles in length, and that on the farthest extremity was no less than $52\frac{1}{2}$ miles. At meridian the nearest distance was about 6 miles.

On Sunday the 19th, the weather was moderate and hazy. At noon the dulness of the hemisphere, and the sun appearing very faintly, made many suppose land to be in sight; but, on sounding 120 fathom, no ground was found: at 10 o'clock the sun shining bright, all parties were convinced it was an ice-bank; this large field or body, by the different bearings, was thought to be near 18 miles in length, as appeared by the distance run by the log, and by the workings of the different courses that the ship had sailed from 10 A. M. in their their last log until 5 P.M. in this, when the extremes of it bore East about 8 or 9 miles. At 6 o'clock the extremes of the ice in sight bore S. E. $\frac{1}{2}$ S. distance 3 or 4 leagues. This most tremendous field made the twenty-ninth island of ice we had sailed past, from 5 A.M. until 5 P.M. In the course of the day we discovered a number of birds, seals, and porpoises: the evening was very blustering, during the greater part of which the ship lay-to, and every one appeared anxious to know the event of this dismal night.

On the 21st, we had a continuance of dark and dismal weather, attended with heavy gales, incessant sleet, and violent labourings of the ship.—Indeed, all our little comforts were done away by anxiety, sea-sickness, and darkness; the turbulent waves rendering it necessary for the dead-lights to be up on all sides; and the intense cold obliged us to have stoves and hot shot slung to heat the different cabins.

The 22nd. a great swell remained from the last gale; the appearance of ice was seen to windward again E. by S. to N. E. by N. also whales, birds, rock-weed, together with lightning all round the compass.

These heavy seas and hard gales were our chief attendants until the 27th, when the weather became more moderate, and we once more began to entertain the hope of revisiting those friends, whom we had almost despaired of seeing again: but the anxiety of mind, which I had laboured under for some time, would have been much more poignant had I not been participating the fate of so many others whose good example and patient resignation taught me to consider that I was but an insignificant individual amongst them.—Nay, had the danger been inevitable, it would have been some consolation in approaching destruction, to have had a prospect of sharing the same fate with him whose virtues I am left to bewail.

Hazy damp weather continued during the first part of the month of March. We discovered frequent shoals of porpoises, also Cape hens, albertrosses, and other birds. Singular as the circumstance may at first appear, a large shark was caught, on opening of which an old Prayer-book, now in my possession, was taken out of its belly; those who know the ravenous appetite of this rapacious fish, will not be surprised at the explanation—as there was a marine on-board whose name was written in it, but who probably from fear of punishment denied that it was his. It appears to have belonged formerly to a convict, as on one of the leaves was written "TO DIE," and underneath "REPRIEVED," with a space left on purpose to insert the day of the month. The above circumstance is probably *unique*.[42] It was wittily observed, on the occasion, that it would not have been so astonishing if a *Law*-book had been found instead of a *Prayer*-book,—as the shark was always thought more of the *Lawyer* than the *Parson*, being called by sailors a *Sea-Lawyer*; as the following little anecdote, related to me upon this occasion, will fully evince.

A certain Judge, on his passage to the East-Indies, looking in distant amaze at the flouncing of an enormous shark, upon which the sailors were operating, enquired with retiring trepidation, "what the prodigious creature could possibly be?" "*Nothing*," replied a Tar, in a tone of voice better conceived than expressed,—"*Nothing, your Honour, but a Sea-Lawyer*."

The prospect now began to brighten; the expectation of returning safe to the Cape, revived our drooping spirits. Dinner-parties, cards, &c. were once more the pastime of those on-board: even our little birds and plants appeared sensible of the return of sunshine and tranquillity.

Chap. XI.

Arrive at Table-Bay—take up our abode at Mr. Peter de Witt's—mild treatment of the Slaves at the Cape—a Gentoo—a visit to Constantia— return to Cape Town.

On the 12th of March, land was once more in view, and at 6 o'clock in the evening the ship was running into *Table-Bay*, where we found two Dutch frigates, a brig of war, several Dutch Indiamen, and ships of different nations. We saw no one from shore that night. Happy at our safe arrival after so many anxieties, the remainder of the evening passed away very agreeably, and the next morning at an early hour one of our officers went on-shore, and returned, accompanied by Mr. Peter de Witt, with fresh butter, lemons, grapes, figs, apples, meat, and vegetables; refreshments which we began to stand in need of; for, although we did not absolutely want provisions, our stores in general were nearly exhausted; the sheep we took from this place had lost so much that the whole quarter when boiled has not been larger than a fore quarter of lamb.

When we formerly landed at the Cape, my readers will remember, that we lodged at Mrs. de Witt's. We now took our abode at the house of Mr. Peter de Witt's, a son of the good lady above-mentioned. Colonel and Mrs. Gordon lost no time in paying their congratulations upon our return, and renewing their friendly invitations; as did also the Governor, whose name was Monsieur Renies. The Colonel was so obliging as to send his carriage for me; and on my arrival at his villa I had the pleasure of finding all our marine officers, and such of our gentlemen as could be spared from the ship; for, although safely landed in this healthful and plentiful country, we all had sufficient reasons for wishing to proceed on our voyage.

We found the family in good health, nor was their polite attention in the least diminished; nay, after our being confined on-board for three months, even the villa itself appeared, if possible, more beautiful than before.

The lady of Mr. de Witt was extremely attentive to us, and endeavoured to render our abode as comfortable as possible. According to the best of my recollection there were thirty slaves belonging to this house.

The beauty of one of the females particularly struck my attention; the elegance of her deportment, the symmetry of her features, and the pleasing curl of her fine dark hair, could not pass unnoticed by any, excepting those who were unwilling to pay that tribute to the simplicity of nature, which all the assistance of art could not place them in the possession of.

With satisfaction I noticed that the slaves were treated at the Cape with the greatest humanity: and only in name bore the degrading distinction.

They are let out by the month, week, or day, during which time they are obliged to earn for their masters a certain fixed sum. The male slaves wear their own hair, upon which they set a great value, wrapped up in a handkerchief, somewhat like a turban; the females wreath up theirs, and fix it on their heads with a large pin. Trowsers constitute the other part of their dress; and as a token of their servile condition, they always go barefooted, and without a hat.

Previous to sitting down to meals, it is the custom of the Cape for a female slave to bring a bason and a towel for the company to wash their hands; which is repeated on rising from table. In the houses of the wealthy, every one of the company has a slave behind his chair to wait upon him: this slave has frequently a large palm-leaf in his hand, by way of a fan to drive away the flies, which are extremely troublesome in these climates.

The company's gardens, at a small distance from Cape Town, are very pleasant, and the chief resort of persons of respectability in that country. Mrs. Gordon has frequently called upon me in her carriage, and obliged me with a ride to see them; and nothing could be more refreshing than the fragrant evening breezes that generally prevail in these hot climates.

Our time was now taken up in visiting and receiving visits; we had several invitations from the Governor, where the entertainments were elegant, and the company numerous, consisting chiefly of marine officers, and those belonging to our ship.

On the 18th, a Dutch Indiaman arrived from Batavia, and shortly after we were gratified with the company of Captain Edwards, of his Majesty's ship the Pandora, who a few days after landing embarked, and afterwards pursued his voyage in our ship: the convicts also who had escaped from Port Jackson were taken up at sea by the Pandora, and returned to England in the Gorgon.[43]

About this time I had the pleasure of receiving a visit from Mrs. Johnson, a lady who had arrived at the Cape on her return from the East Indies. I was also introduced, by Colonel Burrington, to the acquaintance of a lady, who was so obliging as to favour me with the sight of a Gentoo,[44] which is indeed singular in every respect; they having a gold ring upon almost every toe, also in their ears and noses, and large silver rings round the ancles; they wear the hair fastened with a silver pin and a curious piece of India muslin, which negligently, though not inelegantly, almost covers their bodies.

A party of us had fixed a day for a jaunt to Constantia, a little district at the Cape of Good Hope, consisting of two farms, which produce the wellknown wine so much prized in Europe. It is situated at the distance of a mile and a half from *Alphen*, in a bending, formed by and nearly under the ridge of hills, which comes from Muysen-Mountain, and just where it strikes off towards *Houtbay*. One of these farms is called Little Constantia: here the white wine is made; the other produces the red.

On the morning of the day appointed we set out in two carriages, each containing four persons, and the gentlemen on horseback. We had rode but a very little way before we were overtaken by a smart shower of rain; and as the front seats of the vehicle were not sheltered from it, we were sprinkled in a short time to such a degree that, when we arrived at the end of our journey, we found ourselves necessitated to refer for a change of cloathing to the good people of the house, who willingly granted our request although we were entire strangers to them.

We met here the Governor of Cape Town, with some captains and officers belonging to the Dutch Man of War then lying at Table-Bay. It being the usual compliment in that Country for the Lady of the house to resign her seat at the table, I was invested with that honour, and accordingly placed at the head of a numerous party, (mostly strangers,) deprived of all the decorations which vanity, a few hours before, had induced me to bestow upon myself; for, my coat and hat being wet through, I was furnished with a large white jacket belonging to the lady of the house, one half of which I could have spared with great convenience.

We were received and entertained with attention and respect, and tasted the different sorts of the famous wine which borrows its name from the spot where the grapes grow; although I think I have eaten a similar grape in the Mediterranean; which conjecture is in some measure confirmed by the great quantity of wine that appears under this name;—if I am wrong in my suspicions, these small vineyards must afford a profusion indeed!

The weather continued much the same during the remainder of the day; however, as we were none of us strangers to a watery element, it rendered it less troublesome to all, and we returned in our borrowed garbs to Cape Town, well pleased with our visit; and affording no small amusement to our friends, from the laughable appearance which we made.

This excursion served us frequently for conversation, and was nearly the last we took during our stay.

Chap. XII.

Some account of Cape Town—departure from the Cape—Ascension Road—the voyage continued—reach Saint Helens—land at Portsmouth—arrive in London—Conclusion.

On our return to the Cape, I took several opportunities of walking about the town, in which there are many excellent gardens laid out in the neatest taste, and producing fruit and culinary vegetables in great abundance.

The extensive and beautiful garden belonging to the Company is always open to the publick; and it is from this garden that the stranger, on his arrival, meets with his first refreshments.

The town is adorned with three large squares, in one of which stands the Protestant church; it likewise has a fountain in it, which furnishes the inhabitants with water. In the other is the Town-hall. The third is laid out for the convenience of the country people, who bring their goods to market.

While I was passing my time thus agreeably at the Cape, Captain Parker and the officers were more essentially employed in the necessary preparations both for our safety and support. The Governor and Colonel

Gordon's family seemed to study what presents might be most acceptable for us when we next embarked; owing to their goodness, we added, to our stores, wine, goats, liquors, and many other refreshments which were likely to be serviceable to us.

The Ostrich feather is one of the most gaudy and valuable purchases that can be made in this country; and, to those who are amateurs of birds, I can, from experience, recommend the Cape Canary; the plumage of which is much like our green linnet, the breast more yellow, and the colour, if any thing, more lively; it has a very pretty note, and, what renders it still more agreeable, is its being rather louder, though similar to that general favourite and winter companion, the sprightly Robin. One morning I purchased *sixteen*, and the cage containing them, for the moderate sum of *four* shillings and *six* pence.

On the 31st, we took our final dinner at the hospitable villa before mentioned, and reluctantly bade adieu to the good Colonel and his lady, whose attention to strangers I have signified in the former part of this narrative.

The last farewel being taken, accompanied by a considerable number of our friends, we once more repaired on-board, after having passed a month at the Cape with much satisfaction and pleasure. I began now to turn my thoughts towards Old England, and encouraged the pleasing expectation of being shortly in the company of a mother and two dear children, from whom I had been so long absent.

Our birds, &c. being replaced and lashed as before, we set sail on the 6th of April. With moderate weather we continued our voyage to Saint Helena, which Island was first seen on the 18th at midnight, and by $\frac{1}{2}$ past 7 in the morning we could perceive three ships in the road, viz. 1 Swedish, 1 English Indiaman, and a Whaler. The necessity of returning with the dispatches of the Colony as speedily as possible left us no time for delay at this island; we therefore contented ourselves with viewing the shore at a considerable distance; thus, favoured with pleasant breezes and trade-winds, we rolled merrily on till the 23d, when we anchored in 15 fathom, at *Ascension Road*. At this uninhabited Island we found the *Betsy*, an American schooner, with the master, his wife, and four or five men on-board, without a grain of tea or scarcely any provisions. Our boats were sent on-shore, with men, to try if it were possible to procure some turtle; they shortly returned with a sufficient quantity, which was of infinite service to numbers on-board.

The sea continued tranquil and the ship still, which made our short stay very agreeable. After leaving the body of a child on shore for interment, we again set sail on the 25th.

The moderate weather, and fine trade-winds, added to the pleasing hope of seeing our friends in a little time, made the remainder of our voyage appear short. The beginning of the month of May, we had light winds and frequent calms, which tended to prolong our journey, and to do away the expectations we had formed of returning to Spithead about the 6th of June.

However, the intrusion of calms was easily endured by us; for, after sailing so many thousand miles together, our little parties were, if possible, more agreeable than at first setting-out, and for this reason it must not be supposed that our friendship for each other had in the least degree diminished, but much the contrary.

About the middle of June, we reached Saint Helens: Captain Parker and the other gentlemen, intrusted with government dispatches, fixed the same evening for their departure for London. Captain Edwards accompanied me on-shore, and after four hours rowing against wind and tide, we landed at the *Salley Port*, at Portsmouth, where we were met by many, who, astonished at the speedy return of our ship, cheerfully congratulated us on our arrival.

We repaired to the Fountain Inn, and, after seeing the above gentlemen set off for London, I retired to rest. Early the next morning, accompanied by one of our officers, I took chaise, and arrived in town at 8 o'clock the same evening, where I had the happiness of again embracing an affectionate mother, and a little daughter, who is at this present time one of my greatest comforts; my other child, a boy, had died during my absence. This vacancy in my family did not, however, remain long after my arrival; for on the Thursday *following*, Captain Parker had luckily taken lodgings in Frith-street, Soho, *in the morning*, where, after a short ride from my friend's house, I was safe in bed at 4 o'clock in the afternoon. This little boy is of the number of those for whose *benefit*, by the advice of my friends, I have taken the liberty to set forth this narrative; humbly hoping that my kind readers will pass over the many faults with which it abounds, when they reflect that it was written under the pressure of mind, occasioned by the unexpected loss of him, who was indeed an indulgent husband, and a tender parent. The youngest of these fatherless children is an infant of *seven* months, who has chiefly been on my left arm, whilst the right was employed in bringing once more to my recollection the pleasing occurrences of *fifteen* months, spent in the company of *him*, whose kind attention supported me under all my affliction:—but the scene is changed—a retrospect of the *past* tends only to augment my present calamities; whilst the *future* presents nothing to my view but the gloomy prospect of additional misfortunes and additional sorrows!

FINIS.

EDITOR'S NOTES

1. John Parker (1749–1794), appointed Lieutenant 1783, promoted to commander in 1790.

2. In 1789 the soldier Francis Grose (1758?–1814) was appointed Lieutenant-Governor of New South Wales and Commandant of the New South Wales Corps which he had helped to raise. The Corps were to replace the First Fleet marines.

3. Philip Gidley King (1758–1808) was the first navy officer in charge of the new settlement at Norfolk Island. He served there from 1788 until 1790, when he returned to England, married Anna Josepha Coombe in March 1791, then embarked a few days later on the *Gorgon*. His 'family' at this stage consisted of two illegitimate boys born on Norfolk Island to the convict Ann Inett. The first child of his marriage was born December 1791, and named Phillip Parker King, after Captain Parker. Philip Gidley King was later to be Governor of New South Wales from 1800 to 1807.

4. David Burton (d. 1792) was appointed superintendent of convicts, but was paid privately by Sir Joseph Banks to collect seeds and botanical specimens; the *Gorgon* left carrying 60 of his tubs of plants and sundry other boxes. Charles Grimes (1772–1858) was deputy surveyor of roads on Norfolk Island; the chaplain James Bain (*fl.* 1789–1794) served first at Parramatta, then at Norfolk Island.

5. Teneriffe, now one of the Canary Islands, in the North Atlantic Ocean, about 70 miles west of the Moroccan coast of Africa.

6. Puerto Oratava, about 34 kilometres south west of Santa Cruz.

7. Peter Rye, *An Excursion to the peak of Teneriffe, in 1791; being the substance of a letter to Joseph Jekyll . . . from Lieutenant Rye, of the Royal Navy* (London: R. Falder, 1793). An excerpt from this appeared in the *Lady's Magazine*, June 1794. I am grateful to Anette Bremer for locating this magazine excerpt.

8. From Nicholas Rowe's play, *The Ambitious Step-Mother: A Tragedy* (London: Peter Buck, 1701).

9. For a lively account of some of the homoerotic horseplay associated with this ceremony, see John Nicol's account of the *Lady Juliana*'s crossing in 1791 in *John Nicol, Life and Adventures, 1776–1801*, ed. T. Flannery (Melbourne: Text Publishing, 1997), p. 127. Greg Dening describes crossing the line as 'play of a serious and disturbing sort'. For an illuminating analysis of why Captain Bligh denounced the custom as 'most brutal and inhuman', see Dening's *Mr Bligh's Bad Language: Passion, Power and Theatre on the Bounty* (Cambridge: Cambridge University Press, 1992), pp. 77–80.

10. William Paterson (1755–1810), soldier, explorer, amateur botanist and friend of Banks. In 1789 he was gazetted Captain in the New South Wales Corps, which he also helped to recruit. Upon arrival in Port Jackson, he was sent to Norfolk Island where he served from 1791 to 1793. King appointed him lieutenant-governor of the colony in 1800. Four years before sailing in the *Gorgon* he married Elizabeth Driver (1760?–1825), described by Ralph Clark as 'a good

coasy Scott Lass and fit for a Soldiers wife'; see Ralph Clark, *The Journal and Letters of Lt. Ralph Clark, 1787–1792* (Sydney: Australian Documents Library, 1981), p. 221.

11. George Johnstone (1730–1787), British Commodore and Member of Parliament. After The Netherlands entered the war against Britain in 1780, Johnstone was given command of a squadron in 1781, with instructions to attack Cape Town. Control of the Cape was considered vital for protecting the sea route to India, but Johnstone's mission failed.

12. In the 1790s Batavia was the declining centre of the Dutch East India Company's operations. Pollution of its canals and drinking water made it an unwholesome place to visit. Batavia is now Jakarta, capital city of Indonesia.

13. Sir William Draper (1721–1787), lieutenant-general, served in Madras, Brittany and Spain. The lines are probably from the cenotaph he raised on his family estate for the 30 officers and 1000 soldiers who died in the East Indies in the period 1758–1765. Like Captain Parker, many of these men had died of fever.

14. A sweet and heavy dessert wine.

15. The year 1790 saw the publication of several narratives concerning Captain Edward Riou (1762–1801) and the wreck of the *Guardian* on an iceberg in December 1789. One of these narratives claimed to print 'authentic copies' of Riou's letters to the Admiralty; see J. A. Ferguson's *Bibliography of Australia*, vol. 1, *1784–1830* (Canberra: National Library of Australia, 1941), p. 37. Riou's name was synonymous with heroism in this period; he did his best to repair the ship's damage, and would not leave until the very last.

16. Robert Jacob Gordon (1743–1795) was an explorer, and colonel in charge of the Cape Garrison. He was the author of extensive travel diaries, maps, charts and diverse scientific writings, including detailed descriptions of the mode of living, religion, customs and language of the Bushmen and Hottenots, none of which were published until this century. After his death in 1795, the British Government asked Riou to value his collection for purchase.

17. Mrs Gordon was Susanne Marguerite Nicolet, from Lignerolle, Switzerland. The couple had four sons.

18. Paterson first visited South Africa in 1777, and made four journeys into the interior over the next few years. In 1789 he published *Narrative of Four Journeys into the Country of the Hottentots and Caffraria* (London: J. Johnson, 1789), which he dedicated to Sir Joseph Banks; a second edition appeared a year later in 1790, to be followed by one German and eight French editions. Some of Colonel Gordon's extensive knowledge about the country interior of the Cape passed into Paterson's book.

19. Mount Dromedary is approximately 300 kilometres south of Port Jackson.

20. This account of the lightning strike is taken more or less verbatim from Captain Parker's log.

21. 'The Supply wanted wood for a mast, and more than forty of the choicest young trees were cut down before as much wood as would make it could be procured' (Watkin Tench, *A Complete Account of the Settlement at Port Jackson, in New South Wales* (London: G. Nicol, 1793), p. 164; hereafter *Complete Account*).

22. This excerpt is from Captain John Parker's report to Admiralty, 2 July 1792. According to David Collins, the colony's legal officer, when two transports of the Second Fleet arrived together at Port Jackson at the end of June, 1790, the lifting out of the transports' dead and living 'exhibited more horrid spectacles than had ever been witnessed in this country' (David Collins, *Account of the English Colony in New South Wales* (London: T. Cadell, 1798), p. 122).

23. Native Sarsaparilla (*smilax glycyphylla*), drunk by the early settlers as a substitute for tea, and highly prized as a remedy against scurvy. It was also believed to enhance fertility. John Nicol, steward aboard the *Lady Juliana* transport (1790), recalled: 'There was an old female convict, her hair quite grey with age, her face shrivelled, who was suckling a child she had borne in the colony ... Her fecundity was ascribed to the sweet tea' (Nicol, *Life and Adventures*, pp. 130–131).

24. John Hunter (1737–1821) was an explorer, and later Governor of New South Wales 1795–1800. He published *An Historical Journal of the Transactions at Port Jackson and Norfolk Island, with the discoveries that have been made in New South Wales and the Southern Ocean* (London: John Stockdale, 1793).

25. David Collins (1756–1810), deputy judge-advocate, was responsible, under the Governor, for the colony's entire legal establishment. In 1798 he published his illustrated *An Account of the English Colony in New South Wales: with remarks on the dispositions, customs, manners &c. of the native inhabitants of that country* (London: T. Cadell, 1798).

26. John Palmer (1760–1833) came out on the First Fleet as purser of Governor Phillip's flag-ship, *Sirius*. He had only just been made commissary, an important post in which he was responsible for the reception and issue of all Government stores.

27. 'The general face of the country is certainly pleasing, being diversified with gentle ascents, and little winding vallies ... a variety of flowering shrubs abound ... among these, a tall shrub, bearing an elegant white flower, which smells like English May, is particularly delightful, and perfumes the air around to a great distance ... Grass ... grows ... with the greatest vigour and luxuriancy, though it is not of the finest quality, and is found to agree better with horses and cows than sheep' (Watkin Tench, *A Narrative of the Expedition to Botany Bay* (London: J. Debrett, 1789), pp. 118–19; hereafter *Narrative of the Expedition*).

28. Reverend Richard Johnson (1753–1827) was a Church of England clergyman. He came out on the First Fleet as Chaplain to the settlement.

29. The more usual spelling is Parramatta, an aboriginal word meaning head of the river, or the place where eels lie down.

30. In March 1791, Elizabeth Macarthur wrote that the harbour was 'universally allow'd to be the finest in the known World ... it is so beautifully form'd that I can conceive nothing equal to it, branching out into a number of Arms, and Coves, forming little Islands, and points of Land, so agreeable and romantic that the most fanciful imagination must tire, and I think allow himself to be outdone and yield the palm to reality and simple nature'; see *The Journal and Letters of Elizabeth Macarthur, 1789–1798*, ed. Joy N. Hughes (Glebe: Historic Houses Trust of New South Wales, 1984), p. 26.

31. A few months later, in an admiring description of the gardens at Government House, Rose Hill, Tench commented on the excellent condition of the small fruit trees brought in the *Gorgon* from the Cape (*Complete Account*, p. 143).

32. In Tench we read of the 'greasy filth their skins are loaded with', the 'fish bone struck through the gristle of the nose' (*Narrative of the Expedition*, pp. 78–79).

33. Of their huts Tench writes: 'nothing more rude in construction, or deficient in conveniency, can be imagined. They consist only of pieces of bark laid together in the form of an oven, open at one end, and very low, though long enough for a man to lie at full length in. There is reason, however, to believe, that they depend less on them for shelter, than on the caverns with which the rocks abound' (*Narrative of the Expedition*, p. 80).

34. 'Their honesty, when tempted by novelty, is not unimpeachable; but in their own society, there is good reason to believe, that few breaches of it occur' (*Complete Account*, p. 190).

35. William Cowper, 'The Negro's Complaint', *The Poetical Works of William Cowper*, ed. H. S. Milford (London: Oxford University Press, 1934), p. 371.

36. The marines included James Scott, together with his wife and two young children. See James Scott, *Remarks on a Passage to Botany Bay, 1787–1792* (Sydney: Trustees of the Public Library of New South Wales in association with Angus and Robertson, 1963).

37. Such was the beauty of these pigeons that the anonymous Sydney Bird Painter used gold paint to suggest their brilliant and beautiful bronze feathers, which change into red, copper and green in different reflections of light.

38. Scott was so eager to secure some birds to take back to England with him that he offered a guinea for a pair of 'live pidgons' when the cutters went on shore at Lord Howe Island (*Remarks*, p. 70).

39. Willoughby was the commander of an expedition to discover and explore a north-east passage to the far east; two of his three ships had to seek refuge in a bay on the coast of Lapland, but perished in the long Russian winter. In the spring of 1554, Russian fishermen found the two vessels, with all the frozen men aboard.

40. Constantine John Phipps (Baron Mulgrave), *A Voyage towards the north pole: undertaken by his Majesty's command, 1773* (Dublin: Sleater, William &c., 1775).

41. 'The Ice lookd beutifull. When close to. it. forming Many, Angles, Concaves Convexes. Cones &c. &c. some part resembling. fortifications. Houses, &c—' (Scott, *Remarks*, p. 73).

42. Lt Ralph Clark records the shark and Bible incident (*Journal and Letters*, p. 233).

43. This short paragraph is silent about a number of quite remarkable events. Captain Edward Edwards's mission had been to round up the Bounty mutineers in the South Seas. The wreck of his ship, the *Pandora*, with the loss of almost 40 people, had been told in 1793 by George Hamilton, the ship's surgeon, in *A Voyage round the World, in His Majesty's Frigate Pandora. Performed under the Direction of Captain Edwards in the Years 1790, 1791,*

1792. With the Discoveries made in the South-Sea; and the many Distresses experienced by the Crew from Shipwreck and Famine, in a Voyage of Eleven Hundred Miles in open Boats, between Endeavour Straits and the Island of Timor (London: B. Law & Son, 1793). The 'convicts' were Mary Bryant (b. 1765) and four others, survivors of a remarkable escape from Port Jackson; see Tench, *Complete Account*, p. 108. For the story of these escapees, see C. H. Currey, *The Transportation, Escape and Pardoning of Mary Bryant* (Sydney: Angus and Robertson, 1963).

44. Gentoo: Hindu.

BIBLIOGRAPHY

WRITINGS BY ANNA MARIA FALCONBRIDGE

Two Voyages to Sierra Leone during the years 1791–2–3, In a Series of Letters. To which is added a Letter from the Author, to Henry Thornton, Esq. M. P. and Chairman of the Court of Directors of the Sierra Leone Company (London: Printed for the Author, and sold by different Booksellers throughout the Kingdom, 1794).

Narrative of Two Voyages to the River Sierra Leone, during the years 1791–2–3, performed by A. M. Falconbridge. With a succinct account of the Distresses and Proceedings of that Settlement; a description of the Manners, Diversions, Arts, Commerce, Cultivation, Custom, Punishments, etc. And Every interesting Particular relating to the Sierra Leone Company. Also the Present State of the Slave Trade in the West Indies, and the improbability of its total Abolition, 2nd edn (London: L. I. Higham, 1802).

WRITINGS BY MARY ANN PARKER

A Voyage Round the World, in the Gorgon Man of War: Captain John Parker. Performed and Written by his Widow; for the advantage of a numerous family (London: John Nichols, 1795).

A Voyage Round the World, facs. ed. by Gavin Fry (Potts Point: Hordern House for the Australian National Maritime Museum, 1991).

WORKS CITED OR ALLUDED TO IN THE ORIGINALS

Falconbridge

John Nicholson Inglefield, 1747–1828, *Captain Inglefield's Narrative of the Loss of the Centaur, in 1782 ... a literal extract of his letter to the Admiralty, written from Fayal in 1782. Also, a copy of the ... court martial ... officers of the Centaur* (London: J. Murray and A. Donaldson, 1783).

Matthews, John, *A Voyage to the River Sierra-Leone, on the Coast of Africa; containing an Account of the Trade and Productions of the Country, and of the Civil and Religious Customs and Manners of the People; in a series of Letters to a Friend in England, during his Residence in that Country in the Years 1785, 1786 and 1787. With an additional letter on the African Slave Trade* (London: B. White and Son, 1788; 2nd edn 1791).

Parker

William Cowper, 'The Negro's Complaint', *The Poetical Works of William Cowper*, ed. H. S. Milford (London: Oxford University Press, 1934).

Constantine John Phipps (Baron Mulgrave), *A Voyage towards the north pole: undertaken by his Majesty's command, 1773* (Dublin: Sleater, William &c, 1775).

Nicholas Rowe, *The Ambitious Step-Mother: A Tragedy* (London: Peter Buck, 1701).

Lt. Peter Rye, *An Excursion to the peak of Teneriffe, in 1791; being the substance of a letter to Joseph Jekyll ... from Lieutenant Rye, of the Royal Navy* (London: R. Falder, 1793).

Watkin Tench, *A Narrative of the Expedition to Botany Bay* (London: J. Debrett, 1789).

WORKS CITED BY THE EDITOR

Manuscript

Abolition and Emancipation, Part 1: Papers of Thomas Clarkson, William Lloyd Garrison, Zachary Macaulay, Harriet Martineau, Harriet Beecher Stowe and William Wilberforce, from the Huntington Library, San Marino, California, 9 microform reels (Adam Matthews Publications, 1996).

Clarkson Papers, British Library, MS Add. 41262A, Add. 41262B, Add. 41263, Add. 41264.

DuBois, Isaac, Journal, British Library, Clarkson Papers, MS Add. 41263, vol. 3.

Printed Works

Abbott, G. J., 'The Botany Bay Decision', *Journal of Australian Studies*, 16 (May, 1985), pp. 21–45.

An Abstract of the Evidence delivered before a Select Committee of the House of Commons in the years 1790, and 1791; on the part of the Petitioners for the Abolition of the Slave-Trade (London: J. Phillips, 1791).

Afzelius, Adam, *Adam Afzelius: Sierra Leone Journal, 1795–1796*, ed. A. P. Kup (Uppsala: Studia Ethnographica Upsaliensia, 1967).

Altick, R. D., *The Shows of London* (Cambridge, MA: Belknap Press of Harvard University Press, 1978).

Astley, Thomas, *A New General Collection of Voyages and Travels ... in Europe, Asia, Africa, and America*, 4 vols (London: Thomas Astley, 1745–47).

Atkinson, Alan, *The Europeans in Australia: A History*, vol. 1. (3 vols planned) (Melbourne: Oxford University Press, 1997).

Bakhtin, Mikhail, *Rabelais and His World*, trans. Helene Iswolsky (Bloomington: Indiana University Press, 1984).

Barbauld, Anna Laetitia, *The Correspondence of Samuel Richardson*, 6 vols (London: Richard Phillips, 1804).

Beaver, Philip, *African Memoranda: relative to an attempt to establish a British settlement on the island of Bulama, on the western coast of Africa, in the year 1792* (London: C. & R. Baldwin, 1805).

Braidwood, Stephen, *Black Poor and White Philanthropists: London's Blacks and the Foundation of the Sierra Leone Settlement, 1786–1791* (Liverpool: Liverpool University Press, 1994).

British Critic: A New Review, 42 vols, 1793–1813.

Carretta, Vincent (ed.), *Unchained Voices: An Anthology of Black Authors in the English-speaking World of the 18th Century* (Lexington: University Press of Kentucky, 1996).

Clark, Ralph, *The Journal and Letters of Lt. Ralph Clark, 1787–1792* (Sydney: Australian Documents Library, 1981).

Clarkson, John, *Sierra Leone after a Hundred Years*, ed. E. G. Ingham (London: Frank Cass, 1968).

Clarkson, John, 'Diary of Lieutenant Clarkson, R. N.', *Sierra Leone Studies*, n. s., vol. 8 (March, 1927), pp. 1–114.

Coleman, Deirdre, 'Conspicuous Consumption: White Abolitionism and English Women's Protest Writing in the 1790s', *English Literary History*, 61 (Summer, 1994), pp. 341–62.

Coleman, Deirdre, 'Sierra Leone, Slavery, and Sexual Politics: Anna Maria Falconbridge and the "Swarthy Daughter"of Late 18th Century Abolitionism', *Women's Writing*, vol. 2, no. 1 (1995), pp. 3–23.

Coleridge, Samuel Taylor, *Lectures 1795: On Politics and Religion*, eds. L. Patton and P. Mann (Princeton: Princeton University Press, 1971).

Collins, David, *An Account of the English Colony in New South Wales: with remarks on the dispositions, customs, manners &c. of the native inhabitants of that country* (London: T. Cadell, 1798).

Cook, Elizabeth, *Epistolary Bodies: Gender and Genre in the Eighteenth-Century Republic of Letters* (Stanford: Stanford University Press, 1996).

Cugoano, Ottobah, *Thoughts and Sentiments on the Evil and Wicked Traffic of the Slavery and Commerce of the Human Species* (London, 1787).

Currey, C. H., *The Transportation, Escape and Pardoning of Mary Bryant* (Sydney: Angus and Robertson, 1963).

Darwin, Erasmus, *The Botanic Garden; A Poem, in Two Parts. Part I. Containing The Economy of Vegetation. Part II. The Loves of the Plants. With Philosophical Notes* (London: J. Johnson, 1791).

Davis, David Brion, *The Problem of Slavery in the Age of Revolution, 1770–1823* (Ithaca: Cornell University Press, 1975).

Defoe, Daniel, *A New Voyage round the World by a Course never sailed before* (London: A. Bettesworth, 1725).

Dening, Greg, *Mr Bligh's Bad Language: Passion, Power and Theatre on the Bounty* (Cambridge: Cambridge University Press, 1992).

Dorjahn, V. R. and Fyfe, C., 'Landlord and Stranger', *Journal of African History*, 3 (1962), pp. 391–97.

Edwards, Paul, 'Three West African Writers of the 1780s', in *The Slave's Narrative*, ed. C. T. Davis and H. L. Gates (Oxford: Oxford University Press, 1985).

Edwards, P. and Dabydeen, D. (eds), *Black Writers in Britain, 1760–1890* (Edinburgh: Edinburgh University Press, 1991).

Edwards, P. and Walvin, J., 'Africans in Britain, 1500–1800', in *The African Diaspora: Interpretive Essays*, eds M. Kilson and R. Rotberg (Cambridge, MA: Harvard University Press, 1976).

Edwards, P. and Walvin, J., *Black Personalities in the Era of the Slave Trade* (London: Macmillan, 1983).

Equiano, Olaudah, *The Interesting Narrative of the Life of Olaudah Equiano, or Gustavus Vassa, the African* (London, 1789).

Falconbridge, Alexander, *An Account of the Slave Trade on the Coast of Africa* (London: J. Phillips, 1788).

Ferguson, John Alexander, *Bibliography of Australia*, vol. 1, *1784–1830* (Canberra: National Library of Australia, 1941).

Ferguson, Moira, *Subject to Others: British Women Writers and Colonial Slavery, 1670–1834* (London: Routledge, 1992).

Fry, Gavin (ed.), *A Voyage Round the World* by Mary Ann Parker, facs. 1st edn (Potts Point: Hordern House for the Australian National Maritime Museum, 1991).

Fryer, Peter, *Staying Power: The History of Black People in Britain* (London: Pluto Press, 1984).

Fyfe, C., 'Thomas Peters: History and Legend', *Sierra Leone Studies*, vol. 9 (1953), pp. 4–13.

Fyfe, C., *A History of Sierra Leone* (London: Oxford University Press, 1962).

Fyfe, C. (ed.), *Sierra Leone Inheritance* (London: Oxford University Press, 1964).

Fyfe, C. (ed.), *'Our Children Free and Happy': Letters from Black Settlers in Africa in the 1790s* (Edinburgh: Edinburgh University Press, 1991).

The Gentleman's Magazine, 70 vols (1731–1800).

Gibson, Ross, *The Diminishing Paradise: Changing Literary Perceptions of Australia* (Sydney: Angus & Robertson, 1984).

Gillen, Mollie, 'The Botany Bay Decision, 1786: Convicts, not Empire', *English Historical Review*, vol. 47, no. 385 (October, 1982), pp. 740–66.

Guest, Harriet, 'The Great Distinction: Figures of the Exotic in the Work of William Hodges', in *New Feminist Discourses: Critical Essays on Theories and Texts*, ed. I. Armstrong (London: Routledge, 1992).

Guest, Harriet, 'Looking at Women: Forster's Observations in the South Pacific', in *J. R. Forster, Observations made during a Voyage round the World*, ed. N. Thomas, H. Guest and M. Dettelbach (Honolulu: University of Hawai'i Press, 1996).

Hamilton, George, *A Voyage round the World, in His Majesty's Frigate Pandora. Performed under the Direction of Captain Edwards, in the Years 1790, 1791, 1792. With the Discoveries made in the South-Sea; and the many Distresses experienced by the Crew from Shipwreck and Famine, in a Voyage of Eleven Hundred Miles, in open Boats, between Endeavour Straits and the Island of Timor* (Berwick: W. Phorson; London: B. Law & Son, 1793).

Hansard, *The Parliamentary History of England from the Earliest Period to the Year 1803*, vol. 3 (London: T. C. Hansard, 1817).

Hoare, Prince, *Memoirs of Granville Sharp* (London: Henry Colburn, 1820).

Hughes, Robert, *The Fatal Shore: A History of the Transportation of Convicts to Australia, 1787–1868* (London: Collins, 1987).

Hunter, John, *An Historical Journal of the Transactions at Port Jackson and Norfolk Island, with the discoveries that have been made in New South Wales and the Southern Ocean* (London: John Stockdale, 1793).

Ingham, E. G. (ed.), *Sierra Leone after a Hundred Years* (London: Frank Cass, 1968).

Inglefield, John Nicholson, *Captain Inglefield's Narrative of the Loss of the Centaur, in 1782 ... a literal extract of his letter to the Admiralty, written from Fayal in 1782. Also, a copy of the ... court martial ... officers of the Centaur* (London: J. Murray and A. Donaldson, 1783).

Kilson, M. and Rotberg, R. (eds), *The African Diaspora: Interpretive Essays* (Cambridge, MA: Harvard University Press, 1976).

Long, Edward, *History of Jamaica*, 3 vols (London, 1774).

Macarthur, Elizabeth, *The Journal and Letters of Elizabeth Macarthur, 1789–1798*, ed. Joy N. Hughes (Glebe: Historic Houses Trust of New South Wales, 1984).

Matthews, John, *A Voyage to the River Sierra-Leone, on the Coast of Africa; containing an Account of the Trade and Productions of the Country, and of the Civil and Religious Customs and Manners of the People; in a series of Letters to a Friend in England, during his Residence in that Country in the Years 1785, 1786 and 1787. With an additional letter on the African Slave Trade* (London: B. White and Son, 1788; 2nd edn 1791).

Monthly Review; or, Literary Journal, 108 vols, 1790–1825.

More, Hannah, 'The White Slave Trade', *The Works of Hannah More*, 11 vols (London: T. Cadell, 1830).

Neville, Richard, *A Rage for Curiosity: Visualising Australia 1788–1830* (Sydney: State Library of New South Wales Press, 1997).

Newton, John, *An Authentic Narrative of some Remarkable and Interesting Particulars in the Life of ********* Communicated in a Series of Letters to the Reverend Mr Haweis*, 5th edn (London: J. Johnson, 1782).

Nicol, John, *Life and Adventures, 1776–1801*, ed. Tim Flannery (Melbourne: Text Publishing, 1997).

Nussbaum, Felicity, 'The Other Woman: Polygamy, *Pamela*, and the Prerogative of Empire' in *Women, 'Race' and Writing in the Early Modern Period*, ed. M. Hendricks and P. Parker (London: Routledge, 1994).

Ogilby, John, *Africa; being an accurate Description of the Regions of Egypt, Barbary, Lybia, and Billedulgerid, the Land of Negroes, Guinea, Ethiopia, and the Abyssines, with all the adjacent Islands, either in the Mediterranean, Atlantick, Southern, or Oriental Seas, belonging thereunto* (London: T. Johnson, 1670).

Paterson, William, *Narrative of Four Journeys into the Country of the Hottentots and Caffraria* (London: J. Johnson, 1789).

Portlock, William Henry, *A New, Complete, and Universal Collection of Authentic and Entertaining Voyages and Travels to all the various parts of the World ... describing in the most accurate manner, upon an entire, new and interesting plan, every place worthy of notice in Europe, Asia, Africa and America* (London: Alexander Hogg, 1794).

Pratt, Mary Louise, *Imperial Eyes: Travel Writing and Transculturation* (London: Routledge, 1992).

Pratt, Mary Louise, 'Scratches on the Face of the Country; or, What Mr Barrow Saw in the Land of the Bushmen', *Critical Inquiry*, 12 (Autumn, 1985), pp. 119–143.

Scott, James, *Remarks on a Passage to Botany Bay, 1787–1792* (Sydney: Trustees of the Public Library of New South Wales in association with Angus and Robertson, 1963).

Sierra Leone Company, *Substance of the Report of the Court of Directors of the Sierra Leone Company to the General Court, held at London on Wednesday the 19th of October, 1791* (London: James Phillips, 1792).

Sierra Leone Company, *Substance of the Report delivered by the Court of Directors of the Sierra Leone Company, to the General Court of Proprietors, on Thursday the 27th March, 1794* (London: James Phillips, 1794).

Sierra Leone Studies, Freetown, vols 1–21, June 1918–January 1939; n.s. vol. 1, 1953–.

Smith, Bernard, *European Vision and the South Pacific*, 2nd edn (Melbourne: Oxford University Press, 1989).

Smyth, W. H., *The Life and Services of Captain Philip Beaver* (London: John Murray, 1829).

Stockdale, John, *The Voyage of Governor Phillip to Botany Bay; with an account of the establishment of the colonies of Port Jackson & Norfolk Island; compiled from authentic papers* (London: John Stockdale, 1789).

Tench, Watkin, *A Narrative of the Expedition to Botany Bay* (London: J. Debrett, 1789).

Tench, Watkin, *A Complete Account of the Settlement at Port Jackson, in New South Wales* (London: G. Nicol, 1793).

Thompson, George, *Slavery and Famine, Punishments for Sedition; or, An Account of the Miseries and Starvation at Botany Bay. With some Preliminary Remarks by George Dyer* (London: J. Ridgway, 1794).

Wadstrom, Carl, *An Essay on Colonization, particularly applied to the Western Coast of Africa, with some free thoughts on Cultivation and Commerce; also Brief Descriptions of the colonies already formed, or attempted, in Africa, including those of Sierra Leona and Bulama* (London: Darton and Harvey, 1794–1795).

Wadstrom, Carl, Nordenskiold, August *et al. Plan for a Free Community upon the Coast of Africa, under the Protection of Great Britain; but intirely independent of all European Laws and Governments* (London: R. Hindmarsh, 1789).

Walker, James W. St. G., 'The Establishment of a Free Black Community in Nova Scotia', in *The African Diaspora: Interpretive Essays*, ed. M. Kilson and R. Rotberg (Cambridge, MA: Harvard University Press, 1976).

Walvin, James, *Black Ivory: A History of British Slavery* (London: HarperCollins, 1992).

White, John, *Journal of a Voyage to New South Wales* (London: J. Debrett, 1790).

Wilberforce, William, 'Debate on Mr. Wilberforce's Motion for the Abolition of the Slave Trade, 1791', in Hansard, *The Parliamentary History of England from the Earliest Period to the Year 1803* (London: T. C. Hansard, 1817), vol. 29, pp. 250–359.

Wilson, Ellen Gibson, *The Loyal Blacks* (New York: Putnam, 1976).

Wilson, Ellen Gibson, *John Clarkson and the African Adventure* (London: Macmillan, 1980).

Wilson, Ellen Gibson, *Thomas Clarkson: A Biography* (London: Macmillan, 1989; 2nd edn 1996).

Winterbottom, Thomas, *An Account of the Native Africans in the Neighbourhood of Sierra Leone, to which is added An Account of the Present State of Medicine among them*, 2 vols (London: C. Whittingham, 1803).

INDEX

Abbreviations
AMF: Anna Maria Falconbridge, *Two Voyages*
BB: Botany Bay
MAP: Mary Ann Parker, *Voyage*
SL: Sierra Leone
Italicized page number: illustration

abolition, abolitionists, abolitionism
    AMF no longer 'bigoted for the
        abolition'   134–5
    connections with slave trade
        insinuated by AMF   10, 118, 126,
        131, 145
    emblem of kneeling slave   14–19, *17*
    emblems in coins, seals of SL
        Company: hand-shake of black
        and white   *16*, 19
Adam's Town, gramatto town on Bance
    Island visited by AMF, Adam's
    House, Capt. Tittle's grave   56–7
adultery   24, 77
    see also red water ordeal or trial
Afzelius, Adam ('Botanist')
    arrival SL   103
    experimental garden   108
    slave traders, 158–9n.34
    Sierra Leone Journal (1795–96),
        156n.12, 158n.31, 164n.107
    student of Linnaeus   163n.90
amusements and pleasures, of Cape
    Town   196
Amy, SL Company ship, embarks/
    arrives on 2nd voyage   95–7
    crowded with discontents   131–2

Falconbridge held responsible for its
    cargo   140, 151–2
Anderson, Isaac, Deputy for SL settlers
    to Court of Directors in London
    21, 138, 141–3, 145, 146–7
    see also Petition to SL Company
Anderson, John and Alexander, slave-
    traders *see* Bance Island
ants, and other insects
    most formidable enemy of fowl
        (AMF)   120
    a 'torment' (Clarkson)   163n.88
authorship, female
    AMF, knee serves as writing desk   7,
        65
    MAP writes with infant on left
        arm   4, 220

Bakhtin, M. M.   27, 41n.73
Banana Islands, Matthews, *Voyage to
    the River Sierra-Leone*
    (1788)   162n.74
    visited, described (AMF)   101
Bance Island (slave) Factory   24, 28, 73,
    129, 158–9n.34
    AMF fraternizes with slavers   53,
        56–8, 66, 68

Bance Island – *continued*
  John and Alexander Anderson,
    owners 48, 156n.4
  slaves in slave yard 58
Banks, Sir Joseph and Lady Banks,
  subscribers to MAP 34, 172
Barbauld, Anna Laetitia, on epistolary
  mode 7
Bar (nominal currency) 67
Beaver, Lieut. Philip (1766–1813)
    39n.47, 106, 162–3n.84;
  see also Bulama
Bennelong, Banalong (*c*.1764–1813) 33,
    42n.91
  dressed in European fashion, 34
  in London 42n.91, n.93
  'tear of sensibility' 33, 210
birds (MAP)
  emu and other birds noticed on
    excursion to Rose-Hill 204, 206,
    208
  Ostrich (Cape Canary) 219
black jury 130
  Captain Newcomb denies SL settlers'
    court competent to try sailors 130
  castaways on St. Vincent banished by
    black Governor of Mayo 86
  sailors of *African Queen* tried for
    killing settler's duck; white man
    whipped 129–30
black gentlemen/white rogues: African
    conundrum 74
  see also rogue
black loyalists from Nova Scotia 1, 36
  feel like slaves with SL Company as
    overseer 145
  frustrations over quit-rent, surveying
    of their land 125–7; *see also*
    petition to SL Company
  hopes for children central to
    Petition 144, 148
  hopes of independence and equality
    with whites in SL betrayed 21
  land allotments in SL 164n.100
  petition of settlers to Directors of SL
    Company: authenticity contested
    by Macaulay 166n.116
  religious sects, godly practices 122
    Methodistical 163n.94

viewed as infants 149
vindication by AMF 7
black poor in SL 2, 10, 35
  'Committee for the Relief of Black
    Poor' 10, 35n.5
  defections, coercion 8, 35–6ns.6, 7
  survivors assembled by Falconbridge,
    Granville Town 69–70
  wretched exiles in SL 63–4
'Black Prince', John Frederic Naimbana
    (1767–93)
  courted in London; appearance,
    disposition, capabilities
    (AMF) 93–4
  death 94, 161n.61
  life by Macaulay, *The African Prince*,
    published 1796 159n.36
  Naimbana sheds tears when shown
    his protrait 97
  Old Queen affected by his
    departure 82
  pledge or hostage; to England for
    education 68, 82, 87
'Botany Bay' (colony)
  in connection with SL 4, 7–21,
    35ns.1 & 2, 38n.32, 50, 157n.21
  publications on 29, 41n.79
  vogue for 'histories of new
    countries' 4
  see also infant colony (Botany Bay)
Bristol 22, 46, 95, 103, 121, 129, 138,
    140, 151–2, 154
  Coleridge's anti-slavery lecture,
    1795 8
  slaving port 99
  see also Falconbridge, Anna Maria
British Government 48, 70, 111, 196
Bulama 14, 162n.83
  John Clarkson's opinion of
    settlers 19, 39n.45
  rival settlement to SL 19–21, *20*,
    105–6
  see also Beaver, Lieut. Philip;
    Dalrymple, Henry Hew;
    Wadstrom, Carl

Cape Town
  MAP arrival on homeward
    journey 216

castaways
  Capt. Inglefield, his escape,
    sufferings 90–1, 161n.57
  D'Auvergne 191
  St. Vincent island, banished by black
    Governor of Mayo 86–7
  failure to relieve haunts AMF
    87–8
children *see* infants and children
Clara, daughter of Naimbana and Old
    Queen, married to Griffith 61
  AMF tries her disposition, is glad to
    be rid of her 69
  see also dress
Clarkson, Lieut. John (1764–1828) 21,
    22, 23, 25, 40n.66
  description of his first meeting with
    Naimbana, parallels AMF 25–8
  Governor of Sierra Leone
    aspersions against his character
      and attempts to 'singe his
      reputation' 123
    diary/'Journal' 4–5, 39n.45
    lack of sympathy for SL Company
      emphasis on trade, 162n.80
    resented by Thomas Peters
      39n.55
    settlers' dissatisfaction, 39n.56
  identification as *anon.* 'gentleman'
    AMF cites 149: 'obliged to be
    silent' 36n.18
  promises made to settlers in Nova
    Scotia: 'no distinction between
    black & white' 123
  repatriates loyalist blacks from Nova
    Scotia 3–4, 36n.13, 93, 97
Clarkson, Thomas (1760–1846), brother
    of John, distinguished
    abolitionist 4, 21, 23
  enlisted Falconbridge in cause of
    abolition 93
'Clarkson's Plantation' tract of land on
    Bulom shore, for white settlers
    leaving Free Town in 1792 115,
    118, 123
Cleveland, or Cleaveland, father & son,
    Portuguese mulatto rulers 101
Cocks, James, SL Councillor, colony's
    original Surveyor, nicknamed

'Captain of the soldiers' 101–2,
    103, 104, 162n.76
  made a monkey of 101–2
  replaced by Pepys as Surveyor 103
Cola, or Kola
  ceremonial use in 1st Palaver 66, 67
  symbolic significance, white and red
    tokens of peace or war 158
Coleridge, S. T.
  anti-slavery lecture, Bristol 1795 8,
    37–8n.30, 166n.123
  'Kubla Khan', *cf* Darwin's 'Visit of
    Hope to Sydney-Cove' 11
Collins, David (1756–1810) Judge
    Advocate BB 31, 204, 222n.22
  An Account of the English Colony
    (1798) 42
Congo Bolokelly
  AMF told he will succeed King
    Naimbana 122
Constantia (at Cape of Good
    Hope) 217
  remarks on wines of 217, 218
convicts 32, 157-8n.21
  convict's prayer-book found in belly
    of shark 215
  at Parramatta, or Rose-Hill 206
convict colony as despotism
    (AMF) 113
Cowper, William, 'The Slave's
    Complaint', quoted by MAP 210
cry or lamentation 56, 118, 162n.73
  rum for 56
  see also rum
Cugoano, Ottobah (*c.*1757–91) 1, 21
  author 38n.33
  'Son of Africa', ex-slave, friend of
    Granville Sharp, initial enthusiast
    for 'Province of Freedom' 10
curiosity 65, 81, 120, 211
  collecting and commerce,
    Gorgon 33–4, 42n.94, 211
  clay from Botany Bay 34
  concept in travel literature 41n.77
  female
    AMF 28, 58,
    MAP 29, 194
  slave yard at Bance Island
    Factory 58

curiosity – *continued*
  of native Africans towards
    Europeans 63
  natural curiosity at Fyal 89
  'raree-shows' 27, 33

Dalrymple, Henry Hew, relations with
    SL Company, involvement in
    Bulama settlement 105–6,
    162n.83
Darwin, Erasmus, 'The Botanic Garden'
    (1792) 19, 38n.36, 39n.44
  'Botany Bay', 11–14
  Wedgwood cameo engravings
    11–14, *12*
Dawes, William (1762–1836) officer of
    marines, scientist, astronomer,
    administrator 3, 36, 39n.51,
    163n.94
  BB service prejudicial in SL 21, 113
  character, manners 116
    hardening of John Clarkson's
    opinion 40n.58
  connection with BB, the bad father
    figure 22, 113
  'Fort Mad' extravagance 117–18,
    164n.100
  proposal for palisade thwarted by
    black settlers 122
  settlers threaten him with fate of
    Louis XVI 130
  subscriber to MAP *Voyage* 175
  trading activities, meanly 'engrossing'
    economy, attacked, satirized
    117–18
  unpopular with black settlers, his
    mortification 122–3
De Witt, Mrs, MAP's hostess at the
    Cape, satirized 30, 193
De Witt, Peter, son of Mrs, host of MAP
    on return journey 216
Defoe, Daniel, *A New Voyage Round
    the World* (1725) 14, 38n.38
delicacy 24–5
  delicacy of gentlemen at slave
    yard 58
  offense of nakedness against 24, 53
  supposed indelicacies for eye of
    Englishwoman, on board slave

    ships 133
Domingo, Signor 74, 118, 120
  Anthony (son) educated in
    England 157n.16
  as injured father, kills Captain
    Tittle 56–7
dress, costume
  Bennelong in European dress 34
  English convicts, free English in New
    Holland 32, *203*
  MAP caught in rain, deprived of
    decorations of vanity 218
  Naimbana 58
    changes of dress 60, 61
    dishabille 58
    gold-laced hat 59; worn at 1st
    Palaver 66
    stockings, 'harlequined' 58, 60
  Naimbana and John Clarkson for
    ceremonial meeting 25
  national modes of dress
    European mode of native men,
    observed by Winterbottom
    157n.20
    men at Porta Praya 84
    native, mulatto and European
    women, at Porta Praya 84
  Pa Boson, has a reverential
    appearance 63
  petticoats and trousers sent for naked
    castaways on St Vincent 85
  Queen Naimbana and Clara 63
    AMF tries to refashion Clara, the
    Ethiopian princess 69
  SL Council members, pompous
    uniforms satirized 96
  slave women on *Nassau* as decent as
    in Africa 133
  women and satirical play on notions
    of dress and delicacy in AMF
    24–5
DuBois, Isaac
  dismissal 5; protest of Clarkson
    at 40n.60
  'Harmony Hall', mess house, later
    burnt, built by him 106, 163n.87
  Journal 37n.22, 40n.60; *see also*
    Clarkson, John
  nurses AMF 132

education
    importance given by Naimbana,
        other natives   25, 61, 68, 74;
        see also rogue
    rigid military education of
        Dawes   113
epistolary mode
    advantages of for women travel
        writers   5
    AMF returns to old epistolary
        mode   125
    Barbauld, Anna Laetitia   7
    as facade in AMF   5, 37n.22, 156n.5
    notion of the 'citizen-critic'
        (Cook)   7, 37n.24
    publication, construction of
        categories public and private   7
Equiano, Olaudah (*c.* 1745–97),
        author   1, 21, 38n.33
    'Commissary on the part of
        Government' to Sierra Leone, and
        dismissal   38
    letter to Privy Council, 1788
        38–9n.43
    remarks on old settlers taken to SL;
        complaint that 'unauthorised
        persons' taken on board   36n.7
    'Son of Africa', ex-slave, friend of
        Granville Sharp, initial enthusiast
        for 'Province of Freedom'   10
evangelical philanthropists   3
excursions   29, 30, 31, 89, 108, 185, 189,
        194, 206
    of Bennelong, Capt. Parker,
        remembered   210
    MAP to Constantia   217–8
    MAP to Puerto Oratava   187–8
    to Parramatta, or Rose-Hill   206
    to Peak of Teneriffe, by Burton and
        Rye, an excursion published   188,
        221n.7; *see also* Rye, Lieut. Peter
    improved by a little difficulty   188
    up the country, by Col Gordon   196

Falconbridge, Alexander
    Account of the Slave Trade (1788):
        AMF aims to subvert   23–4,
        40n.65, 133–4
    bad husband, counterpart to bad

fathers of AMF's tale   23, 40n.59
    character, opinions   5, 36n.12,
        161n.63
    conduct as Commercial Agent   151–
        4, 161n.63
    conduct as first husband of
        AMF   53–4, 110
    good doctor   91, 93
    illness and death, 'a very happy
        release' (Clarkson)   163n.93
Falconbridge, Anna Maria
    apologist for slave trade   133–36
    Capt. Morley, her brother   24,
        40n.64, 121, 165n.109, 166n.118
    dedicates her book to inhabitants of
        Bristol   46
    elegance, variety and richness of
        wedding dinner   121, 165n.110
    female spectator, transformed to
        spectacle   24
    hasty first marriage   7, 23, 48
    hasty second marriage   125, 165n.11
    infant pen   5, 46–7
    Mr. S— identified as Horwood her
        brother   166n.118
    native of Bristol   46, 95
    opinions on SL Company officers,
        'parcel of hypocritical puritans'
        undermining colony   116
    SL Directors as hypocrites   109
    presented with two beautiful
        pineapples by Naimbana   61
    suggestion that AMF book
        'sponsored' by pro-slavery
        faction   37n.25
    thatched house burns down   120–1
Falconbridge, William, brother of
        Alexander
    quarrels with Alexander, goes into
        employ of Bance Island Factory,
        dies of fever 72
fathers, Father   22–3
    Governor Phillip as 'Father of his
        People'   211
    John Clarkson likened to kind and
        tender Father by Nova
        Scotians   22
    King Naimbana, father of 'Black
        Prince'   68, 82, 97

fathers, Father – *continued*
  Monarch of Great Britain is Father of his People 211
  Pa or Father, title for senior native men 63
  Signor Domingo as injured father 57
France, French
  abolitionist inflection given to emblem of revolutionary France, 'La Nature' 14, *18*
  citizenship conferred on Thomas Clarkson, Wilberforce, Paine, by Revolutionary Convention, Oct. 1792 132, 166n.120
  ferocious appearance and accoutrements of French republican privateer sailors on slave coast: 'Republican ragamuffins' 129
Free Town (Freetown, SL) 97, *98*, 106, 119, 141–7
  called a 'camp' by natives 121
  renamed 'Town of Slavery' 21

George III
  Accession Day celebrated in Port Jackson 211
  see also Bennelong
  King Naimbana 'ostensible to King George', his good friend 59, 60
  Monarch of Great Britain is Father of his People 211
Gilbert, Rev. Nathaniel 101, 119, 162n.72
Gooreedeeana 33
Gordon, Robert Jacob and Susanne 195–7, 216–19, 222ns.16, 17
Gorgon (Captain Parker) 33
  carrying supplies to relieve starving colony at Port Jackson, New South Wales Corps 2, 196, 199
  congratulations on arrival in Portsmouth 220
  loaded with curiosities on return journey 211
Gree Grees, or native fetishes (*gree gree, grisgris, grigris,* or *gregory*; and *Gree-Greeman*) 62, 158n.23
  AMF thoughtlessly tries to examine in Robana Town 61
Green Point, 'hospitable villa' of Gordons at Cape Town 196
Griffith, Elliott, Naimbana's secretary, translator, and son-in-law, as *Elliotte Griffiths* (AMF) 54, 58–63, 66–9
  thought to be rogue by DuBois and Clarkson 164n.104
Grose, Francis (1758?–1814) 186, 220–1n.2
Guardian, shipwrecked by iceberg 29, 196
  MAP views remains at False Bay, reflects on parallel with *Gorgon* 194
  supply ship intended to relieve colony at Port Jackson 2
  see also Riou; shipwrecks

harlequin figure 27
Horne, Rev. Melvill
  preaches sermon to natives ('dry palaver') 121, 165n.108
  Thornton's opinion of 163n.94
Horwood
  AMF's brother, identified as Mr. S—, the Surgeon 166n.118
hospitality
  shown to AMF
    Bance Island House 68
    Hibernian 101
    Jamaican 136
    other 81, 83–4, 89
    SL natives 74–5
  shown to MAP
    Colonel Gordon sends his carriage 216
    Constantia, MAP placed at head of table 218
    Governor Phillip 206, 211–12
    Green Point, as 'hospitable villa' of Gordons at Cape Town 196, 219
    Peter De Witt in Cape Town 216
    to strangers 218, 219

hostage taking or pawning 68
  AMF agrees to be hostage for King
    Jemmy 97
  importance in slave trade 41n.75
  Naimbana's son offered as hostage in
    land sale 68
Hottentot song, MAP finds it impossible
  to describe 196
Hummums
  AMF and DuBois' house, later
    disparaged by Macaulay 128,
    166n.117
  from Turkish 'hammam', jokingly
    named 166n.117
hysteria, unknown among native African
  women 158n.32
hysterics
  AMF 'swoons into hysterics' at first
    palaver 27, 67
  as delirium 50
  John Clarkson's, brought on by
    palavers 25

'infant colony' (Botany Bay) 2, *13*, 199
'infant colony' (Sierra Leone) 2, 4, *95*,
  100, 103, 115, 149
  refractory rather than docile child 22
  Sharp's 'ill-thriven swarthy
    daughter' 22
infants and children 4
  bandy-legged (SL) 74
  black and white *18*
  child buried in Cape Town 219
  MAP fatherless children, her chief
    comforts and beneficiaries of her
    book 220
  MAP's reunited with one child, other
    died in her absence, gives birth to
    a third 220
  of marines, terrible mortality on the
    Gorgon 30
  women in canoes at BB hold them
    up 210

Johnson, Rev. Richard, chaplain
  appointed to First Fleet to
  BB 206

kangaroo, MAP eats with glee 206

King Jemmy
  burning of settlers' town 3, 51, 59,
    156n.8
  flirtatious relationship with
    AMF 28, 96–7, 117–19
  partly defended by Naimbana and by
    AMF 59, 119
  vociferation at 1st Palaver 67
King Jemmy's Town, disturbing to
  settlers 74, 106, 118–19
King, Philip Gidley and Anna Josepha
  depart for Norfolk Island,
    farewells 211
  fellow travellers of MAP 186
King of Kings
  Bakhtin's notion of carnival-
    grotesque 27
  invoked by Falconbridge, in
    negotiations with Naimbana
    59

land tenure (African) 60, 157n.17
  Naimbana's exposition of 60
Lapwing, cutter of SL Company
  nearly shipwrecked on AMF's first
    return journey 87–8
  rubbishy goods sent out on it *59*,
    71
  'tub' and floating prison or cage of
    AMF 53, 54, 58
  see also shipwrecks
Liberty (concept and principle)
  British liberty infringed in SL 70
  Liberty and Equality as basis of SL
    colony 23, 113
  revolutionary figure of Liberty *14*
  see also Free Town; 'Province of
    Freedom'
Louis XVI, King of France 23
  death, news of in SL 128
  fate used to threaten Dawes 130

Macarthur, Elizabeth 31, 42, 223
Macaulay, Zachary (1768–1838)
  Councillor, later Governor of SL
    (as *McAuley* in AMF) 21,
    39n.51, 119, 164n.105
  one of Clapham set of evangelical
    abolitionists 161n.60

Marre Bump, or, Marabump 65, 67,
    158n.29
  frightening encounter at secret or
    reserve slave factory 65
Matthews, John 40–1n.69
  apologist for slave trade 7
  conference with natives, 26
  influenced by Long's racist
    theories 41n.74
  A Voyage to the River Sierra-Leone
    (1788) 29, 37n.26, 47, 101, 107,
    158n.31, 163n.89
monkeys, AMF's 73, 102
More, Hannah
  one of Clapham set of evangelical
    abolitionists 161n.60
  'The White Slave Trade' 40
Morley, AMF's brother, Captain of
  Bristol slave-ship, *Nassau* 24,
  40n.64 , 121, 164n.109
mother country 2, 34, 70, 202

Naimbana, *or* Nemgbana, Regent of
    Koya Temne (ruled 1775–93) 54,
    58–63, 66–9, 74, 94, 111–12, 117,
    157n.13
  clever and experienced
    negotiator 25
  death 124
  'ostensible to King George', his good
    friend 59, 60
  pantomime figure: his lack of
    regality 27, 58–60
  physical description 61, 63
  and wives 26
  see also dress
Naimbana, John Frederic (1767–93), son
    of Naimbana and Queen
    Naimbana, the 'Black Prince', *see*
    'Black Prince'
Nassau slaving ship
  AMF travels to Jamaica on 24, 121,
    122, 131–4
natives of SL, appearance 74
natives of NSW
  MAP describes 33, 209–10
natural beauties
  BB 204
  SL 51

Nature (concept of) 135, 210
'La Nature', engraving, *c*. 1790 14, *18*
Newcomb, Captain, of frigate *Orpheus*,
  see black jury
Newton, John, *An Authentic Narrative*
  (1782) 40n.63
Nordenskiold, Augustus
  'Mineralist', arrives SL 103
  as Nordenschold, illness and
    death 115, 163n.90
  preparing to make excursion into
    interior 108
  Swedenborgian, in collaboration with
    Wadstrom, *Plan for a Free
    Community upon the Coast of
    Africa* 2, 35n.4, 163n.90, 164n.98
novelties, amusements of Cape Town,
  do not efface sense of perils, in
  MAP 196
'novelties of Sidney Cove' 205

Old England 219
oysters 19, 120
  AMP dines on, placed round sailors'
    hats in lieu of plates 209

Pa Boson
  character, appearance, dress, good
    deeds 63–4
  courteous bows 64
Pa Bunkie
  believed likely to succeed Naimbana
    as King 120
  offered rich present or *Dash* by
    Dawes 120–1
Paine, Thomas 23, 134, 166n.120
Palaver, or African Court 57, 59, 119,
  111
  1st Palaver 66–68; called 'mock
    judiciary' 68
  2nd Palaver 111
  stressful for Europeans 25
palm tree, palm-nut oil 60–1, 74,
  158n.24
Palmer, John, the Commissary at
  BB 204
Panyarers, or man thieves 72
Parker, Captain John (1749–94) (the
  Gorgon) 220n.1

account of prospects of Whale-
fishery, given by MAP 2, 201–2
Report on high mortality on
transport ship *Queen* 11, 30,
200
Parker, Mary Ann
custodian of curiosities and birds on
Gorgon return voyage 215
debts to Tench's books 31, 33,
42n.90
fluency in Spanish and role as
Interpreter General at
Teneriffe 30, 187, 188
Spanish compliment *di los
manos* 186–7
mother, wife, and author 4
parties, dinners, pastimes
in NSW, comprising Mrs King,
Mr Johnson and the Ladies 206
on board ship: 'chearful parties
. . . within our wooden
walls' 212, 215, 220
previous travels in France, Italy and
Spain 29, 185, 195
sees ice-islands near Falklands 29,
213-15, 224n.41
see also amusements; authorship,
female; birds, in MAP; *Gorgon*;
hospitality; widows
Parramatta, *or* 'Rose-Hill' 14, 206
description of Governor's
House 15, 206
Tench's comparison with Pall-Mall,
Portland Place 14
Paterson, Elizabeth (1760?–1825)
'wife fit for a soldier' 221n.10
Paterson, William (1755–1810), soldier,
explorer, amateur botanist and
friend of Banks 190, 196–7,
221n.10
peginine (piccaninny) 77
Pepys, Richard
speech defaming Clarkson 123–4,
65n.113
'Surveyor' 116, 164 n.100
Perkins, Cato, Deputy for SL settlers to
Court of Directors in
London 138, 141–3, 145, 147–8
see also Petition to SL Company

Peters, Thomas, ex-slave and
spokesperson for the Nova
Scotians 39n.55
Petition to SL Company by black
loyalists 7, 124, 138
AMF quotes in full 125–7
grievances ignored 141–8
Phillip, Governor Arthur 33, 204
'Father of his People' 206, 211
Voyage to Botany Bay
(1789) 36n.14
polygamy 24, (Nussbaum) 37n.25
in Africa honorable and confers
status 74
Winterbottom's observations
on 157n.19
poor blacks, *see* black poor
present, or *Dash* 120
as unasked for present, offered to Pa
Bunkie by Dawes 121
presents
AMF granted 50l. to buy presents for
Naimbana and Old Queen 94
from Naimbana and Directors to
dead Falconbridge, appropriated
by Dawes 117
to Naimbana 117
'Province of Freedom' 2, 3, 10, 98, 119,
161n.59

Queen Naimbana, the 'Old
Queen' 140, 152
appearance, temper, manners, mode
of dress 63
at dinner at Queen's House, sits
outside tent with her
daughters 158n.26
Queen stood behind the King
eating an onion 61
'Canny old woman', according to
Winterbottom 157n.20
first meeting with 58
much affected at parting from Black
Prince 82
Queen of Portugal 89
Queen Yamacubba or Ya-ma-cooba,
queen or head woman, her
Town 74, 62
quit-rent 21, 39n.50, 146, 148, 167n.133

raree-shows   27, 33, 158n.25
  AMF tours 'all the raree-shows of
    Robana town'   60–1
  Harlequin the 'white-negro'
    woman   41n.72, 158n.25
  spotted negro boy at Bartholomew
    Fair   41n.71
Ravenet, Juan (*c.* 1766–?)
  'Convicts in New Holland'   *32*
  'English in New Holland'   *203*
red water ordeal or trial   77, *78*,
    165n.114
  of favourite of King Jemmy   120
  witnessed by Afzelius   164n.107
religion in SL
  of coastal Africans, influenced by
    Portuguese   40–1n.69
  of white employees, 'parcel of
    hypocritical puritans'   116
Renaud, slave trader at French factory
    on Gambia Island, as
    Rennieu   68, 79–80, 82, 118, 122,
    159n.35
reviews
  Two Voyages   5, 37ns.20–1, 165n.115
  Voyage   28–9, 41n.80, 42n.83
revolutionary figure of Liberty   14
Robana (Robanna) Island and
    Town   58, 66, 68–9, 73, 82, 111,
    124, 157n.18
  AMF examines African plants in
    garden   61
  compared with Adam's Town   60
rogue
  AMF considered as   24
  'rogue so well as white man', as
    conundrum of coastal people
    about Europeans   27, 74
Rowe, Nicholas, *Ambitious Step-
    Mother: A Tragedy* (1701) quoted
    by MAP   188, 221n.8
rum, rum-drinking, presents of rum, in
    SL   39n.56, 56, 59, 64, 66, 107
  dram of rum the slave's snack on
    Nassau   134
  settlers' rum watered down by
    Dawes   126
Rye, Lieut. Peter   188, 221
  Excursion to the Peak of Teneriffe

(1793)   188, 221n.7

Sandy Bay, landmark   213
scenery, Port Jackson harbour, North
    Branch   206, *207*
Sharp, Granville (1735–1813)   35, 38,
    92, 157n.16
  Granville town named in his
    honour   70, 73, 80
ships
  Amy, SL Company ship, embarks/
    arrives on 2nd voyage   95–7
    crowded with discontents   131–2
    Falconbridge held responsible for
      its cargo   140, 151–2
  Betsy, American schooner, at
    uninhabited island Ascension
    Road   219
  Calypso, dreadful mortality on   105,
    163n.85
  Duke of Buccleugh, slave ship   10,
    48, 51, 118, 140, 152
  Lapwing, cutter of SL Company; *see*
    Lapwing
  Orpheus, HM frigate, Capt.
    Newcomb, engaged in privateering
    war with France   129–30
  Providence, trading cutter of SL
    Company   118
  Sirius, supply ship, lost 1790   31
shipwrecks
  spectre of   186, 196, 199
  of Lord Mulgrave   214, 224n.40
  of *Pandora* (Capt. Edwards)   217,
    224n.43
  Riou & *Guardian*   2, 194, 199,
    222n.15
  of Sir Hugh Willoughby   214, 224n.39
Sierra Leone   73
  climate   72
  natural history, 'animal and vegetable
    productions of Nature':
    musquettos, serpents, variety of
    beautiful lizards, stinging insect,
    chameleon, etc.   72–3
Sierra Leone (colony)
  AMF's animadversions on
    Council   96
  'Province of Freedom'   119

Sierra Leone (colony) – *continued*
see also 'Botany Bay (colony)
Sierra Leone Company
1791 'Substance of the Report' 2,
35n.7, 39n.49
1794 'Substance of Report' 23, 36n.19
blames Falconbridge for faltering
progress of colony 5, 109, 161n.63
incorporation by Act of
Parliament 164n.103
Sierra Leone River 73
slave factories
French, on Isles de Loss 129; on
Gambia Island 80
see also Bance Island; Marre Bump
slave ships
French Guineaman with 1200 slaves
on board reported 129
Duke of Buccleugh (Capt. McLean)
with 300 slaves for Jamaica 118
see also ships, *Duke of Buccleugh;
Nassau; Zong*
slave trade
Bance Island House slave yard 58
'genteel' employment 40n.63
Marabump secret or reserve factory
(Marre Bump) 65, 67, 158n.29
see also Falconbridge, Anna Maria
slaves
AMF sees King's slaves preparing
palm-nut in Robana town 61
in household of Peter De Witt in
Cape Town 216
old, refuse female slaves employed in
salt mines of Robana 69
starvation, want
BB 2, 31, 196
Betsy at Ascension Road 219
first return voyage of AMF 82–3, 88
SL settlement 99, 103–4
Stockdale, John, publisher 38
sugar, tea, coffee not served at
Naimbana's for lack of 63
'Surveyor' see Cocks, first Surveyor;
replaced by Pepys 103
Swedenborg, Emmanuel, 'A New
Jerusalem in Africa' 2
utopian 'Plan for a Free Community'
(1789) 35n.4

Tasso Island, opposite Bance Island 64
Tench, Watkin (1758?–1833) 14, 31,
40, 204
*Complete Account of the Settlement
at Port Jackson* (1793) 36
MAP debts to 31, 33, 42
Thompson, George, author, and George
Dyer, radical, editor, *Slavery and
Famine* (1794) 37n.27
Thompson, Capt. Thomas Boulden
(captained 1787 ships to SL, and
negotiated for land there) 59, 60,
68, 111, 156n.8, 157-8n.21
connected with St. George's Bay
Company 59
Thornton, Henry, Chairman of Court of
Directors, Sierra Leone Company
behaviour towards SL settlers'
Deputies 141–2
home centre for Clapham set of
evangelical abolitionists 161n.60
marks of attention to AMF, the
chaise, etc. 95
Tilley, John, slave-trader, Bance
Island 158–9n.29
AMF finds him 'genteel' 56, 158n.34
Tittle, Captain, murders son of
Domingo, and is killed by father;
his grave in Adam's Town 56–7
transportation
high mortality on Third Fleet
transport ship *Queen*, Parker's
Report 11, 200–1
Slavery and Famine (1794), by
George Thompson and George
Dyer 8, 9
likened to slavery 8–10, 37n.29
see also *Zong*, slave ship
travellers, travelling
always agreeable to meet
compatriots 196
MAP remarks on usual sights on
return journey 213
travel writing published 188; see
also Matthews, John *and* Rye,
Lieut. Peter
see also excursions
turtle 117–18, 191, 212, 219
'turtle in high perfection' 137

vindication
 of black loyalists by AMF 7, 127
 for Clarkson in settlers' Petition 142
 of injured woman by AMF
  in Letter to Thornton and 1794
   Appendix 151–5
  in Preface 47

Wadstrom, Carl
 comments on white women, and
  black poor, settlers of Sierra
  Leone 35n.7
 An Essay on Colonization (1794–5)
  14, *16*, 19, 35n.7, 164n.103
 utopian sketch of Bulama 19–21,
  20
 'Nautical Map' and abolitionist
  emblem of kneeling slave 14, *17*
 as Swedenborgian 35n.41
 see also Bulama
Wallace, as *Wallis* in AMF, Commercial
  Agent of SL Company replacing
  Falconbridge 109
 ex-slaver, an unseemly choice
  163n.92
Watt, James, original Councillor, SL,
  made plantation manager of
  'Clarkson's Plantation', later slave
  trader 115, 164n.99
Wedgwood cameos
 medallion of Hope 11–14, *12, 13*, 19
 'fetter'd SLAVE on bended
  knee' 14–19, *12*
 revolutionary inflection given
  38n.42
 seal for Bulama *16*
white men
 but English honestest 59
 white man whipped by a black
  man 130
 see also rogue 25
white women in SL
 coercion of, married to black men 70
 controversy over 2, 35–6n.7
 cf. plan for Polynesian
  women 159n.38
Wilberforce, William (1759–1833) 22,
  132, 163, 166n.120

associated with Tom Paine and burnt
  in effigy at Kingston 23, 143
 Director of the Sierra Leone
  Company 167
 'immaculate Member of the House of
  Commons' 149, 168n.134
 member of Clapham set of
  evangelical abolitionists 161n.60
 quoted by AMF against himself and SL
  Company Directors 138, 167n.127
Wilson, Captain T. W., *Harpy*, and Mrs.
  Wilson 95–6, 163n.96
 disputes boisterously with Clarkson
  and Dawes, is arrested 111–13
 retakes *Harpy*, sails her away 113–14
Winterbottom, Thomas, doctor 4 years
  in SL 120, 162n.73
 *An Account of the Native Africans in
  … of Sierra Leone* (1803) cf.
  AMF 41n.75, 157ns.19, 20, 22,
  23, 158n.31
 'Physician', cures AMF 104
wives 34, 49, 91, 160, 224
 Elizabeth Paterson, a 'wife fit for a
  soldier' 221n.10
 Naimbana's Pegininee woman 60
 Naimbana's wives, servants occupy
  Robana Town 60
widows, widowhood
 AMF on her widowhood 125
 AMF persona as widow 138, 141
 MAP persona as widow 4, 34, *169*,
  171, 220
wives, accompanying travelling
  husbands of later period
 how AMF unlike 24
wives, and children 159
 of marines, returning in *Gorgon* 211
wives, daughters, and attendants 66
women
 of the Cape 195
 Englishwomen, comparative liberty
  of 91
 native women of BB 209
 of SL, AMF observations on 74
 Spanish ladies at Santa Cruz 187

Zong, slave ship 38n.35

reflections of Portuguese lady on
Fyal   91
of two nuns, at Fyal   90
native women of BB   209

of SL, AMF observations on   74
Spanish ladies at Santa Cruz   187

Zong, slave ship   38n.35

Please remember that this is a library book,
and that it belongs only temporarily to each
person who uses it. Be considerate. Do
not write in this, or any, library book.